Designing Online Information Literacy Games Students Want to Play

Designing Online Information Literacy Games Students Want to Play

Karen Markey, Chris Leeder,
and Soo Young Rieh

ROWMAN & LITTLEFIELD
Lanham • Boulder • New York • Toronto • Plymouth, UK

Published by Rowman & Littlefield
4501 Forbes Boulevard, Suite 200, Lanham, Maryland 20706
www.rowman.com

10 Thornbury Road, Plymouth PL6 7PP, United Kingdom

British Library Cataloguing in Publication Information Available

Library of Congress Cataloging-in-Publication Data

Markey, Karen.
Designing online information literacy games students want to play / Karen Markey,
Chris Leeder, and Soo Young Rieh.
    pages cm
Includes bibliographical references and index.
ISBN 978-0-8108-9142-5 (pbk. : alk. paper) — ISBN 978-0-8108-9143-2 (ebook)
1. Information literacy—Study and teaching. 2. Educational games—Design and
construction. 3. Educational games—Case studies. I. Leeder, Chris, 1967–. II. Rieh,
Soo Young, 1965–. III. Title.
ZA3075.M36 2014
028.7071—dc23

                                                                2013039210

∞™ The paper used in this publication meets the minimum requirements of American
National Standard for Information Sciences—Permanence of Paper for Printed Library
Materials, ANSI/NISO Z39.48-1992. Printed in the United States of America

Contents

Illustrations

FIGURES

TABLES

Preface

The likelihood that today's high school and college graduates will enter the workforce with ineffective information literacy skills is very real. Such individuals will be unprepared to fully participate in our information-rich society, putting themselves, their families, their fellow workers, and the institutions they work for at a disadvantage. Incorporating information literacy instruction into K–12 and postsecondary education is a necessity to ensure that young people develop a level of competency in information literacy that helps them succeed in school, thrive in the workplace, and lead fulfilling lives.

Information literacy is a set of acquired abilities that enables individuals to recognize when information is needed and to effectively locate, evaluate, and use the information they find (American Library Association 1989). It is the poor stepchild of the K–12 curriculum. Failing to fit neatly into a core-curriculum subject such as language arts, social studies, science, or technology, it is not guaranteed instruction in today's classrooms. When teachers do find a place for information literacy instruction, it is under constant threat due to pressures teachers experience preparing students for high-stakes tests, budget cuts that eliminate school librarians and school libraries altogether, and teachers' reluctance to teach something they are not prepared to teach.

A similar fate awaits information literacy at the postsecondary level. Only a minority of institutions feature first-year experience programs or similar orientation activities in which information literacy content is included. College professors are primarily concerned with disciplinary coverage and are therefore reluctant to cede valuable in-class time to librarians or to discussions of the research process. The importance of information literacy is not apparent to college students, who rarely see a direct cause-and-effect relationship between the sources they select for their assignments and the grades they receive. Truth be told, finding such an effect would be difficult because so many other factors—student knowledge of the subject, student ability to synthesize and write, and inherent time constraints—are in play. Intent on reaping the rewards faculty give them for mastering the core concepts of the academic disciplines, college students focus on their course work rather than on information literacy skills and concepts.

To overcome these barriers to information literacy instruction, librarians try to reach as many students as they can, offering a wide range of venues such as workshops, short courses, virtual reference assistance, Web-based instruction pages, and walk-in assistance at information desks. They approach instructors one at a time, briefing them on information literacy goals, exploring how instruction in information literacy skills and concepts might benefit their students, and customizing instruction to fulfill instructors' learning objectives for their courses and curricula.

In recent years, more has become known about the ways in which students engage with material outside formal learning. For example, video games have become a favorite pastime among today's high school and college students (Squire and Jenkins 2003; Lenhart, Jones, and Macgill 2008). Beginning in 2001, the video game industry began reporting sales that surpassed movie box office receipts (Chaplin and Ruby 2006). As the end of the decade approached, surveys reported that playing video games was "nearly universal among teens with 97% of American youth twelve to seventeen playing computer, console, portable or cell phone games" (Lenhart, Jones, and Macgill 2008, 8) and with 81 percent of adults aged eighteen to twenty-nine playing games (Lenhart, Jones, and Macgill 2008, 1). Young people are attracted to video games because of the combination of fun, fantasy, challenge, curiosity, and competition that they experience during game play. Foremost is the experience of a level of engagement called flow when players are focused single-mindedly on game play to the exclusion of everything else (Csíkszentmihályi 1975).

By mid-decade, educators were extolling the benefits of video games for serious learning (e.g., Prensky 2001a; Gee 2003; Johnson 2006). Best known among them is James Paul Gee (2003), who considers both video games and academic disciplines to be semiotic domains where groups of people share knowledge, expertise, resources, and distinctive social practices. What makes video games so effective for learning is their ability to immerse players in an environment where they learn how to understand and produce meanings that are both recognizable and acceptable to those more experienced and respected in the domain and how to think about the domain at a "meta" level (Gee 2003, 23).

The exuberance over the promise of games for serious learning began to be felt in librarianship by mid-decade, with library practitioners promoting games to teach students information literacy, increase young people's interest in libraries, expand library services, and build new collections (Branston 2006; VanLeer 2006; Levine 2006b; Doshi 2006). The earliest online information literacy games were merely tutorials or tests all dressed up with gamelike features that drilled or tested students on what they already knew (VanLeer 2006, 52; Broussard 2011a, 81–82). Especially needed were online information literacy game design and development efforts that could demonstrate students learned information literacy concepts and skills as a result of game play. Additionally, a successful information literacy game would have to achieve everyone's objectives; that is, instructors would want improved performance on assignments as a result of game play, students would want game play to be fun and contribute to their course work, and librarians would want information literacy instruction to reach as many students as possible.

We proposed games research and development to two funding agencies that supported our efforts in building, deploying, and evaluating the Defense of Hidgeon and BiblioBouts information literacy games. Since we began our investigation, our games-research objective has been to determine the effectiveness of games for information literacy instruction. Specifically, we wanted students to learn the library research process. To achieve this objective, we had students play the games we built and participate in their evaluation. Evaluation results were positive. Students learned information literacy skills and concepts; retained what they learned, including the game's structured research process; used or intended to use the same professional resource discovery tools that had been new to them during game play; and preferred learning about library research via the game format. These research findings were not without qualification, and the games we designed were not perfect. We made and learned from many mistakes along the way. We want to share our games research and development expertise with others who are intrigued by the potential of information literacy games and academic games generally.

This book is about how to design, develop, deploy, and evaluate the online information literacy games that students want to play. It enlists the BiblioBouts game as a case study to show what went right and what went wrong with an actual online information literacy game implementation. Its analysis of game play data reveals what students learned as a result of playing BiblioBouts and how they benefited from game play that gave them additional opportunities to practice what they learned. Our advice to those who are intrigued by the potential of games for learning comes in the form of best practices for the design of information literacy games. We offer these best practices in the hope that they will better prepare everyone involved in the game enterprise to implement games that achieve their stated learning objectives so that students profit long after the games are over.

The story begins with information literacy, giving a short history, definitions, research findings that demonstrate its benefits, speculation about why the game format is suited to information literacy instruction, and a summary of information literacy games research and development to date (chapter 1). Due to the scant amount of research on information literacy games, we summarize research findings from several state-of-the-art literature reviews that have examined the benefits of serious games across a wide array of academic disciplines (chapter 1). Designing a game begins with choosing the information literacy concepts and skills that players will learn as a result of game play, setting the game's learning objectives, and then conducting a needs assessment to determine whether a game is an effective way to teach the particular information literacy needs and skills or whether alternatives to games would be just as suitable (chapter 2). Chapter 2 gets enterprising game designers started on the needs assessment for their project, posing questions that a needs assessment should answer. Using BiblioBouts as a case study, we tell why we built a game for the library research process, what we expected players to learn as a result of playing the game, and how we configured the library research process into an online game (chapters 3 to 5). We enlisted a multimodal approach to evaluate BiblioBouts's effectiveness (chapter 6). We deployed the game in undergraduate classes in colleges and universities, enlisting students, instructors, and librarians in a comprehensive evaluation of the game. Evaluation results were positive, but the game was far from perfect (chapters 7 to 11). These results address the instructional needs players have during game play (chapter 7), how they play the game (chapter 8), how they evaluate sources (chapter 9), and whether the game's focus on quality sources is reflected in the sources players cite in their final papers (chapter 10). Chapter 11 features the benefits of playing BiblioBouts. We present what we learned about the design and development of the BiblioBouts information literacy game as best practices so that designers of future information literacy games and academic games generally can learn from our experience, build games that achieve their chosen pedagogical objectives, and deliver an experience that fulfills players' desires for fun, competition, and challenge (chapters 12 and 13). The book concludes with our speculation about the future of information literacy games, including the changes we would make to BiblioBouts to increase its faithfulness to this book's best practices and suggestions for future information literacy games (chapter 14).

This book's contents will interest the following people:

• Designers and developers of serious games who are contemplating or getting to know the library marketplace prior to taking the plunge

- Library administrators who may be considering games or other media as alternatives or additions to existing methods for delivering information literacy content
- Administrators at high school, college, and university levels who are seeking solutions to the problem of ensuring graduates are equipped with lifelong learning skills to succeed in today's technologically rich workplaces
- Serious games researchers who want to collaborate with learning professionals in a discipline conducive to game design, development, deployment, and evaluation
- Instruction librarians who are seeking alternatives to traditional information literacy training
- Information and library science researchers who study information-seeking behavior and want to know how people assess the credibility and relevance of what they find online
- Academic instructors at the high school, college, or university levels who want to prepare their students to use quality information for their course work and personal endeavors
- Leaders of information industry who welcome exploring connections between their online systems and online information literacy games
- Students in game studies programs who want to apply their energy and creativity to the design and development of serious games for learning

We encourage interested readers to meet at the intersection of games, learning, and information literacy, where they can apply their knowledge, connections, and expertise to the design, development, evaluation, and long-term maintenance and improvement of information literacy games that students want to play.

Acknowledgments

In this book, we describe best practices for online information literacy games and draw on our experience building and evaluating such games in college classrooms to give others guidance for their efforts in this regard. Grants from the Gladys Krieble Delmas Foundation and the Institute of Museum and Library Services (IMLS) supported our efforts. We are especially grateful to Dr. David Stam, Delmas Foundation Trustee, who funded our initial efforts. Building and evaluating the original online Hidgeon information literacy game with Delmas funds resulted in eight premises for the design of information literacy games, which were the impetus for BiblioBouts, an information literacy game that college students played while they wrote their research papers. IMLS funded the design, development, deployment, and evaluation of the BiblioBouts game, this book's case study for the design of future information literacy games and the source of data and analyses that demonstrate how college students assess the online sources they use for their class assignments. We appreciate IMLS for supporting our games research and extend our heartfelt thanks to IMLS program officers Rachel L. Frick and Chuck Thomas, who were always available to answer our questions and discuss project plans and progress.

Helping us to recruit librarians who would deploy BiblioBouts at their institutions was Jenny Levine at the American Library Association, who publicized our games research in her Shifted Librarian blog. We are grateful to our library liaisons Catherine Johnson, head of information literacy and instruction, Langsdale Library, University of Baltimore (UB); Alyssa Martin, instruction/reference librarian, Rosa Parks Library, Troy University Montgomery Campus (TUMC); Averill Packard, former reference librarian, and Anita Dey, head of reference services, Melvin J. Zahnow Library, Saginaw Valley State University (SVSU); and Gabrielle Toth, government information coordinator, University Library, Chicago State University (CSU). They responded to our initial call for partners to deploy BiblioBouts beyond the University of Michigan (U-M). All five library liaisons visited Michigan prior to the release of alpha and beta versions to pretest the game and share their approaches to recruiting instructors who would test BiblioBouts in their courses. We especially recognize Averill and Anita at SVSU, who were the first to identify prospective instructors and classes where BiblioBouts was deployed. At SVSU, they helped us implement the alpha version of BiblioBouts and assisted students when they had difficulties with its complicated registration procedure. Alyssa recruited several TUMC instructors and helped them incorporate BiblioBouts into their syllabus and assignments, deploy BiblioBouts in classes, troubleshoot technical problems, and conduct the evaluation. Catherine incorporated BiblioBouts into her information literacy courses, added the game to her syllabus, helped troubleshoot technical difficulties, and recruited and trained her colleagues to conduct the evaluation. Catherine and Alyssa also drafted applications to their institution's institutional review board and received approval to conduct the evaluation. The BiblioBouts team salutes the contributions of library liaisons generally and especially Alyssa and Catherine, whose dedication and hard work made it possible for UB and TUMC students to have a voice in the evaluation of BiblioBouts.

The first to deploy BiblioBouts was Professor Geoffrey V. Carter at SVSU, who welcomed the opportunity to engage his students in a research project. Following suit were Professor Sara Kosiba at TUMC; Catherine Johnson, library liaison at UB; and Professor Barry Fishman, the late Professor Robert L. Frost, Professor Clifford Lampe, global scholars director Dr. Jennifer Yim, and Dr. Loyd Mbabu at the U-M. Hats off to these faculty who deployed the earliest (alpha) version of BiblioBouts, encouraged their students to participate in the evaluation and were frank with us in postgame interviews about their deployment experiences so we could improve the game and bolster its user support services. It was a rocky road at times, but what we learned from those initial implementations we are able to pass onto future information literacy game designers to streamline their deployment efforts.

We made BiblioBouts' beta versions available to instructors for the asking, and in response instructors from institutions participating in the research project volunteered to implement BiblioBouts in their classes and take part in the evaluation. It was déjà vu all over again for TUMC Professor Kosiba, U-M global scholars director Dr. Yim, and UB library liaison Johnson, who implemented BiblioBouts a second time. Thanks to them and to Dr. Charles Taylor and lecturer Kelly E. Allen at U-M, who welcomed later versions BiblioBouts in their classes, encouraged their students to participate in its evaluation, and took part in postgame interviews with project staff.

We received requests for information about BiblioBouts from instructors in North America and around the world. We struck up a correspondence with several who expressed interest in BiblioBouts above and beyond just implementing the game in their classes and learned from their remarks in postgame interviews. Thanks to Professor Sherry Linkon at Youngstown State University, whose input improved the game's evaluation reports and game logs; Dr. Elaine Khoo at the University of Toronto Scarborough, whose understanding of how her students played the game helped us interpret evaluation results; Professor Roberta Kilkenny at Hunter College, who administered games in several successive semesters; information services librarian Joseph Hartnett at Baruch College's Newman Library, who administered games every year he taught his course; and distance learning librarian Amy Hofer at Portland State University's library, who articulated the librarian-instructor partnership that was required to deploy BiblioBouts. We are grateful to everyone involved in BiblioBouts' deployment and evaluation—students, instructors, library liaisons, and instruction librarians—for making it possible for us to study the game in situ so we could generalize about the effectiveness of online games for teaching information literacy skills and concepts.

Aiding us on home front were University of Michigan School of Information (UMSI) staff. In particular, we thank staff of UMSI's Research Administration and Accounting Offices. Director of research administration Rebecca O'Brien and research process coordinators Jocelyn Webber and Jill Jividen Goff helped us submit grant proposals and navigate the reallocation process afterwards. Hats off to associate accountant Nickie Rowsey and senior accounting clerk Christine Eccleston, who tended to the grants' financial matters and responded cheerfully to our frequent "how much money do we have left?" and "in what categories?" questions. Administrative assistant Bailey Oland helped us set up focus group interviews and library liaison visits. Thanks to transcriptionist Erin Peterson, whose accuracy and precision were so acute that we rarely if ever had to listen to original recordings to understand a passage.

We are especially grateful to our UMSI colleague Professor Kristin Fontichiaro, who read selected chapters, giving us substantive and thoughtful comments so that we could improve their content.

At Rowman & Littlefield, we salute executive editor Charles Harmon, who encouraged our efforts to write a book about designing games for information literacy, and Kellie Hagan and Robert Hayunga, who assisted in this book's final editing and production. At George Mason University's Center for History and New Media, Professor Sean Takats, director of research projects, assisted in the integration of Zotero into BiblioBouts. Freelance artist Brian Walline fashioned a bull's-eye banner that captured the essence of BiblioBouts—playing the game to target the best sources for a research paper.

Thanks to our proofer, Penny Duke, who shouldered the lion's share of the proofing burden.

The core BiblioBouts project team consisted of Andrew Calvetti, Brian Jennings, Chris Leeder, Karen Markey, Gregory R. Peters Jr., Soo Young Rieh, Victor Rosenberg, Beth St. Jean, Fritz Swanson, and Michele Wong. We are grateful to project consultant Fritz Swanson, who led the team's initial design efforts, drafting a game design document that described the new game's objectives, pedagogical goals, and scoring and conceiving a game that was a tournament made up of a series of mini-games or bouts, which would give students hands-on experience and practice conducting library research. Working with our programmer, Greg Peters, was a delight. He was honest, upfront, and articulate about what was possible in a reasonable amount of time and responded to everyone—fellow team members, student game players, instructor users, librarians—cheerfully, immediately, and substantively no matter what their concern, problem, or question. Giving form to everyone's game design verbiage was our team's original graphic designer, Brian Jennings, who transformed ideas into game interfaces and revised them in a workmanlike manner until everyone on the team was satisfied with the final outcome. When Brian graduated, Michele Wong did not miss a beat, adding her distinctive artistry and style to the game's interface. We are grateful to Professor Victor Rosenberg, who advised the team every step along the way and took the lead in the establishment of user support services and technology transfer. Andrew Calvetti handled user support inquiries. Whether responding via e-mail or in person, Andrew was inventive and crafty with troubleshooting tasks, figuring out solutions to problems that had us stumped. Special thanks to doctoral student Beth St. Jean, who came to the rescue of the game's scoring algorithm, building Excel-based scoring models to assess the impact of scoring changes and refine BiblioBouts' scoring algorithm so players who achieved the game's objectives placed atop the leader board. Last and not least, we are grateful for the efforts of masters-level students Caitlin Campbell, Meggan Frost, Sarah Lemire, Adrienne Matteson, Kimberly Miller, Meredith Raymond, and Emily Thompson, who assisted in analyzing data, coding game logs, transcribing interviews, and citing sources. We applaud all BiblioBouts team members, whose dedication to and unwavering support of the research project ensured its success.

Information literacy games are now in their infancy. Instructors, students, and librarians who played BiblioBouts and took part in its evaluation are therefore pioneers in this endeavor. To all, we express our heartfelt appreciation and gratitude. Our games and support services were tested in this research and subjected to a multimodal evaluation. The results enabled us to learn what works and what does not so we could give designers of future information literacy games advice that would be in harmony with player desires, perceptions, and needs.

Chapter One

The Promise of Games for Information Literacy Instruction

This chapter sets the stage for this book's focus on designing, developing, deploying, and evaluating online information literacy games by focusing on information literacy and games. First came calls for hosting video games in libraries, then encouragement for the development of game collections to support game studies programs, and finally interest in the development of online games for information literacy instruction. For a long time, the two developed independently, one hardly cognizant of the other, but the last decade has witnessed the intersection of the two. Even more recently, the development of online games for teaching students information literacy skills and concepts has picked up. Taking a back seat to information literacy game design and development is the evaluation of game effectiveness—demonstrating that students learn information literacy concepts and develop skills as a result of game play. Thus, this chapter includes research findings from the published literature on educational games generally to determine whether online games foster cognitive gains and improve students' attitudes toward and motivation for learning.

DEFINITIONS OF INFORMATION LITERACY

The first documented use of the term "information literacy" applied to work-related skills. Paul Zurkowski, president of the Information Industry Association (IIA), stated in a 1974 proposal to the National Commission on Libraries and Information Sciences (NCLIS) that "people trained in the application of information resources to their work can be called information literates." The report discussed the needs of workers in emerging information technology environments and raised policy questions regarding the relationship between libraries and the private sector (Behrens 1994). It suggested that NCLIS establish the goal of achieving national information literacy in the ensuing decade. In a later report, Eugene Garfield, founder of the Institute for Scientific Information (ISI), which was a partner in creating the IIA, presented a broader version of Zurkowski's definition—"The IIA defines an 'information literate' as a person who knows the techniques and skills for using information tools in molding solutions to problems"—and characterized the content of such training as "methods of information handling" (1979, 210). The focus of both Zurkowski's and Garfield's definitions was on the work-related skills of a successful employee in an increasingly complex information environment.

In the 1970s, several important professional organizations were formed that focused on information literacy: (1) the Library Orientation Exchange (LOEX), a "self-supporting, non-profit educational clearinghouse for library instruction and information literacy information" (LOEX 2013); (2) the Instruction Section (IS) of the Association of College and Research Libraries (ACRL); and (3) the Library Instruction Roundtable (LIRT) of the American Library Association (ALA) (Gilton 2004). These organizations effected a shift in information literacy instruction in academic institutions from library tours and orientations to conceptual frameworks, research strategies, and learning theory (Gilton 2004).

A 1983 report by the National Commission on Excellence in Education titled *A Nation at Risk* decried the contemporary state of American education but ignored the role of libraries in education (Behrens 1994). In response, the ALA formed the 1989 Presidential Committee on Information Literacy, which issued its own charter report bearing a description of information literacy that became the springboard for the field's current understanding of the concept (Eisenberg, Lowe, and Spitzer 2004). The ALA's canonical definition of information literacy—"to be information literate, a person must be able to recognize when information is needed and have the ability to locate, evaluate, and use effectively the needed information" (1989)—underlies the BiblioBouts information literacy game.

In 2000, ACRL, the ALA's academic libraries division, issued *Information Literacy Competency Standards for Higher Education*, providing "a framework for assessing the information literate individual." Referring back to the original ALA definition, the ACRL definition added that information literacy is "a set of abilities requiring individuals to 'recognize when information is needed and have the ability to locate, evaluate, and use effectively the needed information.'" The ACRL definition has been the common starting point for librarians in higher education who design information literacy instruction (Bobish 2011; Allen 2008).

The American Association of School Librarians (AASL), the ALA division that focuses on K–12 librarianship, and the Association for Educational Communications and Technology (AECT) created a set of standards focused on teaching information literacy skills to elementary school students. *Information Power: Building Partnerships for Learning* (AASL and AECT 1998) redefined the role of the library media specialist as actively engaged in education efforts (Eisenberg, Lowe, and Spitzer 2004). The standards included Information Literacy Standards for Student Learning, which state that an information literate student "accesses information efficiently and effectively" (Standard 1), "evaluates information critically and competently" (Standard 2), and "uses information accurately and creatively" (Standard 3). These criteria clearly echo the original 1989 ALA definition. In 2007, the AASL issued the new *Standards for the 21st-Century Learner*, which extended the criteria to a broader educational framework focused on skills, dispositions, responsibilities, and self-assessment strategies. Information literacy elements are now described as "applying critical-thinking skills (analysis, synthesis, evaluation, organization) to information and knowledge in order to construct new understandings, draw conclusions, and create new knowledge" (AASL 2007).

Other professional organizations have also developed standards for skills development. The National Leadership Council for Liberal Education and America's Promise (NLCLEAP) and the Association of American Colleges and Universities (AACU) identified information literacy as one of the essential learning outcomes for all students in the twenty-first century (NLCLEAP 2007). "A coalition of business community, education leaders, and policymakers," the Partnership for 21st Century Skills (2011) advocates "21st century readiness for every student," identifying specific "skills, knowledge and expertise students should master to succeed in work and life in the 21st century" in its *Framework for 21st Century Learning*. These include "Learning and Innovation Skills" (characterized as creativity and innovation, critical thinking and problem solving, and communication and collaboration) and "Information, Media and Technology Skills" (characterized as information literacy, media literacy, and information and communications technology—known as ICT—literacy). The International Society for Technology in Education (ISTE), a professional association for educators using technology in K–12 classrooms, has developed the National Educational Technology Standards for Students (NETS•S). Described as "standards for evaluating the skills and knowledge students need to learn effectively and live productively in an increasingly global and digital world," NETS•S includes subsections on "Research and Information Fluency" (described as applying digital tools to gather, evaluate, and use information) and "Critical Thinking, Problem Solving, and Decision Making" (using critical thinking to plan and conduct research) (ISTE 2007). There is a growing consensus that information literacy and related competencies such as critical thinking and problem solving are essential for individual and community empowerment, workforce readiness, and global competitiveness (Weiner 2012).

In 2010, the Common Core State Standards Initiative (CCSSI) released new English Language Arts and Mathematics Standards for elementary and secondary students. Adopted by over forty states since their issuance, CCSSI standards reference information literacy skills as "key design considerations," representing them as "cross-disciplinary literacy expectations that must be met for students to be prepared to enter college and workforce training programs ready to succeed" (CCSSI 2010, 4). While the CCSSI standards do not use the term "information literacy," K–12 students are expected to be able to conduct original research, engage in credibility assessment, and understand and synthesize information.

THE EVOLVING CONCEPT
OF INFORMATION LITERACY INSTRUCTION

Early "library instruction" efforts focused on teaching young people in academic settings how to locate and use library resources. Librarians at both K–12 and higher education institutions taught students how to access the library's books and other print resources and oriented them to the structural aspects of libraries such as facilities, classification, and organization (Behrens 1994). This form of instruction has been given a number of related names over time, including "library skills," "user education," and "bibliographic instruction." The evolution of these terms reflects the changing focus of information literacy instruction as it has developed through different phases, each with its own definitions and implementations.

Among the earliest ventures are B. Lamar Johnson's establishment of an instruction program at Stephens College in the 1930s, Louis Shores's 1935 publication of an article about "library colleges" in 1935, and Harvey Branscomb's 1940 publication of *Teaching with Books*, which explored collaborations between instructors and librarians (Gilton 2004). Two early groundbreaking initiatives pioneered the practice of library instruction. Patricia Knapp's Monteith Experiment at Wayne State University from 1960 to 1962 integrated library instruction into students' course work and featured problem solving, authentic learning, and instruction that was a series of interventions over time (Thomas 2004, 10). At Earlham College in the 1960s, Evan Farber collaborated with faculty to embed library instruction into academic course work. They implemented a planned sequence of instructional sessions, utilizing a "just-in-time" approach to student learning (Thomas 2004, 11).

Researchers in the field have defined historical trends in information literacy practice by characterizing eras or periods of development. Sundin (2005, 38–39) divides information training into four major periods:

- Pre-1960s: Focus on librarians as experts on information sources
- 1960s and 1970s: Focus on information-seeking behavior as a generic and individual skill or technical practice (behaviorist model)
- 1980s and early 1990s: Focus on the information-seeking process from the perspective of the user (constructivist model)
- 1990s to present: Focus on how information-seeking practices are shaped by social practices (sociocultural model)

Alternatively, Bruce (2000, 92–93) identifies four chronological phases:

- Precursors (1980s): Origins in information skills or bibliographic instruction, focus on educational research and model development
- Experimental (1990–1995): Introduction of the term "information literacy," focus on surveys and curriculum development
- Exploratory (1995–1999): Advocacy for information literacy by librarians and government reports, integration into educational agendas
- Evolving (2000s): Growth in research beyond the educational sector, application of information literacy knowledge and skills to the workplace and community

Each stage represents an expansion and development of the prior stages, and there is always overlap. The field's gradual adoption of the term "information literacy" has been accompanied by a shift in focus from library instruction in the use of particular information artifacts to shaping user behavior (Sundin 2005), from teaching tool-based skills to teaching transferable skills and competencies (Owusu-Ansah 2004; Špiranec and Zorica 2010), and from the traditional definition of librarians as collectors and curators of resources to an identification of them as information specialists and teachers (Thomas 2004). Compared to bibliographic instruction, which focuses on mastery of a discrete set of skills, information literacy has a more theoretical base, assumes lifelong learning, focuses on learners' information needs, and involves the evaluation and use of information (Gilton 2004).

The emergence of the Internet and the World Wide Web have had a profound impact on information literacy instruction. Because the Web is the starting point for most people's search for information (Becker 2003;

Costello, Lenholt, and Stryker 2004; Curtis 2000; Swanson 2005), the online sources they find are likely to be missing conventional quality-control mechanisms and indicators of authority that are built into traditional print-based information materials due to their issuance by publishers (Gasser et al. 2012; Rieh 2002). Quality-assessment protocols based on the material format of documents no longer map onto online resources (Sundin and Francke 2009). The volume of online sources, their diversity, and the proliferation of new formats have also made traditional evaluation protocols obsolete and forced the field to develop new ones (Metzger, Flanagin, and Medders 2010). In the online information environment, the traditional library-based research model based on information scarcity and expert authority has been problematized. The abundance of information sources available online and their lack of traditional markers of authority present new challenges to both information seekers and information literacy instructors.

Meeting these challenges with the development and deployment of online information literacy games makes sense because students now find information online due to their familiarity with Google, Wikipedia, and the Web and because accessing online information is more convenient than fetching materials from a library. Online is also where students have to be (but are often not) especially circumspect about the sources they find because of the absence of traditional markers of authority. The evaluation of online sources figures prominently in the design of the BiblioBouts information literacy game (chapters 3 and 5).

MULTIPLE APPROACHES TO
THE INFORMATION LITERACY CONCEPT

Three distinct approaches characterize the conceptualization of information literacy programs: (1) information literacy as a set of skills and attributes, (2) information literacy as knowledge construction, and (3) information literacy as enabling critical thinking (Kerr 2010).

The most pervasive conceptualization is information literacy as information skills acquisition with the purpose of achieving discrete outcomes. This approach is rooted in library skills instruction, including teaching students about specific library resources. It ascribes a list of discrete attributes to an information literate person, such as the ability to recognize the need for information, formulate questions based on information needs, develop search strategies, access sources of information, and evaluate information (Kerr 2010). Johnston and Webber (2003) criticize this skills approach because it takes a surface rather than a deep approach to the ways in which students make sense of information. Some authors cite limitations to skills-based information literacy programs, especially with regard to enhancing student learning (Limberg 1999; Lupton 2002); others (Kuhlthau 2004; Lloyd 2005; Todd 2000) criticize it because they believe it reduces the effect of information literacy. Instead of skills development, these scholars promote the constructivist approach, which characterizes information literacy as a process of knowledge construction. Kuhlthau asserts that "students should engage in issues and projects that involve them in raising questions, seeking information from a wide variety of resources, changing their questions as they learn, identifying what they need to know more about, demonstrating what they have learned, and sharing their new understandings with a community of learners" (2004, 163). Ultimately, embracing the skills-based approach may be a practical decision on the part of librarians in schools and colleges because the limited contact time they have with students forces them to boil down deep information literacy conceptual thinking into a series of steps that they can teach in a half hour or less.

Other researchers and practitioners see critical thinking as a foundational value in information literacy. The ACRL's Information Literacy Competency Standards for Higher Education include "critical discernment and reasoning" as a component of information literacy (ALA 2000, 3). This approach promotes instructional strategies that include source analysis, reasoning and argumentation, problem-based learning, collaboration, inquiry learning, and scaffolding strategies to assist students in reflecting on their own learning (Kerr 2010).

Presenting a unique approach for teaching information literacy are Bruce, Edwards, and Lupton (2006), who encourage practitioners to introduce students to complex ways of interacting with information within the following frames: knowledge about the world of information (content), a set of competencies or skills (competency), a way of learning (learning to learn), contextual and situational social practices (personal relevance), and power relationships in society and social responsibility (social impact). Others have developed practical guides with lesson plans in order to enhance critical thinking in information literacy programs (Gordon 2000; Thomas 2004).

METHODS OF INFORMATION LITERACY INSTRUCTION

While librarians, administrators, and faculty members support the idea that students need to learn information literacy competencies, there is less consensus about who should teach information literacy and what should be taught and when (Saunders 2012). As a result, students may graduate from high school and even college bereft of formal instruction in information literacy. Below are the major methods used for information literacy instruction at the higher education level.

For-credit or not-for-credit stand-alone courses. The stand-alone course is the most traditional form of library instruction, featuring a full- or half-semester class with a syllabus, learning objectives, assignments, and hands-on experience using information resource discovery tools. Badke advocates teaching information literacy as a stand-alone course, stating that "there is simply too much to learn and too large a learning curve on the way to becoming skillful" (2008, 48). Librarians at the University of Florida created a three-credit course for science students to develop research skills focusing on retrieval and evaluation of information, scientific literature searching, online search tools, scholarly publication models, and open access (Johnson and Gonzalez 2010, 105–6). Librarians at the University of Wisconsin–Madison, teach a one-credit course to College of Engineering students that orients students to literature types, research tools, and information strategies, with the goal of preparing them not only for their course work but also for future job searches and real-life engineering tasks (Wheeler, Vallardita, and Kindschi 2010).

Since the late 1990s, information literacy courses have transitioned either partially or completely online to take advantage of the availability of the Internet and to increase the pool of potential students (Holder 2010). Critics of the stand-alone course method warn that "if students do not immediately apply their information literacy skills to a content-based course assignment, they tend not to recognize the relevance of such skills to other courses" (Jacobson and Mark 2000, 261). To avoid critics leveling accusations of this same shortcoming at information literacy games, we promote games that students play while they complete a related assignment so that they develop their skills right there and then and come to recognize the practical importance of the skills they have exercised (see page 191).

Web-based online instruction. In response to students' calls for flexible and convenient educational opportunities, academic librarians have explored online instruction as an option. Typically, multimodal learning objects such as text, graphic, audio, video, and instant messaging are used. For instance, University of Texas instructor-librarians present materials via a course website containing instructional modules, assigned readings, streaming multimedia lectures, synchronous multiuser and one-on-one chat, discussion boards, and online tutorials for hands-on exercises (Chen and Williams 2009). Librarians at the University of Arizona have developed an online for-credit information literacy course for a freshman writing program (Mery et al. 2010). Writing program staff and librarians have collaborated on the development of online tools and tutorials that feature audio in place of text, an informal tone for the spoken word, interactive tutorials with manipulatable on-screen elements, graphics that illustrate concepts and procedures visually, and self-assessments at key points to maintain students' attention and interest (Mery et al. 2010, 82–83). Critics of this method point out that it might not appeal to students who lack confidence using technology on their own and suggest that such students might take the course but opt out when technologies dominate.

Online tutorial. The online tutorial method features Web-based documentation describing information literacy tools, concepts, and skills (Kerr 2010). Librarians at the University of Illinois at Chicago have developed a highly interactive, animated tutorial that introduces undergraduate students to basic information literacy concepts such as selecting keywords for online searches, identifying synonyms and related terms, using Boolean operators, and understanding cited references (Armstrong and Georgas 2006). The tutorial is economical with regard to text, relying instead on multimedia effects to convey basic concepts and involve users in the ongoing discussion.

Course-related instruction. Course-related instruction depends on librarians' success at convincing academic instructors to incorporate information literacy instruction in their courses. Such instruction is often a single lesson devoted to research skills or strategies, and librarians strive to coordinate the instruction with each course's learning objectives, content, and disciplinary coverage. Typically, librarians introduce students to the library's database portal and demonstrate use of the library catalog and one or two databases that are relevant to the course's discipline. They emphasize portal databases as sources of scholarly information where the need for credibility assessment is less urgent than it is on the open Web. Because class time is limited, librarians are only able to give a surface-level treatment to most topics. As a result, instructional librarians tend to rely on online demonstrations instead of hands-on experimentation by students, and they are limited by time constraints in their ability to engage students in discussions or experiential learning that fosters critical thinking. Both librarians and students are critical of this approach, the former pointing out its inability to make much headway in terms of producing information literate students and the latter wanting instruction that is engaging and customized to their information needs (Kim and Sin 2011; Ward 2006).

Course-integrated instruction. Librarians advocate information literacy instruction that is an integral part of the academic curriculum in the form of individual courses and collaboration between librarians and academic instructors (Anderson and May 2010). Because information literacy instruction is embedded in academic courses, this method enables students to have repeated and meaningful experiences with information sources and search processes in specific disciplines (Kim and Sin 2011). Exemplary in this regard is the University of Baltimore, where students enroll simultaneously in three classes—information literacy, social science, and humanities—taught by three instructors who identify a common theme that unifies the proceedings across the three classes (Johnson et al. 2010). Students immediately put to work what they learn in the information literacy class: conducting library research for assignments in the social science and/or humanities courses, such as creating a business plan that cites published literature to trace industry regulations over time. Another example is King's College (Tennessee), where librarians collaborate with English Department instructors, the latter focusing on writing instruction and the former on reference sources, website evaluation, creation of annotated bibliographies, and citation style (Roberson and Horton 2010).

Web 2.0. Librarians have responded to young people's fondness for Web 2.0 tools by integrating them into information literacy instruction. Web 2.0 encourages and reinforces engagement and interactivity among individuals, thus providing new opportunities for information literacy instruction. Luo (2010) surveys librarians and their adoption of Web 2.0 and enlists a three-level hierarchy to characterize librarians' Web 2.0 usage: (1) 4 percent of survey respondents use Web 2.0 tools to organize and manage course-related material for their own purposes, (2) 84 percent use Web 2.0 tools to facilitate the delivery of content to students, and (3) 38 percent draw upon certain features of Web 2.0 technologies to better illustrate information literacy concepts. Because most students are only adept at Web 2.0 technologies for social interaction and entertainment, Luo (2010) admits that a limitation of this approach is the need to ramp up student use of Web 2.0 tools generally.

A number of studies investigate the impact of different information literacy instruction methods in terms of students' learning outcomes. Results are inconsistent. For instance, Schilling (2002) notes that students using the online tutorial method performed better MEDLINE searches than students who received traditional instructor-led training. In contrast, a second study reports the opposite (Churkovich and Oughtred 2002), and two more studies report no significant differences between alternate methods (Silver and Nickel 2005; Anderson and May 2010).

Students' preference for *online* over classroom instruction seems to be consistent in terms of delivering information literacy instruction (Michel 2001; Silver and Nickel 2005). This book's emphasis on online games for information literacy instruction is in keeping with this finding. It makes sense to put information literacy instruction online, where students do their work.

RESEARCH ON THE BENEFITS
OF INFORMATION LITERACY INSTRUCTION

Details of the few empirical studies that have investigated the impact of information literacy instruction on students' academic performance, self-reported skill usage, attitudes, self-efficacy, and confidence are given here, starting with surveys and self-reports.

Over two thousand students were surveyed after taking a one-credit information literacy course at Louisiana State University. They reported that they continued to use the materials and skills they learned to complete course work and conduct personal research throughout their college careers (Daugherty and Russo 2011). Of the fifty-one incoming Florida State University students participating in a survey, the higher-achieving students (based on high school grade point average [GPA] and SAT/ACT scores) were more likely to have received formal information literacy instruction (Gross and Latham 2007). The self-efficacy scores of eighty-five Rutgers University students enrolled in an introductory English composition course increased after they received instruction in electronic information searching (Ren 2000). About seven hundred Hong Kong University of Science and Technology students who received information instruction reported that they retained and used the information literacy skills they learned and appreciated the usefulness of the instruction (Wong, Chan, and Chu 2006).

Researchers analyzed the sources cited by approximately 140 Florida Gulf Coast University students in their term papers and reported that the students who received information literacy instruction cited more books, more types of sources, and more overall sources than students who did not receive such instruction (Cooke and Rosenthal 2011). A similar analysis of the term papers written by 120 Central Michigan University students concluded that students who had taken an information literacy course cited more scholarly resources, produced fewer incomplete citations, and received significantly higher grades for papers than a comparable group of students who had not taken the course (Wang 2006). A statistically significant improvement in GPA was found for about 240 University of California, Irvine, students who had completed a library instruction course over students who had not (Selegean, Thomas, and Richman 1983). Merely attending information literacy instruction resulted in a positive correlation with final GPA for four hundred Hong Kong University of Science and Technology students (Wong and Cmor 2011). In an experiment at a large research university, about two hundred students were divided into treatment and control groups, with the former receiving information literacy instruction and the latter receiving no such instruction. Treatment group students reported experiencing significantly less overall library anxiety than the control group (Van Scoyoc 2003).

Because librarians have put their energy into the design and deployment of information literacy programs rather than into their assessment, program descriptions and attitudinal studies abound, and experimental studies are few and far between (Walsh 2009; Beile 2003). Urgently needed is empirical research that demonstrates a cause-and-effect relationship between knowledge of information literacy concepts and academic performance so that the profession can make convincing arguments about the need to institutionalize information literacy programs in schools and colleges. Assessing the impact of game play on students' academic performance was an important goal of our games research. Our evaluation involved a comparison of the sources players and nonplayers cited in their final papers and instructors' observations about the papers written by students who did and did not play the game (chapters 10 and 11, respectively).

BARRIERS TO INFORMATION LITERACY INSTRUCTION

Information literacy instruction is not a given in schools, colleges, and universities due to a host of barriers. McCarthy (1985) was among the first to observe the "faculty problem," that is, faculty apathy toward or outright obstruction of information literacy instruction. Several explanations have been proffered for this problem. Many faculty consider librarians as support staff and providers of support services instead of partners in the educational enterprise (Owusu-Ansah 2004; Manuel, Beck, and Molloy 2005; McGuinness 2006); they feel that librarians are not qualified to teach (Saunders 2012); they are unwilling to cede valuable in-class time to librarians (Hardesty 1995; Breivik and Jones 1993; Owusu-Ansah 2004; Hrycaj and Russo 2007); they do not connect with librarians' language, standards, and outcomes and consider information literacy instruction to be an administrative or bureaucratic imposition (Bell 2011). Given these challenges, the onus has been on librarians to initiate and maintain discussions with faculty about information literacy instruction and to be proactive about building collaborative relationships (Saunders 2012).

While college faculty appear to value information literacy competencies, they do not necessarily agree about how students should be taught these skills (Saunders 2012). Some instructors expect that students will acquire the necessary competencies on their own—for example, by writing research papers, by working with other students, or simply through exposure to sources (McGuinness 2006). Others assume that students received instruction in high school, in college orientation, or in introductory courses or that teaching these skills is someone else's responsibility (Saunders 2012). Regardless of the rationale, few instructors actively integrate information literacy knowledge and skills into their courses in a systematic way (McGuinness 2006; Saunders 2012).

Only a small percentage of higher education institutions with first-year experience programs include a required information literacy component (Boff and Johnson 2002). When information literacy instruction is available, it is usually located on the periphery of the curriculum. The lack of consistent, uniform program implementation in the curriculum creates a tension between the official standards and competencies models developed by library leaders, library associations, and national committees on one hand, and the practical experience of librarians who deliver the instruction on the other.

Even when librarians successfully work with faculty to bring information literacy instruction into the classroom, instructors allocate so little time that the instruction becomes a singular event, and efforts to promote conceptual understanding must be reduced to skills demonstrations. Librarians fill the available time with coverage of the most basic topics (van Meegen and Limpens 2010), leaving no time for students to practice what they have learned (Mokhtar, Majid, and Foo 2008; Mery, Newby, and Peng 2012). Students complain that one-shot sessions are boring and do not address their specific needs or interests (Smale 2011; van Meegen and Limpens 2010; Doshi 2006). Because students have inflated views of their own information literacy skills, they disregard information literacy instruction, thinking that it applies to others but not to them (Gross and Latham 2007).

So many obstacles stand in the way of successful integration of information literacy instruction in K–12 and college classrooms. While librarians have been tremendously resourceful in attempting to overcome these obstacles in their efforts to reach as wide an audience as possible for such instruction, the time is right to explore the potential of games for teaching young people information literacy concepts and skills.

GAMES AND LEARNING

Because the literature on "serious," or educational, games is extensive and covers many disciplines and game genres, this discussion is limited to the characteristics of games that promote learning. In his influential and highly cited book *What Video Games Have to Teach Us about Learning and Literacy*, James Paul Gee argues that "games are potentially particularly good places where people can learn to situate meanings through embodied experiences in a complex semiotic domain and meditate on the process" (2003, 26).

Gee (2005) suggests not that what people learn from playing video games is always good but that what they are doing when they play good video games is often good learning. He presents a list of thirty-six principles of learning that are built into good video games, including active and critical learning, meta-level thinking, practice, probing, and the presentation of needed information on-demand and just-in-time (2003, 207–12). Games encourage players to think of themselves as active problem solvers, to persist in solving problems even after making mistakes, and to consider mistakes not as errors but as opportunities for reflection and learning. Gee contends that "the theory of learning in good video games fits better with the modern, high-tech, global world today's children and teenagers live in than do the theories (and practices) of learning that they see in school" (2003, 7).

Another early proponent of game-based learning is Marc Prensky (2001a), who asserts that the cognitive benefits of games, such as establishing objectives, learning rules, perceiving relationships, and determining priorities, are important ways of thinking for learners. Interactive features of games such as practice and feedback, learning by doing, learning from mistakes, and observing expert players at work benefit gamers (Prensky 2001a, 157). Prensky (2001a, 117) also suggests that game play fosters learning because people are likely to put more time, effort, and concentration into playful activities.

Yet another early proponent is Steven Johnson (2006, 14), who argues in *Everything Bad Is Good for You* that games, as well as other forms of popular culture, can be seen as "cognitive workouts" that force players to decide, choose, and prioritize. Critical thinking skills, such as weighing evidence, analyzing situations, and consulting one's long-term goals, are integral to the design of many games (Johnson 2006). Games also allow students to make mistakes in a safe environment and to learn from them (Whitton 2010). Gamers must read, process, and use information to make decisions (Levine 2006b, 14–15). They must form theories and test their thinking against simulated outcomes, reinforcing analytical, critical-thinking, and evaluation skills (Squire and Jenkins 2003). Games encourage collaboration among players, providing a context for peer-to-peer teaching and for the emergence of learning communities (Squire and Jenkins 2003). Martin and Ewing state, "Games excel at engaging and motivating players to learn new skills and knowledge without realizing they are in the midst of the learning process" (2008, 223).

Games also appeal to the technological savvy of the current generation of high school and college students. Born after 1982, they are called "digital natives," "Millennials," and "Net Geners," because, unlike previous generations, they have always had information technology and mass media at their fingertips and in view (Prensky 2001b). Tapscott describes them as a generation that, having grown up on digital media, is "learning, playing, communicating, working, and creating communities very differently than their parents" (1998, 2). The Digital natives are used to receiving information fast, and they thrive on instant gratification, frequent rewards, parallel processing, and multitasking (Prensky 2001a, 2001b). They have little tolerance for delays, expect rapid feedback in learning environments, and prefer teamwork, experiential activities, structure, and the use of technology (Palfrey and Gasser 2008). Gaming fits the learning style of digital natives, who prefer learning by doing over listening to explanations from a teacher in front of the class (van Meegen and Limpens 2010). They do not see themselves as receptacles to be filled with content: they want to be creators and doers (Prensky 2001a). Because commercial games are already a ubiquitous part of digital natives' lives (Shute and Ventura 2013; Leach and Sugarman 2006; Lenhart, Jones, and Macgill 2008), the medium of games offers an opportunity to engage today's young people in learning in ways that are suited to their habits, attitudes, and learning styles.

THE RISE OF GAMES IN LIBRARIES

With a few exceptions, such as Kirriemuir's (2002) review of video gaming and education and Thistlethwaite's (2001) Web-based Data Game, it took until mid-decade for librarians to begin to assess the potential of games in libraries. Christy Branston (2006) hosted a game-themed issue of the *Bulletin of the American Society for Information Science and Technology* in April–May 2006 in which she forecasted three growth areas for games in libraries: offering games and gaming tournaments, teaching information literacy, and building collections to support game studies programs in higher education. Mobilization of the field to commit to games in one or more of these three areas was due to Jenny Levine's pioneering efforts. She promoted games in libraries on her Shifted Librarian blog, focused two issues of *Library Technology Reports* on games in libraries, and hosted conferences on games in libraries in summer 2007 and fall 2008 (Levine 2006a, 2006b; Levine 2008).

By the end of the decade, college librarians routinely supported collection development for game studies programs (Harris and Rice 2008; B. Smith 2008). Available were three books on hosting games and gaming tournaments (Neiburger 2009; Galloway 2009; Nicholson 2010), and the ALA added its endorsement by establishing "national gaming@your library day" and celebrating it on the covers of two issues of *American Libraries* ("Popular Games" 2009; Farmer 2010). By the beginning of the new decade, articles describing the characteristics of games that promote learning and the design of online information literacy games were so commonplace that several literature reviews were available (Broussard 2011a; McDevitt 2011; Gumulak and Webber 2011; Smale 2011).

GAMES FOR INFORMATION LITERACY INSTRUCTION

Levine (2006b) enlists this four-step looping process to capture the essence of playing video games: (1) probing a virtual world; (2) based on such probing, generating hypotheses about how to proceed; (3) simultaneously proceeding and observing the effect of doing so (i.e., the game's feedback); and (4) accepting or rethinking one's original hypotheses. Additionally, she suggests similarities between this looping process and the scientific method. Waelchli (2008) echoes her sentiments, pointing out that successful video game players must determine what information is needed to solve a problem, then locate, evaluate, and apply it to specific game situations—tasks that clearly parallel the traditional information literacy skills that librarians teach. Games encourage iterative probing for information, supporting the development of logical thinking and problem-solving skills (Kirriemuir 2008). Interviews with video game players have shown that players carry out information-seeking and -evaluation activities focused on solving problems (Gumulak and Webber 2011; Steinkuhler 2007). Branston tells how video game players do not shirk from conducting a "vast" search for secondary material to support their game play and improve their standing in the game, and she claims that "the ideal situation would be if we can incorporate information literacy and research skills into a game that teaches information literacy" (2006; 26). VanLeer (2006) describes how the World of Warcraft video game meets all four ACRL information literacy standards. Collaborating with librarians at the New York Public Library, pioneering game designer Jane McGonigal wants people to channel the same energy they experience during game play—curiosity, optimism, pride, a desire to join forces with others, positive emotion, strong social relationships, a sense of purpose—into solving the world's most difficult problems (Hohmann 2011). According to Doshi, the learning potential of games lies in their ability to immerse students in real-world situations where "the concept of information literacy loses its abstract, theoretical quality and becomes a relevant part of their lives" (2006). Robertson and Jones reflect on the parallels between information literacy instruction and video games, especially how they make "independent researchers confident in their abilities to locate and use valid information both in physical and digital formats" (2009, 261). They ask rhetorically, Why not employ games explicitly to teach information literacy?

Games offer several advantages over traditional approaches to information literacy instruction: active learning (Leach and Sugarman 2006), interactivity, (Doshi 2006; van Meegen and Limpens 2010; Martin and Ewing 2008), the opportunity to see experts and more experienced players at work (Markey et al. 2008b), communication with fellow players (Martin and Ewing 2008), reflection (Martin and Ewing 2008), practice and trial-and-error experimentation (Markey et al. 2008b; Martin and Ewing 2008), and unique features such as power ups, fantasy, and feedback (Martin and Ewing 2008). Several writers advocate game-based learning because information literacy skills and research behavior are intrinsic to video games (Branston 2006; Doshi 2006; Martin and Ewing 2008; VanLeer 2006; Waelchli 2008; Smale 2011). Other points on which multiple writers agree include the ability of games to replace student boredom and apathy with fun, enthusiasm, and interest (Doshi 2006; F. Smith 2007; Martin and Ewing 2008) and to dispatch game players into the state of flow, "a psychological state where [players are] . . . so involved . . . that nothing else seems to matter" (Martin and Ewing 2008, 214). By the end of the decade, the field's calls for games for information literacy instruction were met with game design, development, deployment, and evaluation efforts.

ONLINE INFORMATION LITERACY GAMES

Librarians have used both offline and online games to teach students information literacy concepts and skills. Almost all of the information literacy games in the book *Let the Games Begin!* are played offline (McDevitt 2011); other reviews of offline information games are available (B. Smith 2008; van Meegen and Limpens 2010).

To our knowledge, Thistlethwaite's (2001) Data Game was the first online information literacy game. Composed of several mini-games, Data Game was developed and deployed at Colorado State University to teach students basic research skills and informally evaluated for usability. The development and evaluation of *online* information literacy games took off in the second half of the decade. A search of the literature resulted in almost two dozen online information literacy games. Table 1.1 cites these games and characterizes their instructional content in these broad terms:

- Citations: Identifying the elements of bibliographic citations and using these elements to generate new citations
- Library research: Presenting topics such as keyword searching, choosing the right databases, differentiating between scholarly and nonscholarly

literature, finding library materials using call numbers, and assigning tags
or subject headings to sources
- Library orientation: Introducing students to the physical layout and services
  of the campus library
- Plagiarism: Describing what it is and how to avoid it

To characterize the evaluations of online information literacy games, we adopted Mayer's (2011) six categories of educational game research. Because
of their rigor, Mayer recommended evaluations characterized by the first
three evaluation categories only.

1. Value-added: Game features that promote learning
2. Cognitive consequences: What people learn as a result of playing the game
3. Media comparison: Whether people learn better from a game or conventional media
4. Advocacy: Opinion-based scholarship that makes strong claims based on
   weak evidence
5. Anything-but-learning: Players' affective responses to the game
6. Let's-see-what-happens: Analyses of activity logs or player video with no
   theory to guide the analysis

When the evaluation was anecdotal and/or did not investigate the effects of
the game on students, the "evaluation type" cell was left blank in table 1.1.
Table 1.1 lists twenty-two games. Over half focus on library research. Only
seven games enlist recommended evaluation types, and the rest enlist non-
recommended types. What we know about the effectiveness of information
literacy games is specific to each of these seven games.

Saving Asia players competed against one another to achieve the position
of junior advisor to an Asian country that had been hit by a tsunami (van Meegen and Limpens 2010). Citation Tic Tac Toe asks players questions about
citations and rewards correct answers with an X in a box on an online game
grid (McCabe and Wise 2009). Their respective evaluations were the most
rigorous of the seven involving pre- and post-tests to assess learning. Because
player scores exceeded nonplayer scores, the researchers concluded that Saving Asia and Citation Tic Tac Toe players learned more than nonplayers.

The Metadata Game was not an information literacy game per se, but because players had to scrutinize the visual content of images to describe what
they depicted, its content was classified as library research. This game's
evaluation revealed that players ignored the tags they assigned to images,
focusing instead on the "clarity of play, the reward system, competing and
collaborating with friends, and the overall feel of the game play experience"
(Flanagan and Carini 2012, 534).

Table 1.1. Online Information Literacy Games

Game	Citation	Content	Evaluation Type
Data Game	Thistlethwaite (2001)	Library research	
Muckrakers	Brown, Ceccarini, and Eisenhower (2007)	Library research	
Benevolent Blue	Clyde and Thomas (2008)	Library orientation	
Bioactive	Gonzalez et al. (2008)	Library orientation	
Blood on the Stacks	Donald (2008)	Library orientation	Anything-but-learning
Defense of Hidgeon	Markey et al. (2008b)	Library research	Cognitive consequences, let's-see-what-happens
Information Literacy Game	Rice (2008)	Library research	Anything-but-learning
Quarantined!	Gallegos and Allgood (2008)	Library research	Cognitive consequences, anything-but-learning
Within Range, I'll Get It	Beck et al. (2008)	Library research	
Citation Tic Tac Toe	McCabe and Wise (2009)	Citations	Cognitive consequences, media comparison
Head Hunt	O'Hanlon, Diaz, and Roecker (2009)	Library orientation	
Magnetic Keyword	McCabe and Wise (2009)	Library research	Anything-but-learning
Chemical Instrumentation Game	Henderson (2010)	Library research	Anything-but-learning
Saving Asia	van Meegen and Limpens (2010)	Library research	Cognitive consequences, media comparison
Get a Clue/LibraryCraft	Smith and Baker (2011)	Library orientation, library research	Anything-but-learning
Goblin Threat	Broussard (2011b); Broussard and Oberlin (2011)	Plagiarism/citations	Anything-but-learning
It's Alive!	Broussard (2011c)	Library research	Cognitive consequences, anything-but-learning
Nightmare on Vine Street	Baker, Shanley, and Wilkinson (2011)	Library orientation	
Planet in Peril	Sitler et al. (2011)	Plagiarism, citations	
Project Velius	Battles, Glenn, and Shedd (2011)	Library orientation	Let's-see-what-happens
Metadata Game	Flanagan and Carini (2012)	Library research	Cognitive consequences
Secret Agents in the Library	Broussard (2013)	Library research	Cognitive consequences, anything-but-learning

Quarantined! was an adventure game in which players used their information literacy skills to contain a deadly virus outbreak on campus, including avoiding contagious students and professors (Gallegos and Allgood 2008; Gallegos, Allgood, and Grondin 2007). Students' answers to pre- and post-game questions revealed increased understanding of some concepts (e.g., keyword searches, online catalogs, the circulation desk) and continued lack of understanding of others (e.g., citations, genre, call numbers).

To play It's Alive!, students assumed the role of a mad scientist and answered questions about conducting research in biology while collecting body parts to build a monster (Broussard 2011c). When the game ended, students were anonymously surveyed about what they learned from the game. The majority of students indicated that they felt prepared and had learned about databases and other library topics. Only after playing Secret Agents in the Library were students tested about their knowledge of the game's information literacy content (Broussard 2013). They scored high overall (92 percent) but faltered on three questions about library databases, scholarly journals, and Boolean searching.

To advance in the online board game Defense of Hidgeon, players had to consult library sources of various genres to give correct answers to questions (Markey et al. 2008a). Game play logs revealed that players guessed at answers rather than checking sources. The analysis of focus group interviews with Hidgeon players was the impetus for the development team's formulation of game design premises to aid future game design initiatives (chapter 3). Foremost of the premises was game play that contributes in a useful way to the course work students are already doing. This premise guided the design of the BiblioBouts information literacy game (chapter 5), and it incorporates all the best practices in this book's game design discussions (chapters 12 and 13).

EVALUATING EDUCATIONAL GAMES

So few evaluations of online information literacy games have enlisted empirical research methods that we felt compelled to check the extensive literature of educational games generally to determine whether it demonstrates games' effectiveness.

Educational games have been developed in a wide range of disciplines (e.g., biology, math, language, engineering) and in a wide variety of formats (e.g., board game, puzzle, adventure, simulation) with varying forms of assessment (Wouters et al. 2013). Because of the large number of studies, we limited our analysis to the six literature reviews of educational games research that have been published since online games came to the fore.

Hays (2005) reviews forty-eight empirical research articles on the effectiveness of educational games and summarizes twenty-six other review articles and thirty-one theoretical articles on educational gaming. His meta-analysis concludes that games provide cognitive learning and motivation for a variety of learners for a variety of learning tasks. In the studies reviewed, Hays was unable to find support for claims that games are always superior to other instructional methods or that they have a lasting impact, changing later course work or classroom structure or relations. He is circumspect as to whether games change students' affect about the learning domain and learning in general (2005, 46).

Vogel et al. (2006) evaluates thirty-two studies that compare simulations and educational games to traditional classroom teaching. Its meta-analysis reports that simulations and games result in significantly higher cognitive gains and attitudes toward learning with a very significant effect strength.

Ke's (2009) meta-analysis of eighty-nine game effectiveness studies involving a number of game formats in a variety of learning settings concludes that 52 percent of these studies report significant positive effects on cognitive and affective learning. Included under cognitive learning outcomes are basic motor skills, descriptive knowledge, conceptual knowledge, problem solving, and general cognitive strategies. Included under affective learning outcomes are self-efficacy, attitudes toward subject content learning, affective feedback toward game use, and motivation or persistence.

Sitzmann (2011) conducts a meta-analysis of sixty-five studies to determine the instructional effectiveness of computer-based simulation games relative to a comparison group. Declarative knowledge is found to be 11 percent higher for the game group, procedural knowledge is 14 percent higher, retention levels are 9 percent higher, and self-efficacy is 20 percent higher. The author equivocates on motivation because too few studies consider it.

Perrotta et al.'s (2013) meta-analysis of twenty-one studies is split on whether students receive cognitive gains from games versus traditional teaching methods and whether games impact students' attitudes toward learning; however, it reports positive impacts on problem-solving skills, broader knowledge acquisition, motivation, and engagement.

Table 1.2 summarizes the findings of the six meta-analyses. Xs and /s designate studies reporting positive effect and mixed results, respectively. All six probed for evidence of cognitive learning gains as a result of playing education games, five found it, and one reported mixed results. Five analyses sought evidence of affective learning gains; three found it, but both Hays and Perrotta et al. were circumspect about the evidence in this regard. Three studies searched for evidence of increased motivation, two detected such evidence, and Sitzmann reported too few studies examining motivation to be able to say something conclusive about it.

Table 1.2.   Findings about the Effectiveness of Educational Games

Findings	Hays (2005)	Vogel et al. (2006)	Ke (2009)	Sitzmann (2011)	Wouters et al. (2013)	Perrotta et al. (2013)
Cognitive learning	X	X	X	X	X	/
Affective learning		X	X	X		/
Motivation	X					X

Overall, educational games research is more rigorous than information literacy games research. Findings from the former are especially positive with regard to game play resulting in cognitive learning gains and affective learning. More research is needed on the effects of game play on students' motivation. When researchers design evaluations of information literacy games, they can draw inspiration from educational game studies, checking literature reviews to generate hypotheses, single out model studies, and fill needed gaps in our knowledge about games and learning.

SUMMARY

This chapter focuses on the intersection of information literacy, games, and learning. These phenomena were hardly mentioned in the same sentence until the second half of the last decade, when the library field recognized how popular video games had become with young people, responded favorably to published accounts of their potential for good learning from other disciplines, and speculated on their effectiveness for teaching young people information literacy skills and concepts. Since then, almost two dozen online literacy games have been developed and deployed in classroom settings, but only a third have demonstrated their effectiveness. To fill the gap in our knowledge about game effectiveness, this chapter includes an analysis of published state-of-the-art literature reviews of the many studies of games' effectiveness in other disciplines. Evidence of cognitive gains and improvements in students' attitudes toward learning are promising, but more studies are needed that test students' motivation for learning.

Chapter Two

The Needs Assessment

It can be tempting to plunge into game design and development based on hunches; however, this chapter encourages prospective game designers to conduct a thorough needs assessment that provides evidence of the need for and utility of an online game. Some needs assessments might conclude that nongame alternatives are better suited than games for accomplishing information literacy goals. Other assessments are likely to uncover fresh, new ideas for game design and development that improve on original ideas, expand the project's scope, or change the game's overarching objective.

To guide designers, we pose eight questions to consider in a needs assessment for an information literacy game. We had to answer these same questions for BiblioBouts, and we are glad that we did: the answers helped sharpen our vision of the game and convince us that an online game that taught students a structured research process to find quality information for their research papers was very much needed and would be suited to testing the effectiveness of information literacy games generally.

FORMULATING THE GAME'S
OVERARCHING LEARNING OBJECTIVE

Game design starts with formulating the game's overarching objective. If you are reading this book with the idea of teaching students something about information literacy as the result of playing a game, ask yourself what the "something" is. If you are having difficulty identifying the "something," complete this sentence. "As a result of playing the game, students should be able to ____."

In this discussion, we will call your "something" an *information literacy aspect*. When it comes to information literacy aspects, there are so many possibilities! Examples are how to conduct research, how to evaluate sources, how to distinguish between scholarly and nonscholarly sources, how to perform a technical reading of a source, how to cite sources in papers, how to select the right database, how to conduct a Boolean search, how to choose the right keywords, how to find a topic to research, and much more. Each and every aspect might not be conducive to a game format, but that should not stop anyone from brainstorming at this stage of development. BiblioBouts's overarching objective was, "As a result of playing the game, students should be able to use the game's structured research process to find quality information for their research papers."

Once you have formulated your game's overarching objective (even several draft objective statements that you are considering will suffice), it is time to proceed with the eight needs assessment questions.

ASKING EIGHT QUESTIONS FOR THE NEEDS ASSESSMENT

Your next step is to ask yourself why you have chosen to embody this aspect of information literacy in a game. Seat-of-the-pants answers are *not* acceptable. Game development and testing are time-consuming and expensive processes. Doing a thorough needs assessment will convince you—and, perhaps more importantly, funders, administrators, and superiors who can allocate resources—that developing an online game is a worthwhile endeavor that will benefit instructors, students, and librarians. Answers to these questions will get you started on the needs assessment:

1. What is known about students' knowledge or lack of knowledge of this information literacy aspect?
2. What specific difficulties do students have in this regard?
3. Ideally, when *should* and when *do* students learn about this information literacy aspect?
4. At what grade or educational level does their lack of knowledge with regard to this information literacy aspect become crucial for succeeding in academic pursuits?
5. What are existing approaches to teaching this information literacy aspect, and why are they inadequate?
6. At what grade or educational level will you pitch your game? What are other important demographics of your game's prospective players?

7. Is this problem limited to students at your institution, or is it generalizable, characteristic of students in different grades or at different educational levels and across different types of learning institutions?
8. In what academic activities are students in this particular grade or at this educational level engaged that require their competence in this information literacy aspect?

After formulating our game's overarching objective, we sought answers to the above questions to demonstrate that there was a need for an online game to teach students a structured research process to find quality information for their academic papers. Our analysis had to provide convincing evidence that the game's prospective players had difficulties knowing how to find quality sources and evaluate the sources they found, that existing approaches to teaching them how to find and evaluate sources were inadequate or not reaching them, that students at the college level should be knowledgeable in this regard, and that these problems were generalizable beyond students at this level and at one particular institution. Generalizability was especially important to us because we wanted to build an online game that was useful for solving problems across several disciplines, educational levels, and types of educational institutions. Building an online game is a major undertaking in time, personnel, and finances, so you need to make sure from the very start that your game is generalizable beyond your particular setting and circumstances so that others benefit from your efforts by adopting your game.

Answers to question #1 above should rely mostly on published research and research in progress. Also take into consideration anecdotal evidence, your knowledge of your game's prospective users at your institution, its curriculum, and the unfulfilled wish lists of instructors, instructional librarians, and the wide array of academic support specialists who help students navigate the academic enterprise.

Answers to question #8 above are crucial because not only will students receive instruction as a result of playing your game, they can also make significant progress on completing class assignments. Thus, answers will help you visualize game play that enables game players to accomplish both tasks. In fact, while performing the literature review for the needs assessment, you may receive inspiration from the sources you encounter or people you talk to that helps you generate answers to this question, so always keep it in the forefront of your mind.

As games researchers, our primary objective has been to determine the effectiveness of games for information literacy instruction. Against that backdrop, we chose to build a game that taught college students a structured research process for finding quality information for their research papers. Our rationale for choosing this approach over other information literacy aspects was based on our answers to these needs assessment questions. Because our needs analysis took place a half decade ago, we updated the discussion with research findings that have been published in the interim. Helping college students find and evaluate quality information is just as important now as it was then.

UNDERSTANDING WHY STUDENTS
PREFER THE OPEN WEB TO THE LIBRARY

Both high school and college students are bereft of expert knowledge of the disciplines, of an understanding of where to start, how to build on a good start, how to evaluate what they find, and of an awareness of the interrelationships between different research and discovery tools. As a result, the Web is either their starting point or their sole source of information for academic pursuits (Fast and Campbell 2004; Head 2007; Becker 2003; Costello, Lenholt, and Stryker 2004; Curtis 2000; Swanson 2005; OCLC 2002; Kolowich 2011).

Numerous empirical studies report that speed, convenience, and ease of use attract college students to open Web resources. Students perceive library databases to be inaccessible, difficult to use, overly complex, and confusing due to their bloated interfaces (Kim and Sin 2011; Armstrong 2009, 299).

Researchers have characterized three categories of undergraduate library users: avid users, occasional users, and library avoiders. Library avoiders in particular use library resources only when their instructors specifically require them to do so; some even report "feelings of discomfort and intimidation" as a result (Colón-Aguirre and Fleming-May 2012, 396).

Most college students' first experiences with online searching come from using Web search engines. When their college instructors expect them to use library databases, they apply their expectations and understanding of Web searching to the library search task (Rieh, Kim, and Markey 2012). For example, because students find lots of information for their topics on Google, they expect the same of library databases and are surprised when their searches of library databases fail to produce many results (Fast and Campbell 2004).

A comprehensive survey reports that about 40 percent of college students do not use their library's website for their academic-related information needs (OCLC 2006); however, when these same students are asked to compare library sources to open Web sources, they consider library resources to have higher values in terms of trustworthiness and accuracy than open Web resources. In fact, the results of two studies (OCLC 2006, 2011) conducted five years apart show a 12 percent increase (from 31 to 43 percent) in the number of students who rate library sources as more trustworthy than open Web sources. Although these findings demonstrate that students consider the college or university library to be an important source of trustworthy information, they still rely on Web resources for information for their academic pursuits.

A host of studies demonstrate students' unsophisticated online searching skills. Julien and Barker (2009) report high school students begin their online searches by copying and pasting the assignment question into Google's dialogue box, scanning the three or four top-ranked search results, and comparing these retrievals' content for consistency. High school students put little cognitive effort into online searching because they perceive it to be "a simple type-and-click operation" (Chung and Neuman 2007, 1514). Their searches are interactive and serendipitous because they do not have clear ideas about the information they want to find (Chung and Neuman 2007). Because students pay little attention to the *process* of finding information, it is not surprising that they have a hard time recalling what they have done during the information-seeking process or why they have done it. In short, they focus not on searching but on the end *product* of their searches (Julien and Barker 2009). Additionally, students are not overwhelmed or frustrated by the amount of online information presented to them because they believe that they can easily find information for their research tasks (Chung and Neuman 2007).

Students are even more challenged by the research process than by online searching. Course-related research is confusing and frustrating to them. They do not know how to meet their instructors' expectations, how to narrow down a topic, or how to make it manageable (Head 2007). During the research process, students struggle with determining what constitutes quality sources and finding "good, citable stuff" (Head 2007, 7). Students do not know what good sources look like; nor do they know how to evaluate the quality of the sources they cite in their assignments (Kim and Sin 2011). The bottom line is that they lack domain knowledge and expertise that would enable them to know where to start, who does the most respected and groundbreaking research on their topics of interest, what jargon would be fruitful for keyword searches, and so on (Markey 2007).

Research results are clear and unequivocal about the urgent need to reduce college students' reliance on the Web for information for their serious academic pursuits and to improve their online searching skills. Information literacy instruction needs to put students into situations where they experience library databases firsthand so that they can judge for themselves whether their search results yield quality information for academic pursuits. They also need to learn strategies for assessing the credibility of the sources they find online and practice formulating research topics. Responding to these needs with an online game where students learn, experience, and practice how to find information and assess its quality would be a tall order, but that was precisely what we wanted to accomplish with the design, development, and deployment of BiblioBouts.

RESEARCH ON HOW STUDENTS JUDGE
THE CREDIBILITY OF ONLINE INFORMATION

After finding sources, online searchers make a series of judgments to select the information they use. Relevance figures prominently into the selection process. Relevance is defined as "users' perceptions of the potential of certain information to resolve their problems in the context of their information seeking and use situations" (Schamber and Bateman 1996, 218). Empirical studies on relevance criteria demonstrate that searchers are able to articulate the criteria on which they base their judgments of information (Rieh 2002; Saracevic 2007). A comprehensive literature review on relevance criteria concludes that the criteria used by a variety of users—scholars, students, children, and the general public—are quite similar and can be categorized as follows (Saracevic 2007, 1930):

- Content (quality, depth, scope, currency)
- Object (genre, format, representation, organization, availability, accessibility)
- Validity (accuracy, authority, trustworthiness, verifiability)
- Situational match (appropriateness to tasks)
- Cognitive match (understanding, novelty, mental effort)
- Affective match (emotional response to information, fun, frustration, uncertainty)
- Belief match (confidence)

The weights people assign to these criteria differ; for example, scholars give high weights to authority, a criterion that matters very little to children (Saracevic 2007). The weights given to different relevance criteria also change depending on the tasks users engage in. People are more stringent about their relevance criteria when they deal with especially focused and defined search tasks. A study of social science graduate students reveals their attention to various document features when assessing relevance such as abstract, author, content, document type, and journal or publisher (Maglaughlin and Sonnenwald 2002). A survey of about two hundred graduate students reveals that relevance involves three distinct constructs: information quality, information credibility, and information completeness (Bateman 1999). As a result of factor analysis, Bateman concludes that information quality is influenced by judgments of sources being well written, focused, consistent, and current; information credibility involves criteria such as "information being about my topic," accuracy, and credibility; and information completeness is composed of comprehensiveness, level of detail, and the specificity of information.

An investigation of college students' information behavior in a digital library environment concludes that students' relevance judgments and quality assessments are distinct mental processes (Fitzgerald and Galloway 2001). Students might judge a document relevant but of poor quality or mostly non-relevant but of high quality. Subsequently, researchers have agreed that credibility assessment and relevance judgments are related, yet distinct, mental processes (Rieh 2002).

Traditionally, credibility has been defined by two core dimensions: trustworthiness and expertise (Hovland, Janis, and Kelley 1953). Trustworthiness involves the perceived quality and believability of information. Expertise pertains to the accuracy and validity of information based on people's prior knowledge, skills, and experience with sources (Fogg 2003). Therefore, credibility assessment is a highly subjective process that people make based on individual expertise and knowledge (Rieh 2010).

A number of empirical studies have probed credibility assessment and yielded these three important implications for information literacy programs. First, credibility needs to be understood within the particular contexts in which information seeking is pursued and assessments are made. Rieh and Hilligoss's (2008) study of college students' information seeking concludes that students' long-term goals, such as academic achievement, problem solving, and personal information needs, directly influence their credibility assessments. For example, when assessing information in academic contexts, students look for evidence of expertise and authority, but they also feel pressured to find information quickly; thus, they are tempted to yield to convenience instead of making the effort to find more sources and deliberate on their credibility.

Second, studies have investigated using the genre of information sources as a strategy for assessing the credibility of information. For example, high school students are aware of qualitative differences between published printed materials and websites, and they take them into account during their credibility assessments (Sundin and Francke 2009). With regard to Web sources, students are able to differentiate between blogs, discussion forums, student papers, and encyclopedias.

Third, studies show evidence of varied abilities among students in evaluating the credibility of online information. Hargittai et al. (2010) surveyed over one thousand first-year college students and observed and interviewed about one hundred of them to probe how they assessed the credibility of online information. The researchers concluded that students differed in their understanding of the reasons behind search engine rankings, how Web addresses are composed, and whether it was necessary to verify the information they found on websites. The actions students took most frequently for their schoolwork were "checking to see if the information is current" and "seeking out other sources to validate the information."

Prior studies reveal that there is a gap in students' normative perceptions and actual search behavior. On one hand, students understand the importance of finding and using high-quality, credible information. On the other hand, when they need information, they rely on search engines because of their speed, convenience, and ease of use. A study of 2,747 young people, ages eleven to eighteen, concludes that their concerns about the credibility of the information they find on the Internet are driven by the analytical credibility evaluation process, which involves effortful examination of information; however, actual beliefs about the credibility of information are dictated by heuristic process by which decisions are made with little cognitive effort (Flanagin and Metzger 2010). The bottom line is that young people know they must perform credibility assessments of the information they find online, but they lack the ability and, possibly, the desire to take a rigorous approach to performing such assessments (Flanagin and Metzger 2010).

As more attention is given to the problem of credibility in the online environment, researchers and practitioners have begun to discuss how to educate and train users. A typical training program involves checklists to guide users when making credibility assessments, encouraging them to check the information for currency, accuracy, objectivity, and authority (Metzger 2007). Among the several limitations to the checklist approach are student complaints that it is time-consuming and labor-intensive (Meola 2004). In fact, Internet users are more likely to perform easy actions—ones that involve either simple recognition, such as determining whether a website's information is current, or their opinion, such as determining whether the information is well written—and less likely to take actions that require effort, such as verifying the author's qualifications or credentials (Metzger 2007).

Meola (2004) suggests a contextual approach to instructing students on credibility assessment. The approach enlists three strategies that involve wider social contexts and judgments, such as promoting peer and editorially reviewed online resources and involving comparison and corroboration. The first strategy enlists librarians to promote high-quality, vetted resources to students. The second encourages students to examine the similarities and differences between two or more Web-based and/or library-supplied sources. The third actively engages students in the verification of the information they find on the Web using one or more sources, and, in fact, the more sources students use for corroboration, the greater the probability that the information is accurate and reliable. Meola (2004) claims that the contextual approach can promote the library's resources, teach information literacy, and encourage judgments of information quality and credibility.

Metzger (2007) suggests a sliding scale approach to teaching credibility assessment skills. When students are in situations that motivate them to perform credibility assessments, she suggests teaching them the contextual model of credibility assessment. When they are in less motivating situations, they can be taught simple heuristics. Metzger adds that credibility assessment should not be left to the discretion of students because, in most information-seeking and -use situations, they are unlikely to exert the mental effort required to make credibility judgments carefully. An alternative is her suggestion that "energy may be better spent developing tools or systems that are designed to assess credibility for users and then training users how to use those tools and systems" (Metzger 2007, 2085).

Research results are clear and unequivocal about the urgent need for college students to be circumspect about the information they choose for their academic pursuits. Using Web-based information may suffice as long as students think critically about both the relevance and credibility of the information in hand. The problem is that students do not routinely evaluate the information they find online. Information literacy instruction needs to put students in situations that require them to evaluate information, possibly even prompting them to apply certain strategies so that they know what questions to ask and must answer them repeatedly, thereby rendering source evaluation second nature instead of an annoying burden. Again, responding with a game in which students learn, develop, experience, and practice source evaluation skills was precisely what we wanted to accomplish with the development and deployment of the BiblioBouts information literacy game.

DETERMINING THE RIGHT AUDIENCE
FOR A LIBRARY RESEARCH GAME

Ideally, instruction on finding information and assessing its quality should begin in the middle school grades when students complete assignments and participate in activities that supplement textbook learning with external sources. At first, middle school teachers are likely to guide students, recommending specific print and online sources that will address their needs. By high school, students are expected to stretch beyond recommended sources, finding sources on their own and using them to complete assignments and write term papers.

Deciding whether to pitch BiblioBouts to high school or college students was difficult. We chose the latter for several reasons. We knew that many college students would be operating for the first time in a richer information environment than their high schools had provided and would benefit from hands-on experience using the college library's portal and databases. For students whose high school education included information literacy instruction, BiblioBouts might review some material, but it would introduce almost all students, for the first time, to the same rich, deep, diverse information environment that their instructors use to teach the knowledge of the discipline and to extend the discipline's frontiers of knowledge. Even if students' use of library databases was limited to a couple, they could draw on their experience in subsequent classes in which citing scholarly sources was expected and choose discipline-oriented databases from the library portal instead of falling back on their habitual patterns: Google and the Web.

When we designed BiblioBouts, we envisioned a game that students played while they wrote a research paper or worked on a project with a research component. Such tasks are typical of assignments that college instructors give to students. In freshman writing seminars especially, college students are expected to master the kind of analysis and argumentation that characterize specialized academic writing. The pervasiveness of writing assignments at the college level increased the likelihood that BiblioBouts would be generalizable beyond the handful of institutions participating in the game's evaluation. We expected and encouraged instructors at other institutions to adopt BiblioBouts, and they responded in kind (see chapter 8).

Stand-alone information literacy courses and course-integrated instruction are the two teaching methods most likely to provide students with significant opportunities to get hands-on experience finding information and evaluating its quality. Unfortunately, use of these methods for information literacy instruction at the college level is the exception rather than the rule. If information literacy instruction reaches college students at all, it is usually through online tutorials and course-related instruction, and neither method is conducive to hands-on exercises. Why not put this instruction into an online game that gives students hands-on experience finding and evaluating information, as well as opportunities to interact with peers and observe how they perform information literacy tasks, and transforms the experience into mini-competitions that reward high-performing students and enable all students to make progress on their academic assignments while they play the game?

That is precisely what we did in the design of the BiblioBouts information literacy game.

SUMMARY

This chapter encourages prospective game designers to conduct a thorough needs assessment prior to initiating game design and development. The assessment begins with a statement that asserts the game's overarching objective. To jump-start your game's needs assessment, we have presented eight questions that the needs assessment for the information literacy game should address. Our answers to these questions with respect to BiblioBouts are featured. Your needs assessment might not underline the need for an online game, concluding instead that offline alternatives or some other medium would be better suited to accomplishing your overarching objective. If your needs assessment does demonstrate the need for an online game, then it is also likely to have sharpened your vision and advanced your original ideas so that you have a running start on your next step—game design and development.

Chapter Three

The Design of an
Information Literacy Game

The starting point for our new game's design was eight premises for the design of information literacy games. The premises were the result of our experience designing, developing, deploying, and evaluating the Web-based board game Defense of Hidgeon (Markey et al. 2008a). Teaching undergraduate students how to conduct library research was Hidgeon's overarching goal, and we embraced this same goal in the design of the new game.

This chapter presents the eight game design premises and our efforts to remain faithful to them in the design of our new game, BiblioBouts. We sometimes strayed from these premises, changing and adding to them after evaluating BiblioBouts several times and improving the game's design based on input from players, instructors, and librarians. User input was not the sole determinant of the new game's evolution. Technology, time constraints, resource limitations, and course-deployment factors all played important roles in the new game's design. In short, this chapter presents the *moving* picture of the new game's successive designs and describes the reasons why it evolved in the ways it did and what we learned about game design as a result of the experience.

PREMISES FOR THE DESIGN
OF INFORMATION LITERACY GAMES

Hidgeon was the initial test bed for our game design research. This Web-administered board game's backstory set events in the middle of the fourteenth century at the height of the Black Death's sweep through Europe. The game's objective was to be the duchy's richest, fastest, and most accurate research team, landing on various monastery library squares and collecting scrolls, gold, and property for giving correct answers to the questions posted at monastery libraries. Game play introduced students to the general-to-specific model for conducting library research (Kirk 1974), advising them to start their library research with broad *overview tools*, such as the Web and general and discipline-specific encyclopedias, handbooks, and histories, to develop a general understanding of their topics, advancing them to *finding tools*, such as bibliographies, catalogs, and abstracting and indexing databases, for specific information to build on their initial understanding, and culminating with *forward-chaining tools*, such as citation indexes, to find cutting-edge research.

Our evaluation of Hidgeon produced valuable data on how students would interact with information literacy games, which we codified into eight premises for the design of such games (Markey et al. 2008b). Table 3.1 lists the premises that served as the starting point for our design of a new game that taught students how to conduct library research, along with the ways we envisioned the new game's design would remain faithful to them.

Of the eight premises, we took the first one about game play contributing to student course work most seriously. Game play had to not only relate to students' course work but further their progress on a particular assignment. Coming up empty-handed as a result of game play was not an option. The rest of this chapter describes the new game's design and how it evolved as a result of input from students and instructors who played the game.

The premises were not a flash in the pan. They inspired our original vision and guided us as the game evolved due to input from instructors, student game players, and librarians. Chapters 12 and 13 revisit these premises, presenting new premises in the form of best practices based on our experience designing, developing, and evaluating BiblioBouts.

PLANNING THE BIBLIOBOUTS
INFORMATION LITERACY GAME

Because BiblioBouts was a research project funded by a National Leadership Grant from the Institute of Museum and Library Services (IMLS), our game design efforts began with a research proposal to IMLS describing the game in the most general terms, the work effort to design, develop, deploy, and evaluate it, and the responsibilities of team members. The team included game deployment partners at academic institutions where the game would be played. These partners were librarians, and we called them "library liaisons," relying on them to pre-test BiblioBouts during system development, recruit interested instructors at their institutions, help instructors incorporate

Table 3.1. How the New Game Remained Faithful to Our Design Premises

#	Premise	Envisioning the New Game
1	Game play must contribute in a useful way to the course work students are already doing.	Game play and students' library research for a research paper assignment were mutually dependent. Playing the game meant that students made progress on their research papers.
2	Game play that gives players mastery over one key concept, task, or procedure is preferable to comprehensive game play.	The game was conceived as an online tournament, made up of a series of mini-games or bouts that gave students practice with a specific subset of information literacy skills within the overall library research process.
3	Students must have concrete evidence that leaving their computer to do research will have a payoff in terms of improving their research or affecting their grades.	Game play took place on the Web so players did not have to leave their computers.
4	Although students want to be in control during game play, they will collaborate with their peers when the collaboration furthers what they want to accomplish.	Students played the game on their own, collaborating with their peers to build and evaluate a library of sources on a broad-based topic that was the starting point for a research-paper assignment.
5	Students want positive and negative feedback from games to improve their performance.	Player feedback included side-by-side comparisons of everyone's source evaluations, badges for meritorious game play, a leader board, and a dynamic scoring log. Instructor feedback was an evaluation report for monitoring player progress, scoring, and reviewing the sources players submitted to the game.
6	Game play must count toward students' grades in the course.	Instructions to instructors encouraged them to incorporate the game into their course syllabi, grading students on their participation in the game and standing on the final leader board.
7	Game play must foster opportunities for students to reflect on their own research habits and what they are learning.	Instructions to instructors encouraged them to conduct class discussions about the information literacy concepts and skills encountered during game play.
8	Game play must give students opportunities to see other researchers at work so they can connect what they do to what others do.	Instructions to instructors encouraged them to play the game, submit sources, evaluate their students' sources, and debrief students at the end of the game.

BiblioBouts into their syllabi and assignments, deploy BiblioBouts in classes, and help conduct the evaluation (chapters 5 and 7). We recruited library liaisons by posting messages on library-oriented listservs. Especially helpful was Jenny Levine at the American Library Association, who publicized our games research on her Shifted Librarian blog.

Interested librarians contacted us via e-mail, and we followed up with e-mail messages, phone conversations, and face-to-face meetings at American Library Association conferences. We named five liaisons at five partner institutions in our IMLS proposal and earmarked funds in the proposal's budget to help defray the costs of their participation. One library liaison dropped out due to taking a job at a different institution, and a second participated in game testing but did not participate in the evaluation. Library liaisons came from these participating institutions: (1) Chicago University (CSU), (2) Saginaw Valley State University (SVSU), (3) Troy University Montgomery Campus (TUMC), and (4) University of Baltimore (UB).

Upon securing grant funds in fall 2008, we began our game design efforts in earnest and assembled a team with experience in programming, graphic design, game play, information literacy training, user support, and data collection and analysis. Some team members had served on the Hidgeon team, and others joined us for the first time.

At the time, we were riding the momentum of our experience designing, developing, and evaluating the Hidgeon information literacy game. Instead of dropping everything and starting anew, we built on what we had learned, remaining faithful to the eight game design premises and adopting Hidgeon's goal of teaching undergraduate students how to conduct library research in the new game. More specifically, we envisioned a new information literacy game that would usher students through the research process, focusing them on (1) resource discovery, (2) source selection, (3) source evaluation, (4) source content, and (5) best-source selection. The game's winners would have to be active in all phases of the game and exceed the minimal-level expectations set by their instructors.

Team member Fritz Swanson spearheaded the team's initial design efforts, drafting a game design document that described the new game's objectives, pedagogical goals, and scoring (Markey et al. 2009, 13–20). He conceived a game that was a tournament, made up of a series of mini-games, or bouts, that would give students hands-on experience and practice conducting library research. More specifically, students would locate, evaluate, and use online information during the course of the game. These three activities mapped directly onto both the ALA's (1989) and the ACRL's (2000) definitions of information literacy, that is, "the ability to locate, evaluate, and use effectively the needed information." Game play resulted in a bibliography of sources that students could cite in their class assignments, an aspect of the game in keeping with design premise #1. Swanson proposed the name *Bib-lioBouts* to reflect the game's reliance on a series of mini-games, or bouts, that culminated in players' selection of the best sources for their research paper's *bibliography.*

The game design document was a major breakthrough, crystallizing how the game worked from beginning to end. The team's graphic designer, Brian Jennings, referred to the document to design interfaces and fine-tune them based on feedback from team members at weekly meetings. Other team members took ownership of design tasks best suited to their expertise and game design experience, presented their solutions at weekly meetings, and responded to feedback with improved solutions at subsequent meetings. For example, team member Soo Young Rieh drew on her expertise in credibility assessment research to convey to team members her vision of how players would perform credibility and relevance assessments; then, graphic designer Jennings mocked up her ideas in draft interfaces and displayed them for dis-cussion at weekly meetings, where all team members reacted to them.

The game's design was truly a team effort. Accomplished in incremental stages, it involved the design team initially and expanded outward to include programmer Gregory Peters, who built the functionality behind the game's interface, as well as library liaisons, instructors, and student game players, whose participation in the game's evaluation resulted in feedback that the team used to ensure the game's usability and enhance its functionality. Rarely did the programmer dictate his vision to the design team, and if he did, his suggestions almost always simplified, streamlined, or facilitated what the design team wanted done. Team member Chris Leeder took charge of day-to-day operations, especially during the game deployment and evaluation phases of the project. Team leader Karen Markey was responsible for all managerial aspects of the game enterprise and, as final arbiter, made decisions when lack of consensus or conflict stood in the way of meeting deadlines.

Including a graphic designer on the design team right from the start was a masterstroke. The designer was an active participant and good listener who transformed the verbiage into paper or online mock-ups, including some of the latter with limited functionality, so the team could react to them and progress could be made.

BiblioBouts game play began with players searching library databases and the Web for online sources on an assigned topic, collecting promising candidates, and submitting the most relevant ones to the game. To facilitate source collection and submission tasks, the BiblioBouts design and develop-ment team relied on the Zotero citation management tool (www.zotero.org; Zotero 2013). An extension to the open-source Firefox Web browser (www.

mozilla.org/en-US/firefox/new), Zotero allowed players to collect, save, cite, and share sources with other Zotero users and groups. BiblioBouts polled Zotero for sources players shared with their particular BiblioBouts group to build a database of online sources for each class playing the game. We chose Zotero over other citation management tools because Zotero was an open-source tool; it was free to anyone, unlike comparable tools that required users to sign licenses and pay subscription fees; its application programming interface (API) encouraged third-party developers to enhance Zotero; and its functionality was exactly what BiblioBouts needed to build a database of online sources for each class playing the game.

BiblioBouts had four design iterations, one paper version and three online operational versions. The first was an on-paper design document that we used to brief library liaisons and prospective instructors (Markey et al. 2009, 9–16). Based on their input, the team developed the second design iteration, the alpha version of BiblioBouts. An evaluation of the alpha version involving student game players, instructors, and library liaisons resulted in the third design iteration, the beta 1.0 version of BiblioBouts. Finally, an evaluation of the beta 1.0 version involving student game players, instructors, and library liaisons resulted in the fourth design iteration, the beta 2.0 version of BiblioBouts.

Table 3.2 describes the bouts that characterized BiblioBouts's four design iterations. Iterations top the four rightmost columns, and an *X* in a column means that the particular iteration included the bout.

Originally, BiblioBouts was conceived as a game with six bouts. Its final version was a slimmed-down, three-bout game. In short, here is how that happened. The game design team shared an on-paper mock-up of the original BiblioBouts to prospective instructor-users who taught first-year writing classes. They reacted negatively, advising us that the game was too long, especially for classes that were fully scheduled with content, activities, and assignments. As a result, we eliminated the Policing bout and diverted two of its features—checking opponents' sources for correct full-texts and for complete citations—to BiblioBouts's Tagging & Rating (T&R) bout. Later, when some players voiced dismay about nonrelevant sources and missing full-texts, we were reminded of the Policing bout that could have identified and eliminated problematic closed sources (see page 183).

In fall 2009 and winter 2010, classes at participating institutions played BiblioBouts's alpha version, which featured five bouts (table 3.2, alpha column); student-players and instructors also participated in an evaluation of BiblioBouts that enlisted all of the methods described in chapter 6. In summer and fall 2010, game play was suspended so that the design team could analyze collected data, identify problems, and make needed changes. Table

Table 3.2.   The Bouts of the Four Design Iterations of BiblioBouts

Bout	Description	Paper Mock-Up	Alpha	Beta 1.0	Beta 2.0
Donor	Players search the Web and library databases for sources and save them using the Zotero citation management tool.	X	X	X	
Closer	Players choose their best sources to "do battle" in the game.	X	X	X	X
Policing	Players review closed sources, designating sources that lack full-texts, have nonmatching citations, or are not relevant for elimination from the game.	X			
Tagging & Rating (T&R)	Players evaluate the content and quality of their classmates' sources, including rating their credibility and relevance on a one-hundred-point scale.	X	X	X	X
Sorter	Players sort sources into categories that describe the major subjects they cover.	X	X		
Best Bibliography	Players specify a topic and select the best sources that they will use to write their research paper.	X	X	X	X
Post-Game Library	Players search and access everyone's closed sources.			X	X

3.3 describes major problems with BiblioBouts's alpha version and solutions implemented in the beta 1.0 and 2.0 versions.

The design team implemented changes and made BiblioBouts's third iteration available as the beta 1.0 version of BiblioBouts. It featured four bouts (table 3.2, beta 1.0 column) and a Post-Game Library that players could search after their game ended to find sources, including citations and full-texts, for their research papers. Beta 1.0 BiblioBouts was released in winter 2011 and made available to instructors for the asking.

Because players continued to report problems with saving and sharing their sources between Zotero and BiblioBouts, the Donor bout was stripped from the game. On the plus side, such a change meant that players used Zotero

Table 3.3.   Problems with BiblioBouts's Alpha Version and Implemented Solutions

Alpha Version Problems	*BiblioBouts Beta 1.0 or 2.0 Solutions*
Game registration was overly complicated.	The game registration procedure was simplified. (1.0)
The scoring algorithm allowed players to easily build huge scores.	A new scoring algorithm was implemented that rewarded players who were active in all phases of the game and submitted sources on the topic in play, which their fellow players rated highest for credibility and relevance and chose for their best bibliographies. (1.0 and 2.0)
Sorter's easy-to-use and fun interface tempted players to score points mindlessly (Markey et al. 2010, 8–9).	The Sorter bout was eliminated from BiblioBouts, and its "keyword" aspect became the "big ideas" aspect of the T&R and Best Bibliography bouts (figure 5.12). (1.0)
Students were expected to choose sources in the Best Bibliography bout for an assigned topic instead of a topic that interested them.	The Best Bibliography bout was redesigned, prompting students to enter their own research topic (figure 5.12). (1.0)
Players called for more feedback that would enable them to determine if their source evaluations were comparable to opponents' evaluations.	Feedback was added to the T&R bout for opponents' ratings (figures 5.10 and 5.11). (1.0) Links to feedback were added to the player's home page for all of the sources they rated in the T&R bout and all the sources they submitted in the Closer bout (figure 5.5). (1.0)
Players called for more feedback generally.	Badges for high-quality game play and a trophy case for displaying them were added to the player's home page (figure 5.5). (2.0) Badges were added to the T&R bout's displays of opponents' ratings (figure 5.11). (2.0)
Players called for access to everyone's sources after the game ended.	A Post-Game Library that players could search after their game ended to find full-text sources for their research papers was added to BiblioBouts (figure 5.15). (1.0)

apart from BiblioBouts, signing onto BiblioBouts when they had registered in Zotero and saved a minimum number of sources (prescribed by their instructors) in Zotero. Such a change enabled the BiblioBouts team to quickly diagnose whether the problem was due to Zotero or BiblioBouts and respond with remedial action. The change focused students on game play that took place entirely in BiblioBouts: evaluating sources, generating a research paper topic, and choosing the best sources for their paper. It also prepared BiblioBouts for expansion beyond Zotero for source submission—for example, allowing players to use comparable citation managers, such as EndNote, RefWorks, Papers, Mendeley, and so on. On the minus side, eliminating the Donor bout meant that BiblioBouts no longer had access to players' donated sources until the Closer bout began. Thus, during the Donor bout, BiblioBouts could no longer report to players the databases where players were finding potentially relevant sources to donate to the game. To compensate for the loss of the Donor bout, BiblioBouts e-mailed players a list of relevant databases suggested by their instructors and librarians on the same date their instructors assigned students the research paper topic that was connected to game play (figure 3.1). The Donor-less version of BiblioBouts became the fourth iteration of the game (beta 2.0), and it was released in winter 2012 (table 3.2, far-right column). In this version was a new feedback feature: badges for high-quality game play.

The final evaluation of BiblioBouts was in full swing at the time of the BiblioBouts beta 2.0 release. Despite our efforts to keep up with usability concerns and demands for new features from student-players and instructors, the final evaluation revealed many ways in which we could have improved on the BiblioBouts beta 2.0 version. These included *minor changes* that we should have implemented earlier (e.g., reducing relevance and credibility rating scales from 0 to 100 to 1 to 5 and adding pop-up identification and description labels to badges); *major improvements*, such as adding a thumbs-

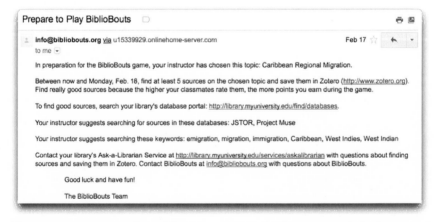

Figure 3.1. Prepare-to-play BiblioBouts message bearing suggested databases and keywords.

up or five-star rating feature to relevance and credibility comments and a keyword search capability to the Best Bibliography bout's Source Library and the Post-Game Library; and *game enhancements* that were forced by technological developments (e.g., releasing a BiblioBouts app for mobile devices). Thus, for game designers, the job never ends because of demands from game-system users and the infinite possibilities for changes, improvements, and advances.

INVOLVING INSTRUCTORS IN GAME PLAY

Both the initial mock-up and the alpha version of BiblioBouts required intervention from instructors during game play. Instructor intervention involved two types of information: (1) broad categories that characterized the subject matter of the sources players submitted to the game, and (2) potential research topics that students could write about, based on the sources they submitted to the game. This meant that after the Closer bout ended, BiblioBouts had to generate a bibliography of players' closed sources and forward it to instructors with instructions to review entries, generate a list of categories and a list of research topics, and send categories and research-topics lists to the game design team before the Sorter and Best Bibliography bouts began so that the categories and research topics could be added to these bouts before students started to play them.

Despite a two- or three-week period between the Closer bout's conclusion and the scheduled start dates of the Sorter and Best Bibliography bouts, priorities unrelated to game play competed for instructors' attention at the same time that Sorter categories and research topics were due. Instructors railed about the boring, tedious, and repetitive nature of both tasks. Although the unsatisfactory nature of how students played the Sorter bout caused its demise, we learned that expecting input from instructors during the course of game play is unwise due to other demands on their attention during the school term.

The only intervention that later versions of BiblioBouts required from instructors was game administration. Game administration occurred before and after game play. Before the game, instructors identified a broad-based topic connected with a related research paper assignment, invited students to games, scheduled bouts' beginning and ending dates, and set bouts' caps or quotas (figures 4.3 and 4.5). Instructors could change their game's parameters during game play, including adding or removing players from the game. Because some instructors wanted to delegate game administration to teaching assistants or librarians, we recommend that game designers add functionality for proxy game administration so that game owners can authorize others to administer their games. During and after game play, instructors could monitor student participation and grade students through the game's evaluation report capability (pages 54–57).

DISCUSSION

We had confidence in our game's overarching game objective—teaching undergraduate students how to conduct library research. We could say what we wanted the game to do, but envisioning it in the form of a game was difficult. To break the impasse, our graphic designer took the initiative. He transformed our verbiage into paper or online mock-ups that elicited reactions from the team, setting in motion a feedback loop that progressed the design of BiblioBouts. What happened to us was akin to a top-first, bottom-up approach to game design; that is, we were certain about the game's overarching and specific learning objectives, having represented them in both the research proposal to IMLS and the design document. The graphic designer's efforts addressed bottom-level specifics, giving form to player actions and game-system responses that coalesced into game play experiences that brought players closer to achieving the game's specific learning objectives. Once we made progress in envisioning player actions, it became easier to generate rules and add feedback and interaction to the game. Chapter 12 revisits how we got started, building on our experience and presenting a systematic approach to the design of information literacy games.

When instructors task students with a research paper, their involvement is often limited to giving students the assignment and reading their final submissions. Some instructors might meet with students to discuss the paper's topic and/or comment on first drafts. For the most part, what happens between the instructor's giving the assignment and grading the final papers can be likened to a black box—an activity that completely occupies the student but is almost entirely inaccessible and unknown to instructors. BiblioBouts is able to peel away some of the black box's packaging, exposing instructors to the sources students find online and how students evaluate these sources, enabling them to observe the trail of refinements students make to their papers' topics, and creating new opportunities for them to intervene and impact students' progress on their written papers.

We observed few instructors involved in game play, including pre-game and debriefing students on the information literacy skills that they encountered during game play. We know that some instructors had to turn their attention to unrelated matters during game play, but we speculated that other instructors, especially those in the academic disciplines, might have felt inadequate to advise students about information literacy. In chapter 13, we revisit this theme, making suggestions about user-support services that could assist academic instructors in this regard.

Because BiblioBouts relied on third-party software for its database building and management functionality, we had to conform to the software's specific requirements and idiosyncrasies. The alternative would have been building functionality that accomplished what Zotero did, a daunting programming task that would have consumed all our resources, or working with one or more vendors of proprietary citation management tools. We chose to integrate Zotero in BiblioBouts because it was an open-source tool; it was free to anyone, unlike comparable tools that required users to sign licenses and pay subscription fees; its API encouraged third-party development; and its functionality was exactly what BiblioBouts needed to build a database of online sources for each class playing the game. Working with third-party software vendors is a risky business. Your application must conform to their software's functionality. Your design team must monitor forums that announce and document changes and be prepared for unannounced and undocumented changes. If you are in charge of open-ended projects with no firm end dates, you might seek alternatives rather than risk working with third-party software vendors whose future viability is beyond your control.

SUMMARY

To design BiblioBouts, the game design team drew on its experience designing, developing, deploying, and evaluating an earlier game that had the same goal as BiblioBouts—teaching undergraduate students how to conduct library research. Our starting point for the new game's design was the eight game design premises that resulted from our game design experience with the earlier game. Most important was remaining faithful to the first premise—that game play must contribute in a useful way to the course work students were already doing—and thus we designed a game that ushered students through the research process while they used professional research tools to find, evaluate, and select high-quality information for their papers.

Table 3.2 presents BiblioBouts's four design iterations using the game's bouts to show how it evolved. New designs were the result of findings from formal evaluations involving students who played the game, their instructors, and library liaisons who assisted both students and instructors in setting up the game, troubleshooting technical problems, and playing the game. Table 3.3 enumerates major problems with BiblioBouts's alpha version, the first online version of the game, and the solutions that the design team incorporated into subsequent BiblioBouts versions. Game design features that required input from instructors during game play were eliminated from BiblioBouts's later versions because of the difficulty of getting instructors' attention during the busy school term. The most conspicuous new feature that was not in our original conception of BiblioBouts was the Post-Game Library. Players wanted this library so that they could access everyone's sources for their assignments after the game ended.

Game designers must keep in mind that their job never ends. Games can always be improved with changes from previous versions that are never quite done to perfection, new features causing entirely new and unexpected problems, and new technological advances that raise the bar for everything.

Chapter Four

The BiblioBouts
Administrator Interface

So much excitement is centered on the game's player interface that the game's administrator interface may be overlooked. It is, however, an indispensable component of the information literacy game. This chapter describes BiblioBouts's administrator interface. Its "super administrator" functionality is reserved for the game development team only and involves player registration, authorization of some registered players as game creators, and diagnostic tools for signing on to player and game-creator accounts to solve technical problems. Administrator functionality is for game owners, and it enables them to create games, monitor students' progress, and view summary game play data for grading students' performance.

To bring these functions to life, BiblioBouts's administrator interface is showcased in this chapter with its instructor tools for creating new games and making changes to existing ones, monitoring player progress, and displaying data on individual players for grading purposes. Included are suggestions for additional tools that game designers can add to facilitate game administration.

SUPER ADMINISTRATOR FUNCTIONALITY

Super administrator functionality is limited to the game's development team. Super administrator functionality for most information literacy games will involve player registration, game creation authorization, and diagnostic tools for development team members to identify technical problems.

If game play requires the game to track "something" about the player and store it for later use, the game needs player registration functionality. BiblioBouts had many "somethings" to track, such as the player's name, alias, e-mail address, registration password, games that the player administered, the game artifacts he had accumulated during game play (such as badges, submitted sources, and best bibliography), data associated with his game play (such as comments, ratings, and selections), and all activity that induced a scoring event. Thus, all BiblioBouts users—players, instructors, and librarians—had to register for BiblioBouts. Because accounts had data that instructors used to grade students, accounts remained private and secure, and super administrator functionality connected with accounts was reserved only for the game development team.

Registered players are authorized as "game owners" who can create games to which they invite other registered players through the super administrator function. Most prospective instructor-users at participating institutions found out about BiblioBouts from library liaisons, whereas instructor-users at nonparticipating institutions found out about it from published articles in the professional literature, the team's presentations at professional meetings, listserv discussions, press releases, blog postings, or librarians at their institution who monitor these communication media. Prospective instructor-users contacted us almost exclusively via e-mail and asked us how they could create games. We responded with information about BiblioBouts generally and instructed them to register for BiblioBouts just like everybody else, then send us a follow-up message asking us for a game administrator account. When they followed up, the BiblioBouts development team upgraded their player account to a game administrator account, which authorized them as game owners and added game administrator functionality to their account. We did not refuse people who asked to become game owners, but when it was not apparent that the person was a serious inquirer—for example, the inquirer's e-mail address did not originate from an educational institution or the applicant did not specify a reason for wanting to use BiblioBouts—we asked for more information, such as the institution the person represented and in what classes they intended to deploy BiblioBouts.

BiblioBouts's super administrator functionality included an account login tool. When instructors or players contacted us with problems, we used the tool to sign onto player accounts to determine the problems players were experiencing and how to solve them. We could also sign onto game administrators' accounts, manage their games, or diagnose their technical problems. There may be super administrator functionality that is unique to your game to support its players and game owners.

GAME ADMINISTRATOR FUNCTIONALITY

BiblioBouts's game administrator functionality was limited to instructors who contacted the BiblioBouts development team asking for game creation

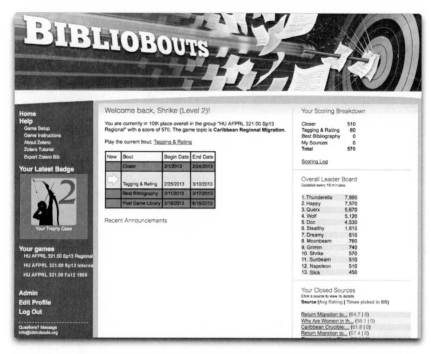

Figure 4.1. Game administrator home page with "Admin" link on the navigation bar.

authorization. In response, the team used super administrator status to up-grade the player's account to a game administrator account.

Figure 4.1 displays the BiblioBouts home page for a game administrator, and in this case, the game administrator is an instructor. On the left is a navigation bar for switching between games, changing one's profile, getting help, or logging off. In the center is a table that displays one of the instructor's games, with an arrow highlighting the current bout. On the far right is current information about this game—for example, a bout-by-bout breakdown of the instructor's score, the leader board, and links to evaluations of the sources the instructor submitted to this game. The navigation bar's "Admin" link distinguishes the game administrator home page from a player home page (figure 5.5).

Clicking on the navigation bar's "Admin" link opens BiblioBouts's administrator interface. Figure 4.2 displays the administrator interface, called "Admin Tools." In the center is a list of the instructor's current and past games, bearing four links that give instructors these tools for making changes to the game or observing player activity:

- Evaluation report: BiblioBouts reports game play data for all registered players that instructors can use to monitor student progress and grade students' game play performance.

- Create/edit news: Instructors fill out a form to create a news item that Bib-lioBouts displays to players on the home page the next time they log into this game.
- Edit player list: BiblioBouts displays a form bearing currently registered players' names that instructors can use to add or remove players from the game and determine who has or has not played the game to date.
- Edit start/end dates and settings: BiblioBouts displays a form that instructors edit to change this game's schedule and/or many parameters.

To create a new game, instructors clicked on the navigation bar's "Create New Game" link. In response, BiblioBouts displayed the "Set Up Your New Game" form that instructors completed to create a new game. Instructors entered four types of information into the form that BiblioBouts used to create and customize the new game: (1) game-content information, (2) players' e-mail addresses, (3) game-scheduling information, and (4) specific parameters particular to each bout. BiblioBouts used players' e-mail addresses to automatically invite players to the game via e-mail messages that contained game-content information (i.e., title, description, assigned topic, relevant databases, relevant keywords, a link to their institution's database portal, and a link to their library's ask-a-librarian service). To register, students clicked on a link in the e-mail message that took them to the game's login page, where they created an account with their e-mail address and a user name. Despite the game's instructions to the contrary, many students inadvertently registered

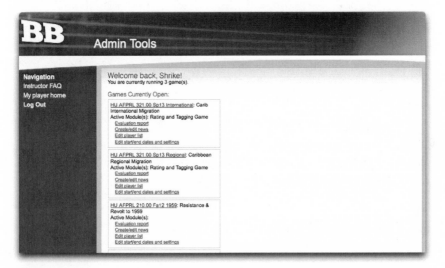

Figure 4.2.   BiblioBouts's administrator interface.

with their personal e-mail address instead of their school e-mail address. Because BiblioBouts linked their game invitation with their school e-mail address, if players signed onto the game using their personal e-mail address, BiblioBouts did not recognize them as authorized to join that game. This was a common problem reported to the game's e-mail support, and it could be eliminated by the game's integration into a course management system (CMS), a topic addressed in this chapter's discussion section.

The "Set Up Your New Game" form is lengthy because BiblioBouts needs a lot of information from instructors to create and customize their games. It links to an Instructor FAQ that gives even lengthier instructions. Figure 4.3 shows the top of the form where the instructor has entered the game's title, topic, and description and is about to enter the URLs of the library's database search page and ask-a-librarian service; below the fold are suggested databases, suggested keywords and phrases, and players' e-mail addresses. The game this instructor is creating is called "Caribbean Regional Migration," and it was a real BiblioBouts game played by undergraduate students at an American university. All figures in chapters 3 and 4 come from this game.

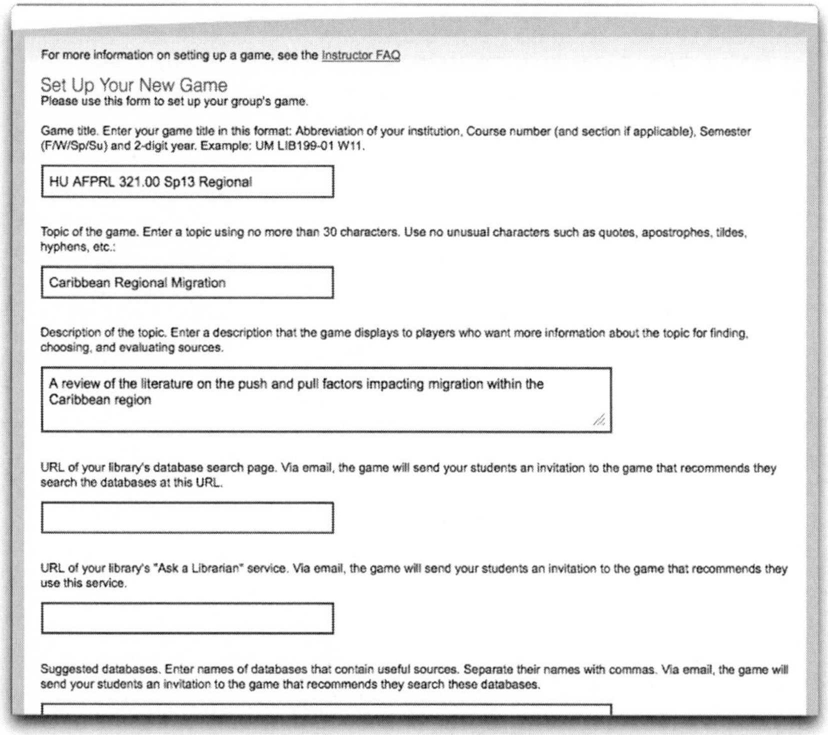
For more information on setting up a game, see the Instructor FAQ

Set Up Your New Game

Please use this form to set up your group's game.

Game title. Enter your game title in this format: Abbreviation of your institution, Course number (and section if applicable), Semester (F/W/Sp/Su) and 2-digit year. Example: UM LIB199-01 W11.

HU AFPRL 321.00 Sp13 Regional

Topic of the game. Enter a topic using no more than 30 characters. Use no unusual characters such as quotes, apostrophes, tildes, hyphens, etc.:

Caribbean Regional Migration

Description of the topic. Enter a description that the game displays to players who want more information about the topic for finding, choosing, and evaluating sources.

A review of the literature on the push and pull factors impacting migration within the Caribbean region

URL of your library's database search page. Via email, the game will send your students an invitation to the game that recommends they search the databases at this URL.

URL of your library's "Ask a Librarian" service. Via email, the game will send your students an invitation to the game that recommends they use this service.

Suggested databases. Enter names of databases that contain useful sources. Separate their names with commas. Via email, the game will send your students an invitation to the game that recommends they search these databases.

Figure 4.3. Entering the game's description on the "Set Up Your New Game" form.

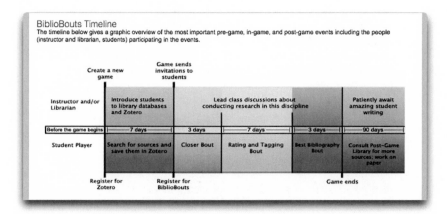

Figure 4.4.   BiblioBouts's timeline on the "Set Up Your New Game" form.

To help instructors synchronize game play activities with the research paper assignment, the form includes a timeline, showing pre-game, in-game, and post-game events graphically, the length of time instructors should devote to each event, and the people participating in the events (figure 4.4).

Under the timeline is the portion of the "Set Up Your New Game" form where instructors enter their game's dates and each bout's quotas or caps (figure 4.5). BiblioBouts automatically enters dates based on the timeline's suggested periods for bouts and the current date. The game also automatically enters default quota and cap values onto the form. The design team established default values based on (1) the minimum game play needed to generate at least three evaluations per source to create average scores, and (2) players' comments in focus group interviews regarding the maximum amount of effort they would put into the game. Instructors can accept BiblioBouts's default values or change them as desired. Added to the form are instructions for filling it out that include advice to instructors about the consequences of changing default values. Figure 4.5 shows dates and parameters for starting the game and for the Closer and Tagging & Rating (T&R) bouts. Scrolling down would reveal more dialogue boxes for entering dates and parameters for the Best Bibliography bout and Post-Game Library. In figure 4.5, the instructor has accepted the game's suggested parameter values for the Closer and T&R bouts but has scheduled more time for them.

When instructors finish filling in the "Set Up Your New Game" form, they click the "Create Game" button at the bottom of the form. In response, BiblioBouts creates a game using the information that the instructor entered onto the form. BiblioBouts lists the new game's title on the home page navigation bar (figure 4.1). Clicking on the title triggers the administrator interface (fig-

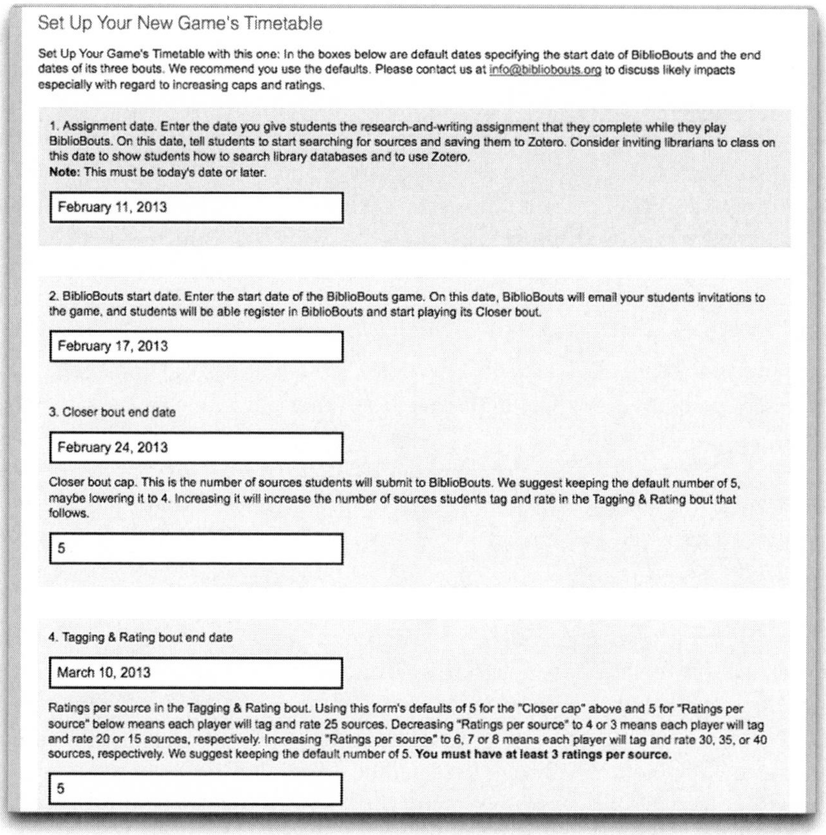
Set Up Your New Game's Timetable

Set Up Your Game's Timetable with this one: In the boxes below are default dates specifying the start date of BiblioBouts and the end dates of its three bouts. We recommend you use the defaults. Please contact us at info@bibliobouts.org to discuss likely impacts especially with regard to increasing caps and ratings.

1. Assignment date. Enter the date you give students the research-and-writing assignment that they complete while they play BiblioBouts. On this date, tell students to start searching for sources and saving them to Zotero. Consider inviting librarians to class on this date to show students how to search library databases and to use Zotero.
Note: This must be today's date or later.

February 11, 2013

2. BiblioBouts start date. Enter the start date of the BiblioBouts game. On this date, BiblioBouts will email your students invitations to the game, and students will be able register in BiblioBouts and start playing its Closer bout.

February 17, 2013

3. Closer bout end date

February 24, 2013

Closer bout cap. This is the number of sources students will submit to BiblioBouts. We suggest keeping the default number of 5, maybe lowering it to 4. Increasing it will increase the number of sources students tag and rate in the Tagging & Rating bout that follows.

5

4. Tagging & Rating bout end date

March 10, 2013

Ratings per source in the Tagging & Rating bout. Using this form's defaults of 5 for the "Closer cap" above and 5 for "Ratings per source" below means each player will tag and rate 25 sources. Decreasing "Ratings per source" to 4 or 3 means each player will tag and rate 20 or 15 sources, respectively. Increasing "Ratings per source" to 6, 7 or 8 means each player will tag and rate 30, 35, or 40 sources, respectively. We suggest keeping the default number of 5. **You must have at least 3 ratings per source.**

5

Figure 4.5. Entering the schedule and bout parameters on the "Set Up Your New Game" form.

ure 4.2), where the new game is listed along with links to four administrator tools. Instructors can immediately use two of the tools (i.e., "Edit player list" and "Edit start/end dates and settings") to add or remove players, reschedule the game, or edit the new game's parameters. Once the new game starts, instructors can use the "Create/edit news" tool to communicate with players and the "Evaluation report" tool to monitor students' game play progress.

The quickest way for instructors to monitor students is to check the leader board on their home page (figure 4.1). Scanning player names reveals which students are playing the game, leading, trailing, or in the middle of the pack. (Note that figures show made-up aliases, not player names or player-set aliases.)

Much more comprehensive for monitoring students' participation in the game and grading them was BiblioBouts's evaluation report. It detailed their participation using four tables (figures 4.6 to 4.9). Figure 4.6 shows the evaluation report's table 1, which lists the game's summary attributes such as its quotas and caps, the group's average number of sources, and the group's highest number of sources.

Figure 4.6 summarizes a BiblioBouts game with thirteen players, sixty closed sources, default cap values for the Closer and Best Bibliography bouts, and a quota of two dozen sources for the T&R bout. The T&R quota depends on the number of closed sources, players, and T&R ratings per source. Scanning figure 4.6 reveals that several of this game's players exceeded the T&R quota because the class averaged thirty-five evaluated sources, and the highest number of evaluated sources was fifty-three.

Figure 4.7 shows the evaluation report's table 2, which lists players and the extent of their game play activity in the three bouts. Cell data are color coded so that instructors can quickly scan game play activity to determine players who have not played the particular bout (pink), players who have failed to meet the particular bout's quota (yellow), players who have met the particular bout's quota (white), and players who have exceeded the particular bout's quota (blue).

Scanning cap and quota columns in figure 4.7 reveals that one player (Slick) failed to play the Closer bout and one player (Napoleon) failed to reach the T&R bout's quota. Trying to make up for his initial nonparticipation, Slick evaluated more than twice as many sources as the T&R bout mandated. Thunderella, Querx, and Grimm also surpassed the T&R bout's quota in a big way. Napoleon's failure to reach the T&R bout's quota probably explains why he was listed at the bottom of the leader board. All thirteen players met the Best Bibliography bout's cap. Twenty-seven and twenty-five players, respectively, cited the sources that Moonbeam and Stealthy donated to the game, and these two players topped the leader board at the end of the game.

Figure 4.8 shows the evaluation report's table 3, which lists average, high, and minimum scores for this game's bouts. Its usefulness becomes more apparent when it is set side by side with the evaluation report's table 4 (figure

---

Group Evaluation Report

HU AFPRL 321.00 Sp13 Regional on broad-based topic **Caribbean Regional Migration**.

Table 1. Quota or cap for minimum-level game play, group average no. of sources, and the group highest no. of sources.

Activity	Closer	T&R	Best Bib
Quota or cap	5	24	10
Group average	5	35	10
Group high	5	53	10

No. players = **13** | No. closed sources = **60** | No. T&R ratings per source = **5**

Figure 4.6.   A game's summary attributes from the evaluation report.

Table 2. Players in the group, number of sources players closed in the Closer bout, tagged/rated in the Tagging & Rating bout, and chose for their Best Bibliography; also the number of times the player's closed sources are cited in best bibliographies and the player's final leader board rank.

■ = No activity   = Below quota   = At quota   ■ = Above quota   ■ = Not open

Names	Closer	T&R	Best Bib	Source #1 Cited	Source #2 Cited	Source #3 Cited	Source #4 Cited	Source #5 Cited	Total Sources Cited	Rank
Grimm	5	48	10	2	1	1	1	1	6	6
Stealthy	5	25	10	9	8	3	3	2	25	2
Sunbeam	5	37	10	8	6	1	1	0	16	5
Napoleon	5	17	10	1	1	1	0	0	3	13
Doc	5	27	10	6	2	1	1	0	10	9
Dreamy	5	25	10	4	1	1	1	0	7	11
Wolf	5	33	10	2	1	1	0	0	4	10
Querx	5	49	10	2	2	0	0	0	4	7
Thunderella	5	49	10	6	2	1	1	0	10	4
Slick	0	53	10	N/A	N/A	N/A	N/A	N/A	0	8
Happy	5	43	10	6	2	2	2	0	12	3
Moonbeam	5	28	10	8	8	5	4	2	27	1
Shrike	5	24	10	2	2	1	1	0	6	12

Figure 4.7.   Extent of game play activity from the evaluation report.

4.9), a display of each player's bout-by-bout scores and final rank on the leader board.

According to figure 4.8, player scores for the Closer and Best Bibliography bouts had little variability, averaging around five hundred and one thousand points, respectively, for players meeting these bouts' caps. Players earned most points for exceeding the T&R bout's quota; in fact, five players accrued over ten thousand points as a result of doing so. Four of these five players averaged about four thousand T&R bonus points, earned by adding comments, opening full-texts, and approximating other players' credibility and relevance ratings during the source evaluation process. BiblioBouts's

Table 3. Group average/high scores per bout including post-bout bonus point scores.

■ = Active scoring   ■ = Not open

Scores	Closer	T&R	T&R bonus pts	Best Bib	Best Bib bonus pts	Cited sources bonus pts	End-of-game bonus pts	Total
Group average score per bout	462	6965	2711	1071	1694	7500	1560	14463
Group high score per bout	510	11800	4200	1700	1900	20250	2050	N/A
Minimum score for meeting quotas/caps	410	3280	N/A	1000	N/A	N/A	N/A	4690

Figure 4.8.   Average, high, and minimum scores from the evaluation report.

Table 4. Players' scores per bout including post-bout bonus point scores.

■ = No activity   ■ = Below quota   □ = At quota   ■ = Above quota   ■ = Not open

Names	Closer	T&R	T&R bonus pts	Best Bib	Best Bib bonus pts	Cited sources bonus pts	End of game bonus pts *	Total	Rank
Grimm	510	11300	4000	1700	1130	4500	1510	24650	6
Stealthy	510	4780	1595	1000	1775	18750	1950	30360	2
Sunbeam	510	6810	3105	1000	1680	12000	1675	26780	5
Napoleon	510	740	960	1030	1395	2250	1410	8295	13
Doc	510	4020	1590	1000	1890	7500	1735	18245	9
Dreamy	490	4520	2025	1000	1810	5250	1700	16795	11
Wolf	510	6610	2610	1010	1750	3000	1820	17310	10
Querx	510	10160	4075	1000	1745	3000	1140	21630	7
Thunderella	490	10610	3940	1000	1760	7500	1600	26900	4
Slick	0	11800	4200	1000	1620	0	0	18620	8
Happy	490	10300	3485	1180	1800	9000	1895	28150	3
Moonbeam	450	4430	1910	1000	1765	20250	2050	31855	1
Shrike	510	4460	1750	1000	1900	4500	1800	15920	12

* End of game bonus pts may be a negative score until after the Best Bibliography Bout has completed.
Evaluation Report FAQ

For in-depth research and analysis only:
Closer (February 01, 2013-February 24, 2013): Download Closer Stats
T&R (February 25, 2013-March 10, 2013): Download T&R Stats
Best Bibliography (March 11, 2013-March 17, 2013): Download Best Bib Stats
Citations to Closed Sources: Download Citations to Closed Source Stats

Figure 4.9.   Player scores and ranks from the evaluation report.

most lucrative scoring opportunity was the 750-point bonus players earned every time an opponent cited one of their closed sources in his or her best bibliography. Moonbeam and Stealthy topped the leader board at the end of the game because their donated sources were cited in the most players' best bibliographies; however, Happy placed third because of the many sources she evaluated during the T&R bout. This is precisely how BiblioBouts's designers wanted BiblioBouts's scoring algorithm to work—placing players who contributed the best sources and participated fully in game play at the top of the leader board at the end of the game.

Instructors can cut-and-paste evaluation report data into a Google Docs spreadsheet to conduct analyses for grading or other purposes. At the bottom of the evaluation report is the "Evaluation Report FAQ" link (figure 4.9), which instructors can click to retrieve detailed explanations of evaluation report data, including suggestions for how to grade students using these data.

Also at the very bottom of the evaluation report are four "Stats" links (figure 4.9), which retrieve data tables that are logs of the sources players closed, rated, and chose for their best bibliographies. BiblioBouts team members were the primary users of these logs for their in-depth evaluation of BiblioBouts player activity, but a couple of instructors used these files to check on individual students—for example, assessing their credibility and relevance comments, comparing their closed sources with the sources they cited in their papers, and responding to challenges from students regarding grades. In our experience, the vast majority of instructors desired to keep most details at arm's length; however, to satisfy the interest of some instructors for as much information as possible, we suggest that information literacy games produce game play logs with sufficient documentation so that interested instructors can analyze logs to assess students' performance and game play behavior.

DISCUSSION

When we designed the BiblioBouts information literacy game, we focused entirely on its interface, features, and scoring. Neither our original proposals to funding agencies nor our on-paper mock-ups of game action included an administrator interface. Only after reaching a consensus on BiblioBouts's overall design did we give attention to this aspect. Designing and developing the administrator interface took much less time and effort than it took to design and develop the game; however, designing and developing both simultaneously, instead of retrofitting the administrator interface into the game, would have been more efficient.

Of all the administrator tools, the "Set Up Your New Game" form was the most complicated, asking instructors to schedule bouts over various time periods and set parameters for caps and quotas and referring to concepts that were unfamiliar to them as first-time users. In response to instructors' requests for more game creation information, we created an Instructor FAQ that gave more in-depth instructions and explanations, but we could have done more, adding tutorial videos and an instructor forum where instructors could share their experiences.

Integrating BiblioBouts into a course management system (CMS) could simplify game administration. For example, the game would be one of several tools that instructors could add to their CMS course site, eliminating the need for additional game registration, accounts, passwords, and game invitations. All students enrolled in a course site would automatically be enrolled in the game. CMS integration could simplify grading student performance, adding and removing players from the game, publishing reminders, and issuing news items connected with the game. Instructors might be more positively inclined to adopt games with CMS integration because it would lessen the burden of game administration. BiblioBouts team members experimented with CMS Learning Tools Interoperability (LTI) with success and reported their findings at an EDUCAUSE meeting (Leeder, Rosenberg, and Severance 2011).

SUMMARY

This chapter describes BiblioBouts's super administrator and game administrator functionalities, which the game development team used to administer the game system and game owners used to administer games in their classes, respectively. It showcases BiblioBouts's game administrator interface, which gives instructors tools for creating new games, editing existing ones, monitoring students' progress, and grading game play performance. Although BiblioBouts's administrator tools are specific to this library research game, information literacy games generally need administrator tools for many of the same functions.

Chapter Five

The BiblioBouts Game

The BiblioBouts game is conceived as a series of mini-games, or bouts. Playing each bout requires players to perform information-seeking tasks that exercise a discrete set of information literacy skills within the overall research process. It also makes them practice tasks over and over again so that they retain what they learn and add new skills to their daily work habits.

The game ushers students through the research process, focusing them on (1) resource discovery, (2) source selection, (3) source evaluation, and (4) best-source selection. Winners of the BiblioBouts information literacy game are players who submitted the sources on the topic in play that their fellow players rated highest for credibility and relevance and chose for their best bibliographies; however, all BiblioBouts players are winners because game play culminates in an actual bibliography of best sources that players can use to write their research papers.

This chapter tours the BiblioBouts game.

THE STRUCTURE OF THE BIBLIOBOUTS GAME

Table 5.1 presents the big picture overview of the beta 2.0 version of BiblioBouts, listing objectives, learning goals, and the number of days that we advised instructors to devote to each bout. This chapter's tour of the BiblioBouts game includes user support services that are available to instructors and students.

Table 5.1. The Bouts of BiblioBouts

Bout	Suggested Duration	Objectives	Learning Goals
Pre-game preparation (formerly the Donor bout)	Seven days	Search for online sources and save their citations and full-texts using the Zotero citation management tool.	Students become experienced users of professional resource discovery tools, finding and saving sources and managing their citation and full-text representations in a citation management system.
Closer	Three days	Choose one's best saved sources to "do battle" in the game.	Students develop proficiency in selecting their best saved sources on an academic topic.
Tagging & Rating (T&R)	Seven days	Evaluate the content and quality of classmates' sources.	Students practice evaluating sources based on indicators of their quality and their relevance to the topic in play.
Best Bibliography	Three days	Practice formulating a research paper topic and building a bibliography of the best sources for writing one's research paper.	Students practice formulating their research paper's topic and choosing the best sources for writing the paper from the BiblioBouts database of all sources players submitted to the game.
Post-Game Library	Ninety days	Refine one's topic and adjust one's selected sources accordingly.	Students practice refining their research paper's topic, assessing the sources they originally chose, and choosing the best ones from the Post-Game Library and other resources.

Preparing for Game Play

To get students started, instructors assign students a broad-based topic to research and specify the minimum number of sources they are expected to find online on the topic. This number is usually five sources, the default number of sources students submit to BiblioBouts at the start of the game.

Later in the game, students specialize, choosing an aspect of the broad-based topic to write about in their papers. The game's instructional material advises students to choose the very best sources they find on the assigned topic because these sources "do battle" in the game against other sources. If fellow students give the student's sources the highest credibility and relevance ratings and choose them for their best bibliographies, there is a good chance the student will place high on the leader board and maybe even win the game.

Pre-game preparation is a combination of offline and online activity. If players do not already have the Firefox open-source browser on their computers, they must download and install it, as well as the free Zotero citation management extension, before they can begin the game. Prior to the start of BiblioBouts, a librarian visits the class to introduce students to the library's database portal, demonstrates one or two relevant databases, and shows them how to use Zotero to save citations and full-texts for the sources they find online. After the librarian's visit, students have at least seven days to register for a Zotero account, find sources on the broad-based topic in play, and save them to Zotero.

Zotero is an open-source citation management system that anyone can use to automatically create citations for online sources, formulate new citations from scratch, and save full-text attachments (usually PDFs or website snapshots). Zotero automatically imports bibliographic metadata from an online source and formats it into a citation, saving students the sometimes difficult task of manually assembling citations. Citations are stored and easily exportable, helping in the assembly of bibliographies. When users save sources in Zotero, they can quickly relocate previously retrieved online sources without having to retrace their steps or devise their own makeshift methods to save these sources. Additionally, users can authorize Zotero to share their Zotero library with third-party applications such as BiblioBouts. Because Zotero is an open-source product, we could enlist Zotero to collect players' closed sources and share them with BiblioBouts. Without Zotero, we would have had to build our own citation management system, a task beyond the scope of the BiblioBouts project objectives, which would have resulted in a system prohibitively expensive to maintain over time.

BiblioBouts suggests databases where students can find relevant sources and keywords they can search with, extracting the information from the instructor's "Set Up Your New Game" form (figure 4.3) and messaging it to players in an e-mail message along with other pre-game details (figure 3.1). Figure 5.1 shows a Zotero user who has searched the ERIC database, found a relevant source, and saved it to her Zotero library by clicking on the "text" icon on the right corner of the URL dialogue box. On top is the citation in the ERIC database, and on the bottom is Zotero's triple-paned workplace.

In figure 5.1, Zotero automatically creates a citation for the source. For some database sources, Zotero also automatically downloads full-text PDFs too, but not for this ERIC source. The user has to manually download the PDF, place it into the "Caribbean" folder (bottom left Zotero pane), and name it ("yelvingtonCrucible.pdf"). This Zotero user is quite advanced, knowing how to manually download PDFs and having several separate folders in her Zotero library (bottom left Zotero pane), as well as several saved sources in her "Caribbean" folder (bottom center Zotero pane), for this game.

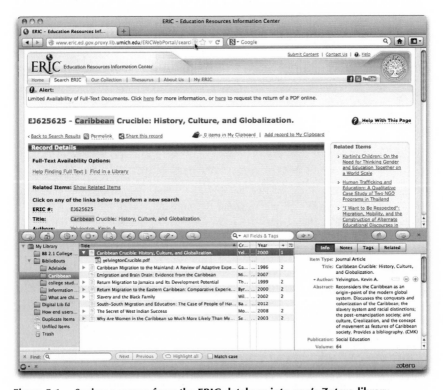

Figure 5.1.   Saving a source from the ERIC database into one's Zotero library.

Zotero has a steep learning curve, and its complexity should be apparent in figure 5.1. The user clicks on the "Zotero" icon on the browser's bottom right corner to open and close Zotero. When Zotero is open, it sits "in front" of the open browser; for example, in the case of figure 5.1, it sits in front of the ERIC database's search-and-display Web page. The user chooses actions listed under the pull-down menu buttons arranged horizontally in a row across the three Zotero panes. As a space-saving measure, Zotero does not name pull-down buttons, forcing the user to mouse over them to display tool-tipped button names and mouse down to browse actions classed under each button.

Manually downloading sources and saving them to Zotero is a multistep process. The user clicks on the database's PDF link, which triggers the "Save As . . . " dialogue box, names the PDF, and places the PDF into a folder on her personal computer. She then opens the Zotero pane, mouses down on Zotero's paper clip icon, chooses the "Attach Stored Copy of File . . . " option, navigates to the folder on her personal computer where she stored the PDF, and chooses this PDF. Players needing assistance with Zotero use can ask a librarian at their institution's library for assistance, consult the Zotero quick-start guide, watch Zotero tutorials, or search the Zotero user forums.

Most instructors schedule the pre-game preparation period to last seven days or longer. Thus, students have a full week to find five or so sources on the broad-based topic in play and save them to Zotero.

Playing the Closer Bout

BiblioBouts sends an e-mail message to students on the day the Closer bout begins. The message invites students to the BiblioBouts game, instructing them first to register for a BiblioBouts account. Students begin game play with five or so sources on the broad-based topic that they have saved in Zotero during the pre-game preparation period.

When a registered student logs on to BiblioBouts for the first time, BiblioBouts polls Zotero, counts the student's closed sources, and checks them for full-text attachments. If BiblioBouts detects sources meeting or exceeding the Closer cap that also bear full-text attachments, the game clears the student to play the Closer bout. If it does not, BiblioBouts displays the sources it detects in two lists, one for closed sources with full-text attachments and another for sources without attachments. It informs the student that she cannot play BiblioBouts until she saves more sources with full-text attachments. The message includes a link to the library's database portal so the student can click the link to search for more sources. Figure 5.2 depicts this scenario.

When BiblioBouts detects the right number of sources with full-text attachments in Zotero, it displays a message telling students how many sources it

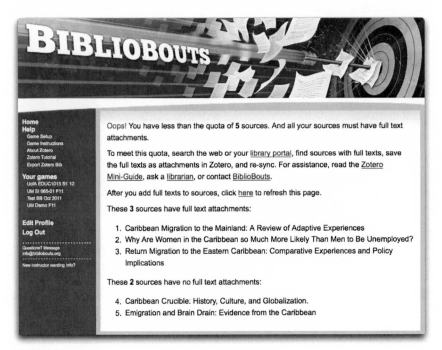

Figure 5.2. Too few saved sources to play BiblioBouts.

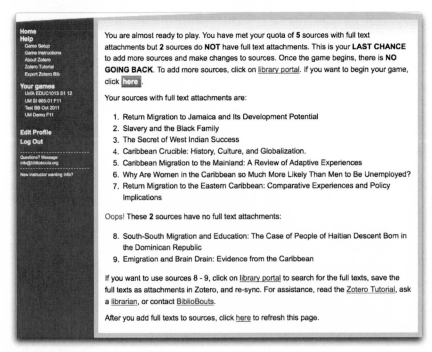

Figure 5.3. The right number of sources to play BiblioBouts.

detects with and without attachments and giving them the choice to add more sources and attachments or play the game. Figure 5.3 shows this message.

Of the several options available to students who have enough sources to play the game, most students click on the "here" button in figure 5.3 to play the game. In response, BiblioBouts polls Zotero for their saved sources and downloads them in the background into BiblioBouts's shared database of all players' saved sources. BiblioBouts's response is to transition to the Closer bout. This bout's objective is for players to choose their best saved sources to "do battle" in the game. Figure 5.4 shows how the player chooses sources in the Closer bout.

On the left side of the page, the Closer bout lists the player's closed sources. The player can scroll through the list to become reacquainted with her sources' content by reading abstracts and clicking on "Full Text" links to read attached full-texts. To choose a source, the player clicks the "Add to

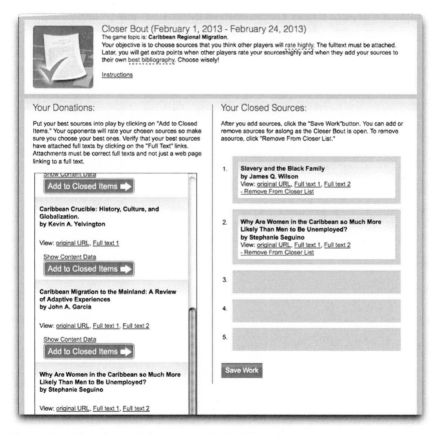

Figure 5.4. Choosing one's best sources in the Closer bout.

Closed Items" button, and BiblioBouts relocates the source from the "Your Donations" list on the left to the "Your Closed Sources" list on the right. In figure 5.4, the player has chosen two sources so far and must choose three more to reach this bout's cap of five closed sources. Clicking on the "Save Work" button locks in the player's closed sources.

BiblioBouts automatically scores student participation in the Closer bout. The player earns a base score of 10 points for each closed source, a 360-point bonus upon reaching the Closer bout's cap, and a 20-point bonus for being the first person to close a source that no one else has closed. Players who give the Closer bout short shrift—for example, by choosing nonrelevant or less-than-credible sources—might not earn bonus points for their closed sources later in the game because their opponents neither give their closed sources high ratings nor add them to their best bibliographies.

Playing the Tagging & Rating (T&R) Bout

Evaluating sources is the objective of the T&R bout. BiblioBouts randomly chooses an opponent's closed source, displays it to the player, and asks the player to assess the source in several ways. Is the source accompanied by a complete and correct full-text? How complete is its citation? What is the source in terms of format or genre? Who published it? What three big ideas characterize the source's content? How relevant is the source vis-à-vis the broad topic in play? How credible is the source? What are the player's reasons for giving this source the relevance and credibility ratings he or she does?

The T&R bout's quota—that is, the minimum number of sources that players are required to tag and rate—depends on the number of ratings per source that the instructor sets during game creation (figure 4.5), the total number of sources players close in the Closer bout, and the number of players in the game. For example, a T&R quota of twenty-five sources is a result of the instructor setting ratings per source at five during game creation and twenty players in the class closing a total of one hundred sources (5 ratings × 100 sources / 20 students).

To play the T&R bout, students sign onto BiblioBouts, which opens their home page, where a table lists bouts and uses an arrow to indicate the current bout. Clicking the arrow starts the T&R bout. Figure 5.5 shows this interaction.

The player home page is very similar to the game administrator home page for instructors (figure 4.1). On the left is the navigation bar for switching between games, changing one's profile, getting help, or logging off. In the center is a table with the current bout highlighted. On the far right is game summary information—in this case, a bout-by-bout breakdown of this

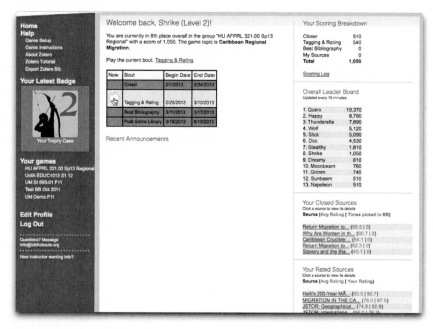

Figure 5.5. Player home page.

player's score, a link to this player's detailed scoring log, this game's leader board, links to other players' evaluations of this player's closed sources, and links to this player's evaluations of her opponents' sources.

To play the T&R bout, the player clicks on the "Tagging & Rating" link in the center table of figure 5.5. In response, BiblioBouts begins the T&R bout, randomly choosing an opponent's source and displaying its title, citation, abstract, and full-text links in the center of the T&R bout's Web page (figure 5.6). At any time during T&R tasks, the player can download and read the source's full-text to double-check its quality and usefulness. The player's first T&R task is to perform two checks of the opponent's source: (1) a full-text check, and (2) a full-citation check (figure 5.6). We purposely omitted the BiblioBouts navigation bar from this chapter's remaining figures to focus attention on the unique content of game play pages. Consult figure 5.5 for this navigation bar.

The T&R bout asks the player whether the attached full-text is correct in view of the source's citation and abstract. In figure 5.6, the player opens the attached full-text to double-check it (bottom right) and responds positively to both the full-text check and the full-citation check questions (center).

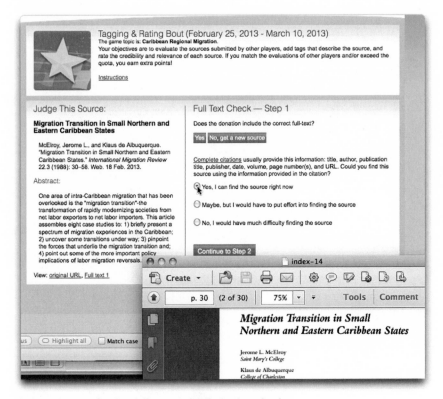

Figure 5.6. Conducting full-text and full-citation checks.

Next, the T&R bout transitions to a three-part tagging task that asks the player to characterize the source's content in terms of three big ideas, information format (IF), and publisher. First, the T&R bout prompts the player for three big ideas that characterize the source's subject contents. A tool tip delivers this definition of a big idea: "a word or a very short phrase that describes a single concept, e.g., Afghan war, deforestation, election reform, redistricting, video games." The player enters each big idea into a separate dialogue box. On the right side of figure 5.7 are displayed the three big ideas for the source on the left.

Second, the T&R bout prompts the player to describe the source's information format. To accomplish this, it asks the player to answer the question "What is this source?" by mousing down on a pull-down menu and mousing up on the IF term that best describes the source. Figure 5.7 shows how a player chooses an IF tag. In the pull-down menu, IFs are grouped according to these purposes and in this order:

- *To inform and/or facilitate learning:* Consumer magazine, consumer newspaper, trade magazine, trade newspaper, research report, conference proceedings, course material, encyclopedia, scholarly journal, dissertation or thesis, public affairs information, book
- *To promote or persuade:* Blog, promotional material, policy statement, public sharing site, informational video
- *To catalog or list:* Database, directory, online repository

In figure 5.7, the player chooses the "Scholarly journal" IF tag. Third, the T&R bout prompts the player to describe the source's publisher (PUB). To accomplish this, it asks the player to answer the question "Who published it?" by mousing down on a pull-down menu and mousing up on the PUB term that best describes the source. The player chooses a PUB in the same way she does an IF, except PUBs are not grouped because there are only six terms: individual person, commercial business, nonprofit organization, K–12 education institution, government organization, and higher education institution.

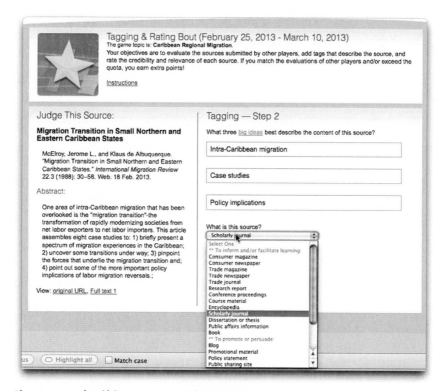

Figure 5.7.   Identifying a source's information format.

When the T&R bout transitions to credibility and relevance assessment, the opponent's source is still positioned on the left side of the Web page, along with its title, citation, abstract, and full-text links, so that the player has full access to both metadata and full-texts to perform the assessment. First, the player answers three questions about the source's credibility. Accompanying each explanation is a tool tip that the player clicks for more explanation. Questions and tool tips are as follows:

- To what extent do you believe that this source is written by an *expert*? (Tool tip: The source provides evidence that its author has expert knowledge, skills, and competence in the subject.)
- To what extent do you believe that this source is *trustworthy*? (Tool tip: The source provides evidence that the information is truthful, fair, and reliable.)
- To what extent do you believe that this source is *scholarly*? (Tool tip: The source is a product of serious academic study and, possibly, original research.)

The player uses sliders to register her ratings on a scale from 0 (not at all) to 100 (to a great extent). For bonus points, the player can enter a comment into the dialogue box that explains why she gave this source these ratings. Figure 5.8 shows the player's credibility ratings and comment for this source.

The player's final T&R task is relevance assessment. The source remains positioned on the left of the Web page so the player can check its title, citation, and abstract and open the full-text. The player answers three questions about the source's relevance. Accompanying each explanation is a tool tip that the player clicks for more explanation. Questions and tool tips are as follows:

- To what extent do you believe that this source contains *useful* information for this topic? (Tool tip: The source specifically relates to the subject at hand.)
- To what extent do you believe that this source has *accurate* information? (Tool tip: After reading the source, you know what it is about, and you could discuss its contents with someone else.)
- To what extent do you believe that this source has a quality *good enough* for you to use in your course work? (Tool tip: The source is appropriate for college-level writing on my topic.)

The player uses sliders to register her ratings on a scale from 0 (not at all) to 100 (to a great extent). For bonus points, the player can enter a comment into

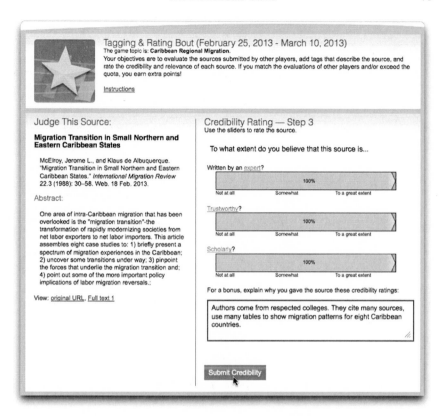

Figure 5.8. Rating and commenting on the source's credibility.

the dialogue box that explains why she gave this source these ratings. Figure 5.9 shows the player's relevance ratings and comment for this source.

At this point, the player is done with the T&R bout's three tasks connected with the displayed source (i.e., checking its correctness, tagging its content, and assessing its credibility and relevance). Under the comment dialogue box in figure 5.9 are three buttons; clicking on any one of them automatically submits the player's evaluation to BiblioBouts and enables the player to (1) evaluate another source ("Submit & Rate Another" button), (2) see other players' evaluations for the source she just evaluated ("Submit & See Others' Ratings" button), or (3) exit the T&R bout ("Submit & Exit" button). In response to the player who chooses the first button, BiblioBouts displays a feedback page bearing the tags and ratings that her opponents gave to this same source. Figure 5.10 shows the top half of the feedback page where the player's credibility and relevance ratings for the source are put side by side

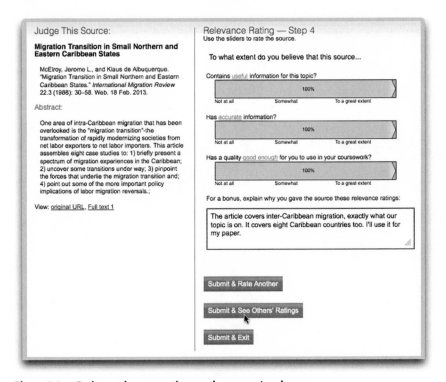

Figure 5.9.   Rating and commenting on the source's relevance.

with the combined ratings of her opponents so that she can easily compare the two.

With respect to both credibility and relevance, the player is generally in agreement with her opponents, but all her ratings are higher than her opponents' ratings. Under ratings are listed the player's tags and opponents' tags, along with the number of players entering the same tags; for example, everyone assigned the "Scholarly journal" IF and "Higher education institution" PUB to this source. Scrolling down reveals the bottom half of the feedback page bearing tabs for the four players who evaluated this source (figure 5.11).

In figure 5.11, the open tab reveals the ratings and comments of the player named Happy. Her "eager beaver" and "cornucopia" badges for exceeding the T&R quota and contributing the most comments, respectively, and her level 4 accomplishment should make other players favorably inclined to her ratings and comments. In fact, both comments about credibility and relevance cite evidence for her assessments, such as the source's JSTOR origins, cited references, and subject content.

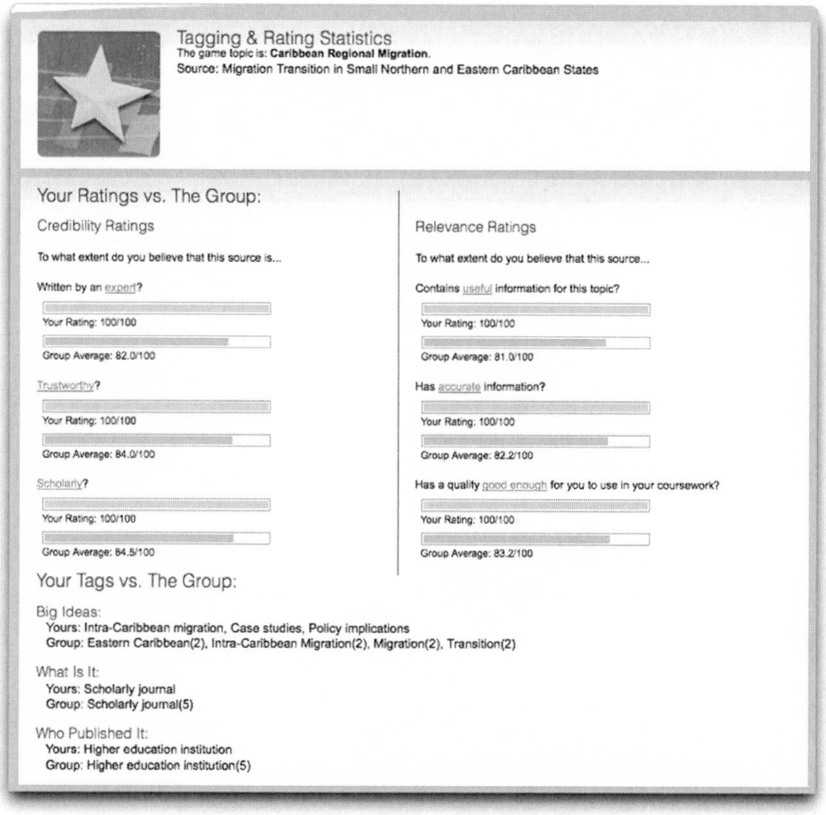

Figure 5.10. Top of feedback page showing credibility and relevance ratings.

BiblioBouts requires instructors to create games in which each source is evaluated at least three times. BiblioBouts's default is five evaluations per source. When players exceed the T&R bout's quota, sources receive more evaluations than the instructor-specified minimum number. Thus, the T&R bout's quota feature ensures that every source is evaluated multiple times so that players can see how others in the class evaluated the same sources they evaluated and earn bonus points based on how closely their ratings match average ratings for a source.

BiblioBouts automatically scores student participation in the T&R bout. The player earns a base score of 10 points for each source she rates and tags up to the quota and a 3,040-point bonus for reaching quota. For evaluating sources above the T&R bout's quota, the player earns 150 points per source for rating and tagging each of the next five sources, 250 points per source for

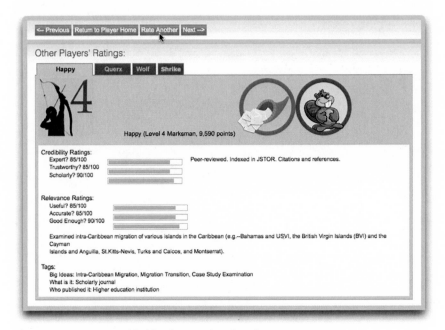

Figure 5.11.   **Bottom of feedback page showing player comments.**

each of the next five sources, 350 points per source for each of the next five sources, 250 points for each of the next five sources, 150 points for each of the next five sources, and after that, 10 points for each evaluated source. The player also earns bonus points for opening full-texts and adding comments about their credibility and relevance ratings. The player earns points during and after T&R game play. With regard to the latter, BiblioBouts has to compare the game play performance of several players to perform the calculations. Thus, the player earns "post-bout" bonus points when her relevance and credibility ratings are close to the average relevance and credibility ratings for the source, and her big ideas, IFs, and PUBs match other players' big ideas, IFs, and PUBs.

Playing the Best Bibliography Bout

The objective of the Best Bibliography bout is twofold: (1) to give students practice formulating a research paper topic within the purview of the broad-based topic that the instructor assigns to everyone in the class, and (2) to give them practice building a bibliography bearing the best closed sources for writing a paper on this topic from the BiblioBouts database of closed sources that everyone in the class contributed to the game. The player's first step is to enter her research paper's topic, describe the paper's argument, and enter three big ideas that she expects her paper to discuss. Figure 5.12 shows this first step. On the right is a list of everyone's big ideas that the player can browse or search to select relevant ones.

The player's paper topic is "Regional migration in the West Indies" and addresses these three big ideas: West Indies, regional migration, and reasons why people migrate back and forth. She enters more details about her paper's argument in the dialogue box. The player's next step is to click on the "Save and Go to Step 2" button. In response, BiblioBouts displays a list of everyone's closed sources, including citations, full-texts, ratings, and tags. The player can search, browse, or sort sources to find the best ones for her best bibliography (figure 5.13).

On the left is the Source Library bearing everyone's sources. Players can sort the list in several ways: (1) by credibility ratings from 100 to 0 percent or vice versa, (2) by relevance ratings from 100 to 0 percent or vice versa, (3) by a combination of the two from 100 to 0 percent or vice versa, (4) by date donated from most to least recent or vice versa, (5) by date published from

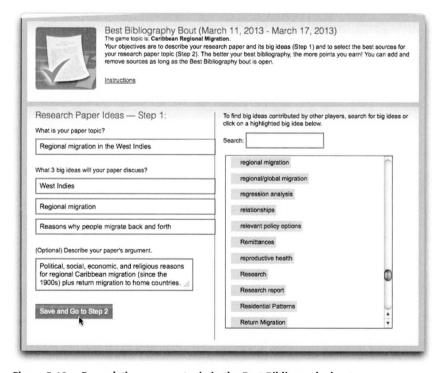

Figure 5.12. Formulating a paper topic in the Best Bibliography bout.

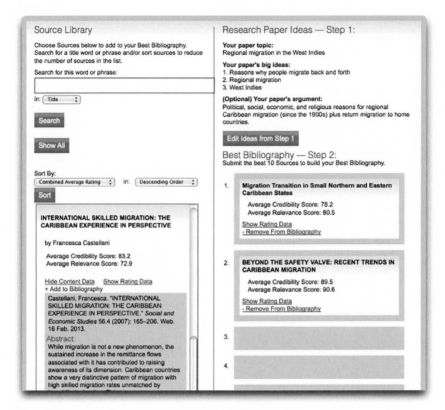

Figure 5.13. Choosing sources for one's best bibliography.

most to least recent or vice versa, or (6) alphabetically by title. They can also search Source Library titles by the initial keyword or title phrase. In figure 5.13, the player has sorted the list by combined average rating in descending order from 100 to 0 percent. On the right are ten slots that the player fills with sources by clicking the "+Add to Bibliography" link accompanying closed sources on the left. (The default number of sources is ten, but instructors can change this on the bottom half of the "Set Up Your New Game" form [figure 4.5]). In figure 5.13, the player has chosen two of ten required sources. She can save her work at any time by scrolling down and clicking on any one of the "Save" buttons under the chosen-sources list. The player can also display her best bibliography and save it to share with her instructor or to remind her of her topic and saved sources. Best bibliographies are a prospectus of the student's paper, bearing its topic and argument, the big ideas the student intends to discuss, and citations to the BiblioBouts sources she may use to write the paper (figure 5.14). BiblioBouts allows players to make changes to their best bibliography as long as the Best Bibliography bout is open.

As soon as the Best Bibliography bout ends, BiblioBouts calculates players' final scores, listing the winner at the top of the leader board and all other players below in rank order from the highest- to the lowest-place finishers. On the player's home page is the leader board that lists all players in the order they finished in the game (figure 5.5).

BiblioBouts automatically scores student participation in the Best Bibliography bout. The player earns a base score of 10 points for each source she adds to her best bibliography and a 900-point bonus for reaching quota. The player earns bonus points for opening full-texts, for adding a source to her best bibliography to which a consensus of players assigned a big idea that matches the big idea that the player intends to discuss in her paper, and for choosing high-quality sources in her best bibliography. BiblioBouts's determination of high-quality sources is based on a consensus of players tagging and rating sources in the T&R bout. Quality indicators are IF tags describing scholarly sources (e.g., book, conference proceedings, scholarly journal,

---

Best Bibliography

Your Research Paper Ideas

Your paper topic:
Regional migration in the West Indies

Your paper's big ideas:
1. Reasons why people migrate back and forth
2. Regional migration
3. West Indies

(Optional) Your paper's argument:
Political, social, economic, and religious reasons for regional Caribbean migration (since the 1900s) plus return migration to home countries.

Your Chosen Sources

1. Seguino, Stephanie. "Why Are Women in the Caribbean so Much More Likely Than Men to Be Unemployed?" *Social and Economic Studies* 52.4 (2003): 83–120. Web. 15 Feb. 2013.
2. Boswell, Thomas D. "The Characteristics of Internal Migration To and From New Providence Island (Greater Nassau), Bahamas 1960–1970." *Social and Economic Studies* 35.1 (1986): 111–150. Web. 17 Feb. 2013.
3. Perusek, Glenn. "Haitian Emigration in the Early Twentieth Century." *International Migration Review* 18.1 (1984): 4–18. Web. 22 Feb. 2013.
4. Roopnarine, Lomarsh. "INDO-CARIBBEAN INTRA-ISLAND MIGRATION: NOT SO MARGINALIZED!" *Social and Economic Studies* 54.2 (2005): 107–136. Web. 18 Feb. 2013.
5. Duany, Jorge. "Caribbean Migration to Puerto Rico: A Comparison of Cubans and Dominicans." *International Migration Review* 26.1 (1992): 46–66. Web. 17 Feb. 2013.
6. Roopnarine, Lomarsh. "UNITED STATES VIRGIN ISLANDS MIGRATION." *Social and Economic Studies* 57.3/4 (2008): 131–156. Web. 18 Feb. 2013.
7. Wiltshire, Rosina. "Caribbean Migration: Challenges to Leadership." *Journal of Eastern Caribbean Studies* 35.2 (2010): 61–79. Print.
8. Castellani, Francesca. "INTERNATIONAL SKILLED MIGRATION: THE CARIBBEAN EXPERIENCE IN PERSPECTIVE." *Social and Economic Studies* 56.4 (2007): 165–206. Web. 16 Feb. 2013.
9. McElroy, Jerome L., and Klaus de Albuquerque. "Migration Transition in Small Northern and Eastern Caribbean States." *International Migration Review* 22.3 (1988): 30–58. Web. 18 Feb. 2013.
10. Duany, Jorge. "BEYOND THE SAFETY VALVE: RECENT TRENDS IN CARIBBEAN MIGRATION." *Social and Economic Studies* 43.1 (1994): 95–122. Web. 18 Feb. 2013.

Figure 5.14. My best bibliography.

trade journal), PUB tags describing a quality publisher type (e.g., government organization, higher education institution), and significantly above-average relevance or credibility ratings. Players earn points during and after Best Bibliography game play. With regard to the latter, BiblioBouts's most lucrative scoring opportunity is the 750-point bonus earned every time an opponent adds one of the player's closed sources to his or her best bibliography.

Consulting the Post-Game Library

As soon as the Best Bibliography bout ends, the Post-Game Library opens to registered game players. The library contains the closed sources submitted

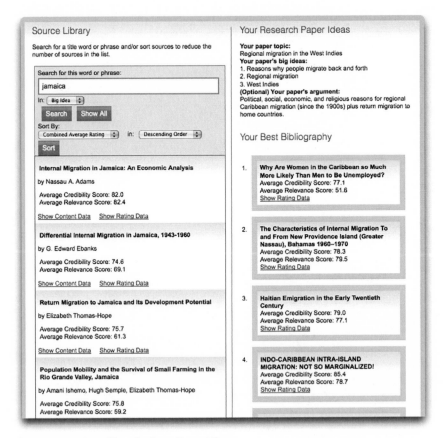

Figure 5.15. Searching the Post-Game Library.

by all players to the game with the addition of consensus big ideas, tags, and ratings from the T&R bout. Using the Post-Game Library is the same as using the Best Bibliography bout's Source Library. Players can sort, search, and browse listed sources; cut-and-paste citations; read abstracts; scrutinize big ideas, IFs, and PUBs; and download and read full-texts. The library is open to registered game users for ninety days, and instructors can extend this period in the game's administrative interface.

Figure 5.15 displays the Post-Game Library on the left side of the Web page along with functionality for searching, sorting, and browsing sources. On the right side of the page is the player's best bibliography. In response to the player's request, BiblioBouts searches for sources to which players assigned the big idea "Jamaica" and sorts retrievals by combined average rating in descending order from 100 to 0 percent.

USER SUPPORT FOR THE BIBLIOBOUTS GAME

BiblioBouts is a complex game for students to play. Right from the start, they have to use professional resource-discovery tools to find and save sources, and some students will be using these tools for the first time. Zotero especially has a steep learning curve, and its full-featured interface is complicated for BiblioBouts players who are using only a fraction of its full-featured functionality to save sources and share them with BiblioBouts. Students have to register to use Zotero and BiblioBouts. Using their library's database portal also requires online authorization.

BiblioBouts is a series of mini-games, or bouts. When one bout ends, the next begins. Game play is different from bout to bout, introducing players to new information literacy concepts and skills and giving them hands-on practice applying concepts and skills in a real information-seeking context. Repetition is an important aspect of BiblioBouts game play. Players practice various information literacy skills so that they become increasingly more familiar with them. Game play is cumulative, adding up to a real bibliography that players can use to write their research papers.

Due to BiblioBouts's complexity, the BiblioBouts team established user support services to assist game players and instructors. Especially helpful in this regard was team member Victor Rosenberg (1987), who drew on his experience establishing such services for the ProCite reference management software. This section reviews BiblioBouts user support services, distinguishing between services that were unique to the research and those that were an integral part of the game to ensure its usability.

Enlisting Library Liaisons

Assisting the BiblioBouts team at participating institutions were library liaisons who participated in all phases of the research project (see pages 35 and 37). They were the linchpin of the research project's deployment and evaluation phases, recruiting interested faculty, helping them incorporate BiblioBouts into their syllabi and assignments, deploying it in their classes, and conducting the evaluation. Some of them were BiblioBouts instructor-users themselves, deploying it in the information literacy classes they taught and participating in the evaluation.

Game deployment included prepping students prior to the start of a BiblioBouts game. Library liaisons visited classes at least two times: on the first visit they introduced students to the library's database portal, suggested one or more relevant databases for searches related to the assigned broad-based topic, demonstrated how to search these databases, and showed students how to use Zotero to save online sources; on the second visit they introduced students to and helped them register for BiblioBouts.

When the registration process for BiblioBouts's alpha version proved especially complicated and error-prone for players, library liaisons were the first line of defense, so to speak, troubleshooting technical problems, identifying recurring ones, and sharing their solutions with everyone. Early on in the project, they had to return to classes a third or fourth time to help everyone get registered in Zotero and BiblioBouts.

Beginning with the beta 1.0 version of BiblioBouts, the team made BiblioBouts available to instructors for the asking. At nonparticipating institutions, there were no library liaisons to assist with deployment. Thus, the team had to put in place specific user support services that would support instructors and students at both nonparticipating and participating institutions.

Using E-Mail

Always present on the player's home page and the BiblioBouts sign-in page was this simple instruction: "Questions? Message info@bibliobouts.org." Clicking the link sent messages to BiblioBouts team members tasked with user support who responded as soon as possible. Questions ranged from instructor inquiries regarding adopting BiblioBouts in their classes at nonparticipating institutions to inquiries from players at both participating and nonparticipating institutions who experienced technical difficulties. Answers to questions ran the gamut. Sometimes we had a ready-made FAQ that we could quickly send to instructors or students. Other times, the initial message ballooned into numerous back-and-forth e-mail exchanges that included players sending us screenshots of their Zotero or BiblioBouts interface to help us diagnose and solve technical problems.

Making Videos Available

Videos were invaluable for giving players a visual representation of the registration process, playing BiblioBouts generally, and playing individual bouts. Videos also described the game's objectives and gave players strategies for achieving them. We used videos to walk students through the registration and setup process and the game play process. The benefit of videos was control. The student could play and replay the videos, stop them, slow them down, and manipulate them while registering or playing a particular bout. Based on our experience, the bare-bones minimum for user support services includes registration and game play videos and an e-mail help line.

Giving Super Administrators an Account Login Tool

To help the BiblioBouts team diagnose players' technical problems, BiblioBouts technical staff built an account login tool that we used to log into a player's account to see for ourselves what the player was seeing. (This super administrator tool is also described in chapter 4.) Mostly the account login tool was used to diagnose problems students encountered when BiblioBouts polled Zotero for students' saved sources to start up the Closer bout. Unfortunately, team members could not see the player's Zotero interface, which might have more sources than BiblioBouts was able to load into the Closer bout; thus, students needed to e-mail us snapshots of their Zotero interface so that we could compare the two. Once BiblioBouts was able to grab enough saved sources from Zotero to begin the Closer bout, most technical problems were solved. We had the account login tool on hand to diagnose problems in the bouts that followed but seldom had to use it.

Publishing FAQs

As a result of post-game interviews with librarians, instructors, and players and the team's troubleshooting experiences, the BiblioBouts team added FAQs to BiblioBouts to provide users with detailed information about certain aspects of the game. Here is a list of BiblioBouts FAQs:

- Instructor FAQ on the BiblioBouts game login page: This FAQ gave instructors an overview of BiblioBouts so they could determine whether the game was right for their course.

- Instructions FAQ on all game play pages: This FAQ gave players a detailed explanation of the bout they were playing and included the bout's objectives and strategies for achieving them.
- Scoring FAQ on the status bar at the top of all game play pages: This FAQ enumerated all scoring opportunities available to players.
- Game creation FAQ on the game creation page: This FAQ gave instructors detailed explanations about completing the game creation form.
- Evaluation report FAQ on the evaluation report: This FAQ advised instructors about using the report's game play data to grade students' game play performance.

Scoring Issues

Post-game interviews revealed what appeared to be students' obsession with scoring. They wanted to know how to score points, why they scored them, what the highest score ever was, and so on. In addition to posting the Scoring FAQ on all game play pages, we responded with these scoring features:

- Leader board on center right of the player's home page (figure 5.5): The leader board ordered all players by score with the current leader on top.
- Scoring breakdown on the top right of the player's home page (figure 5.5): This table was a bout-by-bout breakdown of the player's score.
- Status bar on all game play pages: The status bar was a pervasive feature of all game play pages, displaying the player's score, her progress toward the bout's cap or quota, and a description of her most recent action and the points she earned for it. Figure 5.16 shows the status bar for a player who is playing the T&R bout and has evaluated eleven of the required twenty-four sources; her four last actions—opening a source's full-text to tag and rate it and adding comments for her ratings—earned her sixty points.
- The player's closed sources list: Under the leader board on the player's home page was a list of the player's closed sources (figure 5.5). Accompanying each source were two scores, the combined average relevance and credibility rating for the source and the number of times opponents had chosen the source for their best bibliographies. The player received a whopping 750-point bonus every time an opponent added one of her closed sources to a best bibliography and bonus points for high relevance and credibility ratings. When the Best Bibliography bout began, the player could check this reporting feature to see whether her donated sources were popular with her opponents.
- Scoring log: On the status bar was a link to the scoring log. Clicking the link opened the player's scoring log, detailing every action that earned the

Figure 5.16. Status bar.

player points from the beginning of the game to the end. Figure 5.17 shows the scoring log for a player who has completed the Closer and T&R bouts and is currently playing the Best Bibliography bout. In this example, the log is open to a list of player actions that earned points: 10 points each time she closed a source, 20 points each time she closed a unique source that no other player had closed, and 360 points for meeting the Closer bout's cap.

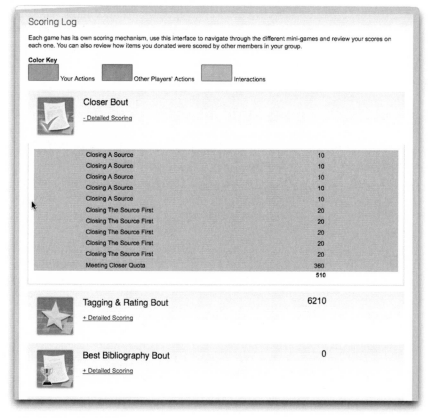

Figure 5.17. Scoring log.

Player actions are color coded in the scoring log. In green are the player's actions and points earned, in blue are other players' actions for which this player has earned points, and in brown are interactions between this player and other players for which this player has earned points. The log displays summary points for each bout. Clicking on the log's "+Detailed Scoring" link lists all scoring events and points earned. In figure 5.17, detailed scoring is enabled for the Closer bout; overall, the log shows scoring due to player actions only.

SUMMARY

The BiblioBouts game ushers students through the research process while they complete a related writing assignment. Game play guarantees that students use professional resource-discovery tools such as the library's database portal, scholarly databases, and citation management software to find and save sources. In the T&R bout especially, repetition is an important aspect of game play. Players practice evaluating sources so that they become increasingly more familiar with the questions they need to answer to identify high-quality sources. Game play exposes players to more sources than they would find on their own, and it is cumulative, adding up to a real bibliography that players can use to write their research papers. BiblioBouts's gamelike features, such as levels, the leader board, and badges, are expected to make library research fun and engaging. The game's features transform source evaluation into a collaborative endeavor that benefits everyone's search for the best sources to complete the related writing assignment.

User support services are an integral part of the game. Instructors want assistance creating and editing games, monitoring players' progress, and grading game play performance. Especially heavy users of these services are students whose game play is fraught with technical difficulties. Students also consult FAQs and videos for information about how to get started, what the game's objective is and the best strategies for reaching it, how scoring works, and what game actions earn the most points.

Chapter Six

The Methods Used to Evaluate BiblioBouts

Two goals drove the evaluation of the BiblioBouts information literacy game: (1) improving the BiblioBouts game system, and (2) determining its effectiveness for information literacy instruction. The evaluation featured a multi-methodological approach for data collection, enlisting both quantitative and qualitative methods so that the BiblioBouts evaluation team could cross-check results from one method with others and use qualitative data to explain quantitative results.

This chapter details the methods used to evaluate BiblioBouts, the data these methods produced, the research questions they addressed, and references to the chapters where research questions are answered. At participating institutions, the evaluation involved undergraduate students who completed game diary forms and pre- and post-game questionnaires; they also participated in focus group interviews immediately on completing the game and/or in follow-up interviews four or more months after playing BiblioBouts; and their activity was also recorded in game play logs. At both participating and nonparticipating institutions, instructors and librarians engaged in pre- and/or post-game personal interviews.

RESEARCH QUESTIONS

The evaluation sought answers to these specific research questions about BiblioBouts's effectiveness:

1. What incentives were needed for students to play BiblioBouts?
2. Did students play BiblioBouts?
3. How did they play the game?

4. What did players learn as a result of playing the game?
5. What did they retain as a result of playing it?
6. How did students benefit as a result of playing the game?
7. Did students prefer playing a game to learn information literacy skills and concepts over other teaching methods? Why?
8. What improvements did players want made to BiblioBouts?

Table 6.1 tells which methods yielded data to answer each of the eight research questions. The evaluation's seven methods are listed in the top row from *a* to *g*. Abbreviated forms of the eight research questions above are listed in the far-left column from 1 to 8, and Xs in columns indicate methods used to answer the particular research question. Capital Xs indicate the methods that were crucial to answering the question. The rest of this chapter gives specifics on each method.

Because human subjects were enlisted in the evaluation, the BiblioBouts team submitted an application to the University of Michigan's Institutional Review Board (IRB). IRB determined the study was "exempt from ongoing IRB review" because it was "research conducted in established or commonly accepted educational settings, involving normal educational practices."

"Participating institutions" refers to academic instructors, undergraduate students, and library liaisons from institutions participating in BiblioBouts's evaluation: Saginaw Valley State University (SVSU), Troy University Montgomery Campus (TUMC), the University of Baltimore (UB), and the University of Michigan (U-M). Participating institutions and library liaisons were named in our proposal to the Institute of Museum and Library Services, the proposal earmarked funds for subject payments, and library liaisons received approval from their university's IRB to conduct the evaluation. "Nonparticipating institutions" refers to academic instructors, undergraduate students, and librarians from institutions that did not participate in the evaluation; however, some instructors from nonparticipating institutions participated in personal interviews, and their participation was covered by the BiblioBouts team's application to U-M's IRB.

GAME DIARY FORMS

Game diary forms included a combination of closed- and open-ended questions that queried players about the one particular bout they had just played. Closed-ended questions asked players to estimate how much progress they had made and to rate their motivation for playing the particular bout and their satisfaction with the progress they made. Open-ended questions asked players

Table 6.1. Methods Used to Answer the Research Questions

Research Question	(a) Diary	(b) Questionnaires	(c) Focus Groups	(d) Follow-Up	(e) Logs	(f) Instructor Interviews	(g) Librarian Interviews
1. What incentives?			X				
2. Did students play?					X	X	X
3. How did they play?			X		X	X	X
4. Did players learn?			X	X		X	X
5. Did players retain?			X	X		X	
6. Did players benefit?		X	X	X		X	
7. Prefer gaming?			X			X	X
8. Improvements?	X	X	X		X	X	X

to describe what went well, what problems they experienced, how they solved these problems, and other experiences, feelings, and ideas about BiblioBouts that occurred to them during game play. Appendix A lists questions on the game diary forms.

The administration of game diary forms was accomplished via an online survey tool. Participation was voluntary, it took place immediately after players completed a bout, and players were paid $5 for each form they completed up to a limit of six forms per game. A total of two dozen forms were collected from players. To streamline payments to survey respondents, diary form administration was limited to game players at U-M.

Because the analysis of diary forms focused almost entirely on improving the BiblioBouts game (i.e., research question #8), diary form administration was limited to the evaluation of the alpha version of BiblioBouts, when game improvement was the BiblioBouts team's first priority. Added to the analysis of diary forms were comments from post-game questionnaires and focus group interviews about improving BiblioBouts. Analysis results fueled the redesign of BiblioBouts in the form of its beta 1.0 and 2.0 versions. How BiblioBouts evolved as a result of the analysis is summed up in table 3.3.

PRE- AND POST-GAME QUESTIONNAIRES FOR STUDENTS

Students completed pre- and post-game questionnaires in classes at participating institutions. The pre-game questionnaire was almost entirely closed ended, beginning with demographic questions (e.g., gender, major, and class). Three questions asked students to rate the specific library research tasks that they would encounter during BiblioBouts game play according to how challenging the tasks would be, how confident they were in performing them, and how well they thought they would do. The pre-game questionnaire also probed students about their existing information literacy knowledge and skills and their interest in playing an online game to learn about library research at the college level.

The post-game questionnaire featured the same closed-ended questions as the pre-game questionnaire plus a few new ones. Post-game questions that were the same as pre-game questions asked students to take their experience playing BiblioBouts into consideration in their answers. Two questions unique to the post-game questionnaire listed specific library research tasks and asked students to rate the amount of practice BiblioBouts gave them with each task and how much they felt their ability to perform each task improved as a result of playing BiblioBouts. The post-game questionnaire ended with an open-ended question that asked students what single improvement they would make to BiblioBouts. Appendixes B and C list questions on the pre- and post-game questionnaires, respectively.

The analysis of questionnaire responses helped answer research questions #6 and #8 (i.e., benefits of playing BiblioBouts and improvements to the game). Improvements to the game also came from diary forms and focus group interviews and figured prominently in the team's improvement of BiblioBouts (chapter 3). To determine whether players' perceptions of their library research skills improved as a result of playing BiblioBouts, we set up an experiment with a pre-/post-test design. Four large U-M classes completed questionnaires. Statistical tests could not be performed on questionnaire data because too few students completed both pre- and post-game questionnaires. We did, however, combine questionnaire responses from the four classes, and we discuss the results on pages 167–73.

FOCUS GROUP INTERVIEWS WITH STUDENTS

After the BiblioBouts game ended, BiblioBouts team members at U-M and library liaisons at SVSU, UB, and TUMC invited students from classes to participate in focus group interviews. Focus group questions were open ended. They probed how prepared students felt they were to play BiblioBouts, what they learned as a result of playing BiblioBouts, what they learned that they would apply to subsequent information-seeking situations, whether they felt an online game was an effective approach for learning how to conduct library research, and if they did, what other aspects of using the library and its resources they would like to learn about through a game or other means. Questions also elicited students' suggestions for improving BiblioBouts. Appendix D lists questions posed to focus group participants.

Because focus group questions were open ended, they addressed almost all research questions but especially questions #4, #6, and #7 (i.e., what players learned, the benefits of playing BiblioBouts, and whether players preferred a game over other teaching methods). Although the analysis of focus group interviews figured prominently in chapters 7 (i.e., pre-game preparation) and 11 (i.e., game play benefits), focus groups also provided insight into the amount of time it took to play BiblioBouts (pages 118–19), players' explanations of their relevance and credibility ratings (pages 150–51), and the sources players cited in their papers (pages 164–65).

A total of twenty-one focus group interviews were conducted at SVSU, TUMC, UB, and U-M, with interview groups averaging eight students from the same class. Students were paid $25 for their participation in focus groups;

plus, pizza and soda pop were served. Audio recordings were made during interviews and transcribed for analysis.

FOLLOW-UP INTERVIEWS WITH STUDENTS

Four or more months after U-M students from selected classes played BiblioBouts, the BiblioBouts team contacted them via e-mail messages and invited them to follow-up interviews. Interviews were conducted via online chat, and all questions were open ended. Generally, questions probed the impact BiblioBouts had on former players' subsequent library research—for example, what they remembered about BiblioBouts, what they had learned that they had since put into practice, whether playing BiblioBouts had changed the way they conducted research, whether they were doing a better job conducting library research as a result of playing BiblioBouts, and whether their experience playing BiblioBouts was the impetus for them to seek additional guidance about conducting library research. Appendix E lists questions from follow-up interviews.

Answers to follow-up questions especially addressed research questions #5 and #6 (i.e., what did players retain and what were the benefits of playing BiblioBouts). A total of seventeen follow-up interviews were conducted with U-M students from a variety of classes, and each student was paid $20 for participation. Results are featured on page 178.

LOGS OF STUDENTS' GAME-PLAY ACTIVITY

BiblioBouts recorded students' game play activity to logs in .csv-formatted data files for export into Excel and other spreadsheet formats for analysis. Common to each bout's log was the unique document identification (ID) number that BiblioBouts assigned to each closed source. Using the document ID number, researchers could track everything that happened to a source—for example, who closed it, when the player closed it, who evaluated it, what IF and PUB tags the player assigned to it, what relevance and credibility ratings other players gave it, when they evaluated it, how many times it was chosen for best bibliographies, who chose it for a best bibliography, and so on.

For each game, BiblioBouts generated one log per bout—that is, for the Donor (BiblioBouts beta 1.0 version only), Closer, Tagging & Rating (T&R), and Best Bibliography bouts—plus a Best Bibliography citations log for the sources players cited in their best bibliographies. Logs were available only to the instructor who created the game and to the BiblioBouts team. Appendix

F lists data elements from the Donor, Closer, T&R, and Best Bibliography bouts and the Best Bibliography citation logs.

Every game generated logs, but the BiblioBouts team's analysis of logged game play data was restricted to logs from games played at U-M. Logs were essential for answering research questions #2 and #3 (i.e., did students play BiblioBouts and how did they play). Also depending on log data are discussions in chapters 8 through 10 about how students played the game, how they evaluated sources, and what sources their papers cited, respectively.

INTERVIEWS WITH INSTRUCTORS

Initially, BiblioBouts team members interviewed instructors from participating institutions before and after their classes played the game. When time constraints and limited resources prevented us from interviewing instructors from all participating and nonparticipating institutions, we consolidated questions into one post-game interview instrument, conducted post-game interviews only, and limited our selection of instructors from nonparticipating institutions to those who had contacted us on numerous occasions with questions, concerns, requests for troubleshooting assistance, suggestions, and so on. Initially, interviews were conducted face-to-face, but eventually we switched to phone interviews to increase the efficiency of the interviewing process.

Some interview questions elicited information about the instructor's integration of BiblioBouts into the course—for example, what the learning objectives were of the research paper instructors assigned to students, what effect BiblioBouts had on these objectives, what instructions they gave to students regarding citing sources in their papers, how much of a role cited sources played in their grading of papers, what incentives they gave to students to play the game, and how they graded their students' participation in the game. Other interview questions probed instructors about students playing BiblioBouts—for example, what students learned as a result of playing BiblioBouts, how students benefited from game play, and what impact BiblioBouts had on written papers. We also asked instructors about their involvement in the game—for example, whether they played BiblioBouts; what improvements they would make to the game, including the pre-game preparation they and library liaisons gave to students; what the prospects were for their integrating BiblioBouts into their classes in the future and recommending the game to their colleagues; and whether they would seek alternatives to BiblioBouts to expose their students in future classes to information literacy concepts and skills. Appendix G lists questions from instructor interviews.

A total of eighteen personal interviews were conducted, thirteen with instructors from the four participating institutions (SVSU, TUMC, UB, and U-M) and five with instructors from nonparticipating institutions. The analysis of instructor interviews addressed research questions #1 to #8. Chapter 7 especially relies on instructor interview data because it describes events leading up to game play—for example, instructors' expectations for the game, their instructions to students about cited sources, and their reactions to students' difficulties playing the game. Chapters 8, 10, and 11 also draw on instructor interviews—for example, echoing player sentiments about the amount of time it takes to play BiblioBouts (see page 112), reflecting on the increase in the numbers of sources to which players were exposed as a result of playing BiblioBouts (see pages 164–65), and enumerating the benefits of game play (see pages 182–83).

INTERVIEWS WITH LIBRARY LIAISONS

Because we considered library liaisons at participating institutions to be members of the BiblioBouts team, we did not immediately formalize their role in the evaluation of BiblioBouts. Over time, we realized that library liaisons were "on the front lines," so to speak, helping instructors integrate BiblioBouts into their syllabi, preparing students to play BiblioBouts, diagnosing technical problems, helping students narrow their paper topics, and answering students' substantive questions about all aspects of the game. Thus, they had much to contribute to the evaluation of BiblioBouts. Using the pre- and post-game personal interview questions for instructors as a base, we developed questions for library liaisons that addressed the support they gave to everyone involved with BiblioBouts—instructors, students, and fellow library staff members. Questions captured their viewpoints on what students learned from playing BiblioBouts, how BiblioBouts specifically and games generally stacked up in comparison to other teaching methods, their suggestions for improving BiblioBouts, and whether they would recommend BiblioBouts to their librarian colleagues locally and elsewhere. Appendix H lists questions posed to library liaisons.

Two personal interviews were conducted with library liaisons (at TUMC and UB). The analysis of library liaison interviews was important for answering questions #2 and #3 (i.e., did students play and how they played the game) but addressed most other research questions. Chapter 7 especially draws on library liaison interview data because it describes the events leading up to game play in which liaisons were directly involved—for example, recruiting instructors and helping them integrate the game into their syllabi, orienting students to the library database portal, and identifying and diagnosing players' technical problems.

SUMMARY

The evaluation of BiblioBouts featured a multi-methodological approach to data collection enlisting both quantitative and qualitative methods so that the BiblioBouts evaluation team could cross-check results from one method with others and use qualitative data to explain quantitative findings. Seven methods were used; this chapter details each one, describing the substantive nature of collected data and the eight research questions they addressed.

Chapter Seven

Preparing Students to Play BiblioBouts

Preparing students to play BiblioBouts is the focus of this chapter. Preparation started with instructors—their expectations for the game, for the research paper and topics they would assign their students, and for the sources that students would cite in research papers. It included students' responses to the information literacy training librarians gave them in preparation for game play. Students used several different technologies to conduct library research and play the game, such as Firefox, Zotero, Web search engines, and library databases; these were also a focus because technical difficulties with one or more sometimes prevented students from starting smoothly and thus may have played a role in dimming their enthusiasm for the game experience. Enlivening the discussion are comments from student game players and instructor-users of BiblioBouts who took part in focus-group and personal interviews at participating institutions.

INSTRUCTORS' EXPECTATIONS

Pre-game interviews probed instructors about their expectations for the BiblioBouts games their students would play. Mostly their responses addressed the library research process and the sources students would use to write their papers. A few other themes were present, but these two points were mentioned repeatedly.

With respect to library research, instructors wanted their students to develop a solid understanding of the library research process. Instructors hoped game play would serve students beyond this particular class, giving them much needed experience and practice that they could apply to future course work. One instructor felt that the experience of playing BiblioBouts would impress on students that library research no longer meant going to the library; instead, students could stay at home and find online the information they needed quickly and efficiently. Another adopted BiblioBouts in his information literacy class because he was teaching students how to conduct library research and was intrigued with BiblioBouts's ability to gamify this process.

When it came to sources, instructors had many expectations for BiblioBouts. They wanted game play to demonstrate to students the importance of using scholarly sources for their papers, give students exposure to more sources than they would have found on their own, and show them how to evaluate sources and how to correctly cite sources in their written papers. Instructors liked the idea of students working collaboratively, pooling sources and seeing what other students had found, discovering new places to search for sources as a result, and having available to all students in the class a database of written literature on the assigned topic.

A few instructor expectations were unique. One instructor anticipated better papers from her students as a result of their playing BiblioBouts, believing that students' exposure to more sources would better prepare them to present an argument and to support it with references to sources. Another instructor wanted his students to become more comfortable with the technology of the library research process. Still another felt that playing BiblioBouts would reduce student procrastination.

RESEARCH PAPER ASSIGNMENTS

Most instructors assigned their students a research paper to work on while they played the game. Alternatives to research papers were producing a video, writing a letter, or drafting a blog post. Regardless of assignment format or genre, instructors wanted students to draw on the sources they and their classmates submitted to the game to advance a causal argument or to persuade the reader to take a particular course of action.

BiblioBouts's design anticipated that instructors would assign everyone in the class the same broad-based topic to research. This was not always easy for instructors because either they did not want to read a huge stack of papers on the same topic or they wanted students to have the freedom to choose a topic that interested them personally, or both. Instructors responded to the game's broad-based topic requirement in one of three ways. First, they defined one broad-based topic for all students in the class and expected students to pursue an aspect of the broad-based topic in their research papers. For example, aspects of the broad-based topic "The effect of social media and other information technologies on the 2012 U.S. election" that students chose for their papers were social media's impact on fund-raising, voter turnout, and independent and third-party candidates. Second, instructors split their class into smaller groups of ten or so students and assigned each group a different topic. For example, one instructor assigned the forty students in her class to one of four games focused on these four topics: (1) achieving strong academic reading/writing and listening/oral communication skills, (2) developing critical thinking and collaborative teamwork skills, (3) managing time and habitual patterns in order to accelerate successful learning, and (4) making the best use of diversity on campus to enhance learning and contribute to the academic learning community. This instructor charged students with writing a three-page paper that convinced their peers to take positive action on developing one of these four skills. Third, instructors assigned students a broad-based topic that included direction on the nature of the aspect they wanted them to explore. For example, the topic "How climate change has brought about a particular adaptation in a particular human population" required students to specialize, choosing a particular human population that interested them.

Some instructors integrated BiblioBouts into their classes in unique ways. For example, an intercultural communications instructor tasked her international students with finding published sources on one of six communication concepts, interviewing an American student, and analyzing their interaction to determine whether the sources' treatment of the concept supported their interview experience with the American.

Almost all instructors gave students instructions about the number of sources their papers must cite. Some instructors were specific, telling their students that citations to Wikipedia, the Web, and even Google Scholar would not be acceptable. Other instructors required students to cite a minimum number of scholarly and nonscholarly sources. Only one instructor put no restrictions on students regarding the number or type of cited sources.

IN-CLASS PREPARATION

Almost all instructors took the BiblioBouts team's advice, inviting librarians to class prior to game play to brief students on the library's database portal, where they would find relevant sources on the broad-based topic in play. Because students did not know where to start searching for quality information on the assigned broad-based topic, they remarked about the helpfulness of these briefings for identifying relevant databases and keywords. Here is a typical student comment in this regard:

> I think the biggest help was when the librarian came in and showed us how to
> use the different databases because I think that there is just so many that I wasn't

really sure where to go. I mean ProQuest was the main one that I used at first because it was just so general, but she showed us these specific business type websites that we could go to. And I liked that. I think that was the most help.

When students were not entirely satisfied, their comments targeted (1) wanting on-the-spot assistance, (2) library anxiety, and (3) frustration with technical difficulties. With respect to on-the-spot assistance, some students preferred just-in-time assistance over the librarian's one-time lecture/demonstration that covered all the bases; however, at such lecture/demonstrations, librarians reminded students to contact them via online chat for immediate assistance. Here is a comment from a student who used this service:

> I used [the ask-a-librarian service] all the time actually. It's really helpful because they IM [instant message] you back immediately. And I don't have to, like, go there and feel embarrassed asking questions.

This student mentioned her reticence about asking for help from a librarian. This was not unusual; other focus group interview participants admitted to having similar feelings.

> Encourage users to ask librarians for help. I personally see them as intimidating. When I see them at the reference desk, I fear that if I asked them questions, they would look down on me for how little I know, or belittle me in their minds because I ask stupid questions or if I'm not 100 percent on what to look for or research. I know that librarians are there to answer questions, but I'm afraid to [ask]. The game could somehow emphasize the importance and reliability of librarians.

Library anxiety is well documented in the professional literature (Mellon 1986; Onwuegbuzie, Jiao, and Bostick 2004; Van Scoyoc 2003) and thus a phenomenon familiar to many practicing librarians. Because students were introduced to librarians during pre-game preparation activities, we did not expect library anxiety to emerge as a theme in the analysis of focus group interviews. For us as game designers, it was a missed opportunity to add links to the library's ask-a-librarian service in the Donor and Tagging & Rating (T&R) bouts, where students could have benefited from a "direct line" to librarians to ask questions about finding and evaluating sources. Designers of future information literacy games should take advantage of the opportunity to introduce students to virtual library reference services so that they can get answers to their questions online instead of avoiding librarians altogether.

When students experienced technical difficulties playing BiblioBouts, librarians sometimes bore the brunt of their frustration. Most problems occurred at the start of the game, when students were searching library

databases and the Web for sources and using Zotero to save and share them
with BiblioBouts. In some ways, the librarians became frontline technical
support for frustrated students, which could become an extra burden for librarians. The next section gives a fuller account of these technical difficulties
and their implications for game design.

Instructors who followed up the librarian's in-class presentation reinforced
the librarian's focus on using quality sources in their papers. Here are examples of instructor follow-up:

- "We did talk in class about the difference between a scholarly resource and
  a resource like SparkNotes or something that's written more for students or
  indeed things that come off the Internet like Wikipedia that aren't really of
  any scholarly value."
- "[We] discuss[ed] what makes for a quality source. [I told them] all of
  you gave me articles from About.com in your first research paper and why
  [that] may not that be appropriate for college-level research?"
- "Every semester I consistently have students who are not willing at all to
  get off of that Google train. . . . So [I ask them] 'When is Google a useful
  tool? When is Google not the best tool to turn to?'"
- "A top-notch citation cites another citation from a good academic journal
  or publisher. [I tell students] they have to cite someone who explicitly cites
  someone else. . . . 'Make sure your sources cite other sources. So don't
  just give me a Wikipedia cite. Don't just give me a website that there's no
  author behind it.'"

Instructors did not grade cited sources per se because citations were but one
of several elements required in research papers. For example, these instructors' comments acknowledged that cited sources were but one of several elements they took into consideration when grading papers:

- "An exemplary paper . . . is one in which the writer uses grammar and sentence structure correctly, organizes their paragraphs, works on clear transitions, manages to isolate the argument that's being presented in these different articles. An ability to summarize them as well as get to critique that
  argument a little bit, to be able to contrast some of those articles together
  or apart against each other a little bit, and then also to have an accurate use
  of citations and an accurate works-cited page."
- "[Sources] were important to the degree that [students] were able to show
  or at least work on their ability to integrate these outside sources and to
  show how they were thinking through this outside perspective. To explore
  it for themselves and what did it mean, how did the reading of the author

change as a result of what they read in a review or in an interview? . . . They had to be good quality sources that we had talked about in terms of relevance and expertise. And had to be relevant to their specific topic. They couldn't just plop it in there."

THE CHALLENGE OF TECHNOLOGY PROBLEMS

To play BiblioBouts, students first had to install the Firefox browser to use the Zotero citation management tool, because Zotero is a custom add-on to Firefox and does not work with other browsers. Installing Firefox on school computers sometimes proved difficult due to schools' information technology policies, and librarians had to negotiate this issue. Once Firefox and Zotero were installed, students used Zotero to save their retrieved sources and import them to BiblioBouts. Saving was usually accomplished with a simple push of this or that button, but sometimes students had to attach full-texts or website screenshots, formulate citations, and insert abstracts manually. Whether Zotero performed saving tasks automatically or users had to perform them manually depended on whether a particular database had formatted its metadata in a way that Zotero could read and capture automatically. Using Zotero entailed a steep learning curve, and at the root of students' difficulties were its complicated interface with three panes and its functionality sensitive to clicking on an enabled entry (figure 5.1). Zotero allows multiple approaches to saving sources, but choosing an approach depends on whether the source is a PDF, text file, or HTML-based Web page. Mousing over icon-based commands produces pop-up command names that may be too terse to adequately describe their function. Figuring out how to get started using Zotero was not intuitive, and experimentation was prone to backfiring because the Zotero user has to be constantly aware of which of Zotero's three panes are enabled when choosing commands from Zotero menus.

When students started to play BiblioBouts, they might have had as many as five different online applications open and working simultaneously: (1) a Web search engine such as Google, Bing, or Yahoo!, (2) the library's database portal, (3) a library database, (4) Zotero, and (5) BiblioBouts. Their "window" to these applications was the Firefox Web browser; thus, this was the sixth application presenting itself to students. Three of these applications required registration and/or authorization (library portal, Zotero, and BiblioBouts). Two applications required downloading and installation (Zotero and Firefox for students using different browsers). For students who had never used the library's digital collection, everything was new except using a Web search engine in a browser.

Let's set BiblioBouts aside for the moment to consider the applications that students routinely use to conduct academic library research. At the very least, they use two applications: a Web browser and a Web search engine. Since their instructors expect them to use quality sources, they should also use the library's database portal and one or more library databases. We had no idea how students kept track of the sources they found to use in assignments, but because Zotero gave students a systematic approach to organizing sources, students told us in focus groups how they had kept track of retrieved sources *before* Zotero.

- "What I usually do is when I am writing a paper and I have my sources, I just have a Firefox or an Explorer window opened up with them all tabbed over, and one time I accidentally closed that, and it was like thirteen sources just gone, and I had to refind all of them and it was a real pain in the butt."
- "I used to do exactly the same thing except one night it happened too many times where I closed it, and I said, 'Well, I'm going to download a program that it'll just capture all of the URLs.' So that's what I would do. I downloaded that and I'd say, 'Copy URLs,' and I'd paste that into a note pad. And then I'd save that."
- "Before Zotero, I tried keeping a list of my sources that I found in databases just . . . you know, copy and pasting in a Word document. That gets really messy. Like you don't really know what's what."
- "I do a lot of research so what I usually . . . do is I just download the PDF and just put it all in one folder, and it's just a mess."

Students' makeshift methods for saving the sources they expected to use in their papers required a certain mastery of their personal computer's file management capabilities. Introducing them to Zotero in the context of the BiblioBouts game would give them a systematic approach to saving multiple sources, relieve them of their makeshift methods, and give them practice using Zotero so they could develop an understanding of its benefits and apply their new Zotero-use skills to future library research tasks.

Troubleshooting reports and the analysis of evaluation data laid bare students' difficulties setting up these six applications properly. For students, instructors, library liaisons, and the BiblioBouts team, identifying and diagnosing technical problems was difficult because multiple steps were necessary for students to set up each application and use it in ways that required interactions with one or more other applications. It took just one misstep for everything to go awry. Students often did not know or were unable to communicate specifically what had caused their problem. Diagnosing the source of the problem and solving it often took repeated efforts from the BiblioBouts team. The confluence of technologies that transferred a student's Zotero source library to BiblioBouts was a sticking point that the BiblioBouts team never successfully resolved.

In focus groups, students described specific Zotero-use problems, such as switching from their preferred browser to Firefox (because Zotero is customized to the Firefox browser), downloading Zotero, selecting the right setup preferences in Zotero, saving sources in Zotero to their BiblioBouts folder, attaching full-texts and website snapshots to Zotero entries, synchronizing their Zotero sources library with BiblioBouts, and much more. Here are sample comments from students about specific Zotero difficulties:

- "Personally, I was a little confused about the whole Zotero thing when I started using it. I for one had to do most of my sources when we were doing the first round by hand because, for some reason or another, Zotero wasn't picking up the sources as an actual source—it wasn't giving me the little icon to click onto automatically, so I thought the whole Zotero thing was shaky."
- "In Zotero, there is one thing that may be confusing. You told us to create a folder that's only for BiblioBouts, and sometimes I clicked the wrong folder and [it was] hard to discern, like, whether the BiblioBouts folder has all of my things or the everything folder has [them all]. . . . Both of the folders have the same thing, and that may be confusing."
- "With the syncing, I don't know if you guys can control this, but with the Zotero part, I wish you could get, like, a confirmation that said, 'Sync complete.' Because you just hit the arrow and then you don't know—did it really sync or not?"

Many students used focus groups to vent their frustration with Zotero. Here are such comments:

- "Zotero . . . is a tough program, and it's not very friendly to use."
- "Zotero. Phew! I've been working on computers since 1976, and I do not like that program. It's poorly done."
- "Zotero . . . The learning curve was kind of steep for me. I don't know if it was I just wasn't getting it or I had a lot technical problems. I don't know if it was me or what."

In response to students' difficulties with the technology of the library research process, the BiblioBouts team focused its game design efforts on simplifying this technology for students. For example, we reduced the number of steps involved in accomplishing certain tasks, such as registering for a BiblioBouts account, tagging sources, and assessing their quality. Another example was spacing out student use of various applications so that they encountered fewer applications simultaneously. This involved a major game-system redesign, removing the Donor bout, substituting Zotero for Donor bout functions, and barring students from game play until BiblioBouts had detected the requisite number of sources with attached full-texts in the student's Zotero source library. As a result, students no longer had to divide their attention between Zotero and the BiblioBouts's Donor bout. They used Zotero to save sources and attach full-texts, and when they reached the requisite number of sources, they synchronized their Zotero source library with BiblioBouts and played BiblioBouts, starting with the Closer bout in which they selected their best saved sources to submit to the game. The final example was eliminating all aspects of the game requiring student interaction that were not used later on, especially in regard to scoring students. For example, players experienced the Sorter categories only one time during game play. We eliminated the Sorter bout in BiblioBouts's beta versions and distributed its categories feature into the T&R and Best Bibliography bouts in the form of big ideas. During bouts played in BiblioBouts's beta versions, players encountered big ideas three times and could win bonus points for completing tasks connected with them; plus, the Best Bibliography bout's Source Library and the Post-Game Library enhanced citations with matching big ideas generated by several players during the T&R bout. Thus, big ideas—a game feature that figured only once in the game's alpha version—were experienced five times by players of BiblioBouts's beta versions.

Our game simplification spawned unexpected and entirely new issues—for example, problems occurred as a result of stripping the Donor bout from the beta 2.0 version of BiblioBouts. In earlier versions of BiblioBouts, savvy students became attuned to the game's objective of submitting the very best sources to the game during the Donor bout as a result of reading game instructions and the Scoring FAQ, monitoring the scoring log, and watching how-to-play videos. The BiblioBouts beta 2.0 version started students with the requisite number of saved sources at the Closer bout, when there was no going back to add more saved sources. We later added warnings, telling students that starting the Closer bout meant no going back for more sources (figure 5.3), but students did not always read or heed these messages. As a result, they were disappointed that they had given short shrift to finding and saving the best sources and were stuck with the first few sources they found.

Technical problems almost always occurred at the start of the game. This was when students were using multiple applications to find, save, and share their best retrieved sources with BiblioBouts, so troubleshooting was difficult. Because students experienced problems right from the start, everyone's confidence in the game was shaken. Users' fears escalated, students worried about grades, and instructors fretted about student evaluations. Fortunately, technical problems rarely occurred after students began playing the Closer bout, but the damage had been done.

When deploying the first instance of BiblioBouts's alpha version, we cautioned everyone that the game was an in-progress research project, and the instructor followed up with reminders to students. In this comment from that first class, a student reflects positively about the research nature of the BiblioBouts assignment:

> It was interesting to play. To be involved in the experiment. It helped you with the research. We knew it was benefiting you. And it was benefiting us because we would get a better grade. And money [for the evaluation]. So why not play?

The instructor from the first class also noticed students' willingness to weather the highs and lows because of the research nature of game deployment.

> I think that [the students] acknowledged that there was a certain bugginess to [BiblioBouts] but that they thought that was part of the process as well. So they were accepting of the steps needed to try to get the game to work.

In hindsight, the BiblioBouts team should have cautioned everyone—no matter what version they were playing—to lower expectations of the game, reminding instructors, students, and librarians that BiblioBouts was a research project. Hence, users could not expect a thoroughly pre-tested, bug-free, and functionality-rich Web-based application; nor could they expect the round-the-clock technical support that for-profit firms would be able to provide for their applications thanks to a steady stream of income from advertisers, the deep pockets of investors, and a dedicated corps of experienced users who would be standing at the ready, monitoring user forums, and quickly responding to inquiries.

The BiblioBouts team applied its limited time and resources to implementing systems that automatically detected and fixed the most frequent problems. Less typical problems were handled individually, on a timely basis, by team members tasked with troubleshooting; however, we could not always help students who played a few hours before a bout's deadline and experienced less typical problems. Such students usually missed meeting the particular bout's cap or quota, but they could play subsequent bouts.

DISCUSSION

In terms of what students usually do to complete research paper assignments, BiblioBouts added a new level of engagement, requiring players to evaluate their opponents' sources. In the process, they learned the right questions to ask themselves to assess a source's credibility and relevance and could discover among the sources they evaluated better sources than they were able to find on their own. Playing BiblioBouts also resulted in a bibliography of sources for their papers, which students had to generate anyway to complete the writing assignment.

All in all, playing BiblioBouts did not add much to what students already had to do to research their papers; plus, there was the benefit of discovering sources better than one's own as a result of game play. Yet, most salient in students' minds was the complicated heap of technology that they had to manipulate at the start of the game. The problems they experienced soured them on the game.

- "I think the game would have been a lot more helpful if it wasn't so confusing."
- "But it's just real confusing and I mean it—it just needs to be more accessible. I don't know what I mean. It just needs to be easier to use and not confusing for everybody like—it's just, like, 'cuz we were only going to write it on, like, one little thingy anyway."

When technical problems marred a smooth start to the game, the BiblioBouts team sought automatic detection and fixes to the most common problems. The confluence of technologies that transferred a student's Zotero source library to BiblioBouts was especially a sticking point that the BiblioBouts team never fully resolved. Due to limited time and resources, we had to handle less typical "transfer" problems individually. If students reported problems at the last minute, we could not always help them due to limited resources and the time it took to resolve particularly vexing problems fully. Ultimately, we did our best to detect and fix the common problems automatically, but the initial setup for each game was always a challenge.

The technical problems that occurred at students' first exposure to the game put them on guard, lessening their confidence in and, perhaps, their goodwill toward the game. Based on our experience in this regard, we caution game designers to be up-front with everyone involved in game deployment, telling them not to expect bug-free game play due to the research nature of the game and limited resources for user support; however, this is not a long-term solution. Open-source applications have been successful in sponsoring user forums in which experienced users lend a helping hand to less experienced ones. Such forums take time to establish, being dependent on a large user base and the goodwill of dedicated users willing to monitor forums and respond to inquiries on a round-the-clock basis.

SUMMARY

BiblioBouts was not plug-and-play. Both instructors and library liaisons had to prepare students to play the game. Instructors had to determine whether BiblioBouts would fulfill their course's learning objectives or introduce new ones. Incorporating BiblioBouts into course syllabi, generating new assignments or making adjustments to existing writing assignments to accommodate BiblioBouts, synchronizing the bouts with course schedules and class activities, and deciding how to grade writing assignments and game play were all tasks that occupied instructors prior to creating a game.

Librarians played an important role, visiting classes to introduce students to the library's database portal, library databases, and Zotero and to help students register for both Zotero and BiblioBouts. Dissatisfaction came from students who wanted on-the-spot assistance, felt anxious about approaching librarians with their questions, or were frustrated by technical problems. When designers plan future information literacy games, they should consider how they might integrate virtual library reference services into the game to serve players wanting just-in-time assistance and stage library reference services so that students experiencing library anxiety can make a smooth transition from virtual to in-person reference services.

Information literacy games that begin with technology problems are doomed, especially in the court of public opinion. Students expect technology to work seamlessly because their favorite consumer electronics work well and provide professional technical support when they do not. Although students will cut research initiatives some slack, information literacy games that enlist technology have to work seamlessly with other applications or be stand-alone applications. Games also require round-the-clock user support services to solve technology problems so that students can complete required game play before deadlines strike.

Chapter Eight

How Students Played BiblioBouts

This chapter surveys the BiblioBouts games students played—how many games instructors created, how many students played the games, the disciplines of the classes playing these games, how often students played the game, whether they were early birds or waited until the last minute, how long they played, and the typical game play styles that emerged. The ways that students played BiblioBouts may give designers of future information literacy games insight into how students will actually play their games.

BiblioBouts's administrative interface—particularly, its game creation forms, player-invitee lists, game play logs, and evaluation reports—provided data for this chapter's analyses. Logs were an especially rich data source because they listed players' contributed sources, the players who submitted the sources to the game, and every action opponents took on their sources, including the time and date of the actions. We called these time-and-date-of-action data "time-date stamps," and they were very important for determining how students played certain bouts.

OVERVIEW OF BIBLIOBOUTS GAMES

From fall 2009 through spring 2010, BiblioBouts was only available to instructors at participating institutions. From winter 2011 through December 2012, BiblioBouts was available to anyone for the asking, and people contacted us from all over the world asking about BiblioBouts. When they requested game creation authorization, we asked them for more information, such as the institution they represented and the classes in which they intended to deploy BiblioBouts. We authorized game owners associated with academic institutions, such as instructors, librarians, and information technology staff.

Game owners set up twenty-six test games involving over one hundred registered BiblioBouts players. These games usually included only a few players and ran for very short periods. Presumably, test game owners were familiarizing themselves with BiblioBouts and trying to determine whether it was appropriate for their classes. We do not know why some test game owners limited their game play to test games or whom they invited to their games because test game owners did not follow up with additional information. About one-third of test game owners followed up with the deployment of one or more actual games in their classes.

Table 8.1 details the number of actual games instructors deployed in classes from fall 2009 through fall 2012 and the number of institutions and players involved. It also shows the extent to which students played individual bouts and met bout caps and quotas.

A total of 1,671 players were invited to sixty-five games at twenty-three different institutions. About three-quarters (74.2 percent) of player-invitees registered to play BiblioBouts. Reasons why a student-invitee did not register were varied: (1) the student did not participate in mandatory game play, (2) playing the game was extra credit and thus not mandatory, (3) the student dropped the course, or (4) technical difficulties prevented the student from registering. We would have liked to know how many player-invitees failed to register due to technical difficulties, but finding out would have involved asking instructors to poll their students about the nature of their playing or nonplaying status, which we considered intrusive and impractical.

Table 8.1. Actual BiblioBouts Games

Game Participation	Alpha	Beta 1.0	Beta 2.0	Total
Number of games	10	14	41	65
Number of different institutions	4	7	12	23
Number (percentage) of invitees	293 (100.0)*	357 (100.0)	1,021 (100.0)	1,671 (100.0)
Number (percentage) of full-game players	91 (31.1)*	113 (31.6)	361 (35.4)	565 (33.8)
Number (percentage) of partial-game players	103 (35.1)*	168 (47.1)	341 (33.4)	612 (36.6)
Number (percentage) of regular nonplayers	13 (4.4)*	10 (2.8)	40 (3.9)	63 (3.8)
Number (percentage) of nonplayer invitees	86 (29.4)*	66 (18.5)	279 (27.3)	431 (25.8)

*Excluded are the first five games because BiblioBouts was not yet programmed to log data on the extent to which invitees played BiblioBouts.

Only 3.8 percent of registered players were nonplayers. Full-game players, those meeting or exceeding their game's caps and quotas, accounted for 33.8 percent of invited players. The highest percentage (35.4 percent) of full-game players played the beta 2.0 version of BiblioBouts in which the BiblioBouts team had done its best to proactively detect and fix the most common technical problems. Overall, the percentage of partial-game players (36.6 percent) was comparable to full-game players (33.8 percent).

Because the BiblioBouts team made changes to BiblioBouts's design intended to reduce technical difficulties at the start of the game, we expected the percentage of nonplayer invitees to decline steadily with each new version of the game. Instead, the percentage dipped to 18.5 percent for BiblioBouts beta 1.0 version and shot up to 27.3 percent for BiblioBouts beta 2.0 version. Reasons for the final upswing could have been an increase in the number of games played for extra credit rather than being required and an increase in the number of games played at nonparticipating institutions where instructors and students might have been reticent about contacting the BiblioBouts team for user support services.

Figure 8.1 shows the disciplines of the classes in which students played the total sixty-five BiblioBouts games. The majority of classes (52 percent) were English and writing classes. In second and third place were history (15 percent) and information studies (14 percent) classes.

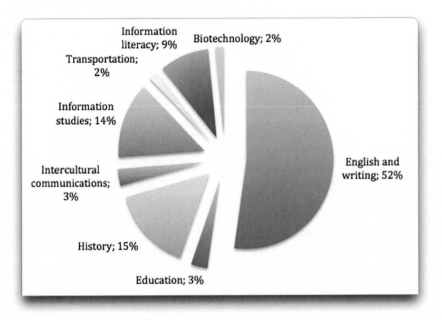

Figure 8.1.   Disciplines of the classes in which BiblioBouts was played.

Most English and writing instructors assigned students current events topics, such as global warming, the Afghanistan War, and health care in the United States. Examples of history topics were Frederick Douglass and the revolt against colonialism and neocolonialism in the Caribbean; information studies topics included archival description and the future of library education. The one science class, biotechnology, researched engineered enzymes. Also represented were classes in the disciplines of education, information literacy, intercultural communication, and transportation.

STYLES OF GAME PLAY

Game play logs contained data that allowed for finer distinctions between partial and full game play. We characterized these distinctions as game play styles and selected one participating institution where three classes played three separate BiblioBouts games to analyze students' game play styles. Two classes were English and writing classes in which students played BiblioBouts while researching the topics "Human adaptation to climate change: how a particular aspect of climate change has brought about a particular adaptation in a particular human population" and "Public sculpture: a close reading of an outside work of art sculpture." One class was an information studies class in which students played BiblioBouts while researching the topic "Social media and the 2012 election: the effect of social media and other information technologies on the 2012 U.S. election." In the subsequent discussions, these games are called "Adaptation," "Sculpture," and "Election."

Game play styles were based on the extent of student participation in the game across all bouts (four bouts in BiblioBouts beta version 1.0 and three bouts in BiblioBouts beta version 2.0). Table 8.2 lists and defines these game play styles.

Distinctions between the five full-game styles pertained to meeting and exceeding quotas for the Donor (BiblioBouts beta 1.0 version only) and Tagging & Rating (T&R) bouts. The bare-minimum full-game style was "quota player," characterized by the player meeting all caps and/or exceeding all quotas in modest amounts. A player who met all caps and modestly exceeded two or more bouts' quotas displayed the "above-quota player" style. To qualify for "superplayer" status, the player had to double either the Donor or the T&R bout's quota or both.

Partial-game play styles involved dropouts, that is, players who played one or more bouts and dropped out entirely, failing to play through the end of the game. There were two types of underperformers: (1) underperforming dropouts who failed to meet one or more caps or quotas and dropped out entirely,

Table 8.2. Game Play Styles and Descriptions

Styles	Description
Full-Game Play Styles	
Quota player	Player meets or modestly exceeds all bouts' caps and quotas.
Above-quota player	Player meets all caps and modestly exceeds one or more bouts' quota (by about ten Donor or ten T&R sources).
Donor superplayer (BiblioBouts beta 1.0 only)	Player is a quota player except in Donor, where he or she more than doubles the bout's quota.
T&R superplayer (BiblioBouts beta 1.0 only)	Player is a quota player except in T&R, where he or she more than doubles the bout's quota.
Superplayer	Player meets all caps and more than doubles two or more bouts' quotas.
Partial-Game Play Styles	
[Donor, Closer, T&R, or Best Bibliography] dropout	The player meets caps and quotas but drops out after playing the [Donor, Closer, T&R, or Best Bibliography] bout.
Underperforming dropout	The player fails to meet one or more caps or quotas and drops out before the end of the game.
Underperformer	The player plays all bouts but fails to meet one or more bouts' cap or quota.
In-game nonplayer	The player fails to play two or more bouts but plays the final Best Bibliography bout.
Nonplayers	
Registered nonplayer	Student registers but plays no bouts.
Nonplayer	Student does not register and thus cannot play at all.

failing to play through the end of the game, and (2) underperformers who played all bouts but failed to meet one or more bouts' cap or quota. Another partial-game style was the in-game nonplayer who failed to play two or more bouts but played the final Best Bibliography bout. There were two nonplayer types: students who did and did not register to play BiblioBouts. Table 8.3 lists game play styles in the far-left column and the number and percentage of students whose game play matched a particular game play style in the "Adaptation," "Sculpture," and "Election" columns.

Percentages of full-, partial-, and no-game styles were comparable across the three classes. A little over half of students played at quota level or higher.

Table 8.3. Game Play Styles from Three Classes

Styles	Adaptation		Sculpture		Election	
	#	%	#	%	#	%
Full-Game Styles						
Quota	11	24.5	18	43.9	47	54.0
Above quota	6	13.3	2	4.9	1	1.2
Donor superplayer	1	2.2	1	2.4	N/A	N/A
T&R superplayer	5	11.1	0	0.0	0	0.0
Superplayer	2	4.4	0	0.0	0	0.0
Subtotal	25	55.5	21	51.2	48	55.2
Partial-Game Styles						
Donor dropout	1	2.2	0	0.0	0	0.0
Closer dropout	1	2.2	2	4.9	2	2.3
T&R dropout	6	13.3	7	17.1	7	8.0
Underperforming dropout	5	11.1	1	2.4	8	9.2
Underperformer	2	4.4	3	7.3	4	4.6
In-game nonplayer	1	2.2	2	4.9	13	15.0
Subtotal	16	35.4	15	36.6	34	39.1
No-Game Style						
Registered nonplayer	1	2.2	0	0.0	5	5.7
Nonplayer	3	6.7	5	12.2	N/A	N/A
Subtotal	4	8.9	5	12.2	5	5.7
Total	45	100.0	41	100.0	87	100.0

Note: Numbers do not equal 100 due to rounding.

Players in the Sculpture and Election classes mostly played to reach quota. Adaptation players were more likely to exceed quota, with 13.3 percent playing above quota and 17.7 percent achieving superplayer status.

Partial-game styles accounted for a little under 40 percent of players in the three classes. Of partial-game play styles, the T&R dropout style was typical across all three games. These were players who met caps and quotas up to the final Best Bibliography bout, when they dropped out. We speculated that T&R dropouts had felt discouraged by being listed at the bottom of the leader board and dropped out because they did not think that they had a chance of winning. To confirm our speculation, we checked these three games' leader boards to determine whether T&R dropouts were listed at the bottom. To our surprise, several T&R dropouts were listed among the top five players when the Best Bibliography bout began, so the explanation for this behavior is unclear. The modestly high percentages of underperforming dropouts in the Adaptation and Election games and of in-game nonplayers in the Election game were troubling. These were players who failed to play one or more bouts or failed to meet bout caps and quotas. Their inconsistent and unpredictable game play might have been due to the many distractions that compete for students' attention during the several weeks they play BiblioBouts. In fact, both instructors and students in these classes said as much.

- "[It is] time consuming . . . to try to do the other things involved in my class and in their cases, my class and their other classes, [and it] presented a huge problem" (instructor of the English and writing class).
- "Because there were other things going on in other classes and also in that class and so it kind of lost that for me. And toward the end it was more of a just, 'I need to get this bout done so that I have completed it for the grade'" (student in the English and writing class).

Full-game styles predominated in the three classes. This was not the case with BiblioBouts games generally, where percentages of full- and partial-game styles were roughly equivalent (table 8.1). These three games most likely produced higher percentages of full- and partial-game players and lower percentages of nonplayer invitees because they were played at the home institution of the BiblioBouts team, where we were on hand to assist, reminding instructors to schedule librarian visits, visiting classes to introduce students to BiblioBouts and Zotero, and meeting one-on-one with students to solve technical problems. Also, these students' familiarity with the team might have made them more likely to contact us when they experienced problems instead of giving up, failing to play a bout, or waiting until the last minute to ask for assistance.

The percentage of nonplayers for the Adaptation (8.9 percent, table 8.3) and Sculpture (12.2 percent, table 8.3) classes was also less than half that for all players (25.8 percent, table 8.1). Adaptation and Sculpture instructors told us nonplayers in their classes were students who dropped the course or skipped the mandatory BiblioBouts assignment. Students in the Election class received extra credit for playing, so there was no way of knowing which Election students did not play due to technical difficulties or disinterest in the extra-credit assignment.

DAILY GAME PLAY ACTIVITY

Generally, instructors heeded our recommendations regarding scheduling BiblioBouts over a three-week period. We examined game logs to determine when students in the Adaptation, Sculpture, and Election classes played each bout. Interestingly, the Adaptation and Sculpture classes were distinctly different, and the Elections class resembled one or the other, depending on the bout.

Let's examine daily game play in each class, starting with the Adaptation class. Except for the T&R bout, about 90 percent of game play activity occurred on the last two scheduled days of the bouts. Activity during the T&R bout was somewhat more protracted, with 86 percent occurring on the final four days of this eight-day bout. Sculpture students' daily game play activity was entirely different. About 6 percent of their activity started on day 1 of the Donor bout; it peaked on day 3 at 16 percent, fell to only 2 percent on day 4, and rose steadily and peaked a second time at 26 percent on day 9, before dropping to 6 and 2 percent on days 10 and 11. Daily activity for the Closer bout amounted to 6 percent or less for the first six days, increased to 17, 11, and 26 percent on days 7, 8, and 9, dropped on day 10, and then peaked at 16 percent on day 11. Daily activity for the T&R bout resembled the Donor bout, rising steadily and peaking at 19 percent on day 4, dropping precipitously until the last two days, when it peaked a second time at 13 and 42 percent. The Best Bibliography bout lasted only two days; half the activity occurred on day 1 and half on day 2. Most activity in the Election game's Closer and Best Bibliography bouts occurred at the end of these bouts. Daily activity during the Election game's T&R bout resembled the Sculpture game's activity for this bout, peaking early (day 3) and late (last day) of the bout.

Differences between the three classes make it difficult to generalize about students' daily game play. Most likely, students played the game when it came to mind as a result of (1) preparing for class the day before or on the day of the class meeting, (2) the instructors' in-class or e-mail reminders, or (3) the game's automatic e-mail message reminders informing them that the current bout was ending in twenty-four hours and the next one was beginning.

TIME SPENT PLAYING THE DONOR BOUT

Checking logs for logon and logoff time-date stamps to determine how long students played a bout was not possible because BiblioBouts only logged player actions pertaining to sources, and logons and logoffs do not pertain to sources. Thus, we had to come up with an alternate approach to determine how long students played bouts. Here is what we did. We examined logged time-date stamps for each player in search of at least four successive time-date stamps for sources. We named such time periods "sessions" and used them to estimate the amount of time it took players to donate sources to the Donor bout and to tag and rate sources in the T&R bout. Intervals between time-date stamps varied—for example, some players donated sources at the rate of one source per minute, whereas other players donated one source per fifteen-minute interval. We considered this variability when making decisions about when a player's donation session ended instead of making a hard-and-fast rule. Usually a thirty-minute period between donations meant that players had stopped donating sources and the donation session had ended; however, this period could have been longer for players whose time-stamps for successive donations were longer than fifteen minutes.

Table 8.4 summarizes donation sessions for the Adaptation and Sculpture games. The Election game was not included in this analysis because it used a later version of BiblioBouts (beta 2.0) and thus had no Donor bout.

Donation sessions came from 90.2 percent of the students in the Adaptation class and 86.1 percent of the players in the Sculpture class. Thus, very few players were omitted from the analysis. Additionally, the majority of sources that players donated to the game were included in the analysis. Most students' donation activity occurred in a single donation session; however, eleven students had two and one student had three donation sessions.

Adaptation and Sculpture students averaged 4.1 and 6.5 minutes to donate a source, respectively. Both instructors set the Donor bout's quota at eight sources. We estimated that it took students in the Adaptation and Sculpture games 32.8 minutes and 52.0 minutes, respectively, to donate eight sources. The average donation time for the two classes was 4.9 minutes per donation.

Some students took a long time to donate a very few sources. For example, one student in the Sculpture class averaged 16.5 minutes to donate each of the four sources in her donation session. Other students took less than a minute to donate their sources. For example, a Sculpture student averaged 0.4 minutes to donate each of the thirty-eight sources in his donation session. Such short average times were due to students' use of Zotero's "select all" capability for search results. Here is how "select all" worked. In response to a student's query to a database, the database reported the number of retrievals and listed the first ten, fifteen, twenty, and so on. Option-clicking in the URL dialogue box produced a list of displayed titles preceded by checkboxes that the searcher could check to save all or selected titles to Zotero. Synchronizing

Table 8.4. Time Spent Donating Sources

Explanation	Adaptation	Sculpture
Number of students who played the Donor bout	41	38
Number (percentage) of students submitting at least four sources (i.e., a donation session)	37 (90.2)	31 (86.1)
Number of donation sessions	46	36
Total minutes for all donation sessions	1,791	1,440
Total number of donations in donation sessions	438	223
Total number of donations in the game	563	365
Percentage of total donations in donation sessions	77.8	61.1
Number of minutes per donation	4.1	6.5
Range of average donation times per session	0.5–15.5	0.4–16.5

Table 8.5.   Donating Multiple Sources on the Same Date and Time

Date	Time	Number of Titles Donated per Batch	One Sample Title per Batch
20110214	11:31	2	Climate change and health research in the eastern Mediterranean region
20110214	11:32	3	Impact of heat on mortality in fifteen European cities
20110214	11:33	3	Impact of heat waves on mortality
20110214	11:34	6	Footprinting of North American emergency medical services systems
20110214	11:39	3	Doctors and climate change
20110214	11:43	5	Public understanding of climate change science

the Zotero source library shared these saved sources with BiblioBouts. Table 8.5 shows that in a thirteen-minute time span, this Adaptation player donated twenty-two sources in six separate multiple-donation episodes.

This player was somewhat selective, placing checkmarks before listed sources instead of selecting all of them. Table 8.5 lists sample source titles so the reader can judge whether the titles are relevant to the Adaptation topic (i.e., "Human adaptation to climate change: how a particular aspect of climate change has brought about a particular adaptation in a particular human population").

Earlier versions of BiblioBouts rewarded players who exceeded the Donor bout's quota with bonus points, tempting players to use Zotero's "select all" capability to quickly and effortlessly receive bonus points. Game players complained that some players were building huge leads on the scoreboard as a result of this "shortcut" action. In response, we reformed BiblioBouts's scoring algorithm, eliminating almost all bonus points for exceeding the Donor quota. This reform was successful because later games featured few Donor superplayers—for example, there were only two Donor superplayers, one each in the Adaptation and Sculpture classes (table 8.3).

TIME SPENT PLAYING THE T&R BOUT

To determine how long students took to play the T&R bout, we examined logged time-date stamps for each player in search of at least five successive time-date stamps for evaluated sources. We named such periods "evaluation sessions" and used them to estimate the amount of time it took players to evaluate sources in the T&R bout. Table 8.6 summarizes evaluation sessions for all three games.

Table 8.6.   Time Spent Evaluating Sources

Explanation	Adaptation	Sculpture	Election
Number of students who played the T&R bout	41	36	70
Number (percentage) of students submitting at least five sources in succession (i.e., an evaluation session)	31 (75.6)	33 (91.7)	68 (97.1)
Number of evaluation sessions	72	65	94
Total minutes for all evaluation sessions	4,822	3,120	5,154
Total number of evaluations in evaluation sessions	1,213	793	1,219
Total number of evaluations in the game	1,469	961	1,438
Percentage of total evaluations in evaluation sessions	82.6	82.5	84.8
Number of minutes per evaluation	4.0	3.9	4.2
Range of evaluation times	0.7–12.6	0.7–13.3	0.8–21.3

Evaluation sessions came from three-quarters or more of the students in the three classes. These sessions accounted for 82 percent or more of the total number of sources evaluated in the three games. Thus, few students were omitted from the analysis, and the vast majority of sources that players evaluated during game play were included in the analysis. Most students' evaluation activity was accomplished in one or two evaluation sessions; nine students conducted three evaluation sessions.

Adaptation, Sculpture, and Election students took 4.0, 3.9, and 4.2 minutes to evaluate a source, respectively. The average time across the three classes was 4.1 minutes. The fastest evaluations took about forty-five seconds and the longest twelve to twenty-one minutes. Longer evaluations almost always involved students writing comments that described the reasons for their credibility and/or relevance assessments.

T&R quotas depended on three game-specific values (number of registered game players, number of donated sources, and number of evaluations per source); thus, quotas were different for the three games. Using an average of twenty-one sources for the T&R quota across the three games resulted in an average 86.1 minutes to play the T&R bout.

TOTAL TIME SPENT PLAYING BIBLIOBOUTS

BiblioBouts recorded only one time-date stamp for actions in the Closer and Best Bibliography bouts—when a user submitted the list of his selected closed or best bibliography sources. As a result, time-date stamps for these bouts disclosed when they ended but not when they began. Thus, no estimates could be made for the time it took students to play the Closer and Best Bibliography bouts.

In the absence of time estimates for these two bouts, we speculated about how long it took students to play them. If students saved exactly as many sources as needed to meet the Closer bout's cap during the Donor bout or the pre-game activity that led up to the Closer bout, then playing the Closer bout was simple. Students merely had to select all of their listed sources and click the "Save Work" button to submit them to the game (see figure 5.4). Such activity should have taken no more than five minutes. If students had saved more sources than needed to meet the Closer bout's cap, then they might have been more selective, reading saved sources' titles and abstracts in the course of making decisions about which to submit to the game. Students who read the Closer bout's instructions about quality full-texts might have lingered, verifying that the sources they put into play had attached full-texts, and this would have taken additional time.

Unlike the Closer bout, the Best Bibliography bout required more of players than merely selecting from a list of their own sources. The Best Bibliography bout prompted a student to enter his or her paper topic, a description of the paper's argument, and three big ideas that the paper discussed (see figures 5.12 and 5.13). Then players chose the best sources for their research papers from the database of all players' closed sources. Most instructors used this bout's default cap of ten sources. On one hand, players who had formulated their research paper's topic would probably not take more than ten minutes to play this bout. On the other hand, players could linger, editing their topics and arguments, changing their big ideas, and sorting and searching this bout's Source Library. Careful players who perused the list, read titles and abstracts, opened attached PDFs, and read individual sources would have taken much longer; however, such activity would have helped them choose relevant sources, a task they would have to do eventually to make progress on their written papers.

Table 8.7 estimates the minimum amount of time it took to play a BiblioBouts game. Numbers of sources are BiblioBouts's defaults except for the T&R bout, which is the average of the quotas for the three games discussed in this chapter.

Table 8.7. Estimated Time to Play BiblioBouts

Bout	Calculation	Time (Minutes)
Donor	8 sources × 4.9 minutes	39.2
Closer	Estimated 5 sources	5
T&R	21 sources × 4.1 minutes	86.1
Best Bibliography	Estimated 10 sources	10
Total	Sum of the above estimates	140

Players averaged two hours and twenty minutes to play BiblioBouts. Obviously, the time spent would be more or less depending on whether a student's game play followed a dropout/underperformer or superplayer/above-quota player style.

Players complained about the amount of time it took them to play BiblioBouts. Of all the bouts, they singled out the T&R bout as being too long and its quota too high. Here is what they said about how long it takes to play BiblioBouts, including the T&R bout:

- "This is a nontraditional school. We all work forty-plus hours a week and then to come in here and do BiblioBouts and a thousand-word essay, that's a lot. And then we've got kids and whew! Like I said, it was just too many steps for BiblioBouts. . . . It took too long for people. . . . We've got so much other stuff going on."
- "Very, very time-consuming. Like, don't think you're just going to go in and it'll get done."
- "I think for rating and tagging . . . was, like, a little bit much. It was really, really time-consuming."

Other players were unperturbed by the amount of time they put into game play, reflecting on how they benefited as a result of everyone's efforts.

The timing of each round and the amount of time that you need to spend to actually hit the quotas and even exceed the quotas was very minimal and uninvasive because I . . . realized, "I don't actually have to spend that much time researching sources and finding sources for a paper." The whole process—the amount of time I actually spent on BiblioBouts—I don't know—maybe like three hours over all of the rounds. But in three hours of game play, I had all of the sources I needed and I had a great bibliography, and from there I was able to just really get right into the work. . . . Even though there [were] the minor glitches [and despite] the disconnect with the [research questions] and my thesis, I thought, "Well, I just really had to augment what I found on BiblioBouts." It was really a great way to just streamline the whole process to three hours for a paper of seven pages. It seemed like a pretty good thing.

Players' comments about the protracted nature of BiblioBouts game play were troublesome.

- "It was so stretched out. Because, I mean, the bouts didn't really take that long. I mean, the longest bout . . . topped an hour and a half really, so. Yeah, we really didn't need a week. And [after] all of that you would forget what you did from the last bout to the next one."
- "It goes on so long, you just lose interest."

- "If you [played] it every two days, like have a bout to do, I think [the instructor] spaced it out because we are in a fifteen-week course and that would make sense, but I don't feel that it adds any to the game. It's spreading it out too much."

Depending on how instructors scheduled the game, some bouts lasted a week or longer. Players who met a bout's quotas and caps could not work ahead but had to wait until the bout transitioned to the next one because the game utilized data from the current bout in the subsequent one. The reason for this was that all players' scores needed to be calculated at the close of each bout before a new one could begin.

Did BiblioBouts's format cause players to lose interest? Were players unable to develop momentum? Did playing in fits and starts obscure the big picture of BiblioBouts's step-by-step approach to library research? How could BiblioBouts have been designed so that early birds could charge ahead instead of having to wait between bouts? We revisit these questions in chapter 12, where best practices #11 and #12 address fits-and-starts game designs, and in chapter 14, where we describe a redesigned BiblioBouts minus the fits-and-starts aspect (see pages 229–31).

DISCUSSION

A total of 1,671 players were invited to sixty-five games at twenty-three different institutions (table 8.1). About one-third (33.8 percent) were full-game players, meeting or exceeding caps and quotas, and about one-third (36.6 percent) were partial-game players, failing to meet one or more bouts' caps and quotas. Very few (3.8 percent) players registered and failed to play BiblioBouts at all. Reasons why the remaining quarter (25.8 percent) of player-invitees did not play BiblioBouts probably involved disinterest, extra-credit grading, course withdrawals, or technical problems. We attributed the lower percentages (8.9 and 12.2 percent; table 8.3) of nonregistrants in the Adaptation and Sculpture courses to students' familiarity with the BiblioBouts team, whose members visited classes to introduce them to BiblioBouts and Zotero and invited them to contact the team for help solving technical problems. Although the optimal solution would be games devoid of technical problems, problems are bound to occur. In response, game deployment teams should offer user support services that enlist a wide variety of approaches so that players feel comfortable asking for and receiving assistance. We have seen that students' reticence about asking questions includes library anxiety (see page 97). Thus, every attempt should be made to provide as many opportunities for assistance as possible so that students feel encouraged to seek solutions to problems.

Daily game play results were a mix of game play activity occurring immediately preceding each bout's deadline or remaining low, with two or three spikes during a bout. Both game designers and instructors have an important role to play in encouraging student participation. Games can be programmed to automatically message players, reminding them of impending deadlines, warning them about complicated or time-consuming game play that may take more time and effort than they expect, and acknowledging meritorious game play with bonus points, badges, and trophies. Instructors can play an even bigger role, actively playing the game, taking a few minutes at the beginning of class to debrief students on their own game play experiences and encouraging students to do the same, speculating on game-winning strategies, defining and expanding on information literacy concepts that students find difficult, discussing game objectives, preparing students for the game play that lies ahead, and much more. We added a "news" capability to BiblioBouts to enable instructors to communicate with students—for example, commenting on lead changes, longtime game leaders, badge holders, and other meritorious game play—but few did. To facilitate instructor-player communication, information literacy games should be integrated into course management systems (CMSs) where game play, e-mail, and other CMS functionalities reside under one umbrella system (see page 57). Game designers need to think creatively about how they can raise their game's salience so that students play and participate at a high level.

That students averaged 4.9 minutes to donate a source seemed rather quick to us. This means that they performed several tasks without a glitch: opened a browser window to a Web search engine or library portal, chose a portal database, entered keywords, scanned retrieved titles in search of potentially relevant ones, scrutinized metadata records and/or full-texts to establish the source's relevance, and saved the source to Zotero. Although use of Zotero's "select all" capability was not typical of game players in this chapter's analyses, it reduced donation times because it performed several steps automatically. We could speculate that students were not especially selective about their donated sources. Game play was giving them their first exposure to sources on the broad-based topic, and most had not yet given much thought to this topic or to how they might narrow it in their research papers. In a sense, our speculation in this regard was confirmed by students playing the beta 2.0 BiblioBouts, the Donorless version of the game. Students first interacted with BiblioBouts during the Closer bout, after BiblioBouts had imported their Zotero sources and there was *no going back* for better sources. After reading the game's instructions, students realized that scoring rewarded them for quality sources. Thus, students complained to instructors that they had given short shrift to source donation and wanted to start over to find better sources than their initial donations. Our response was to add notes to pre–Closer bout screens, FAQs, and videos cautioning players about there being no going back once the game commenced (figure 5.3).

With respect to evaluating sources, average times across the three classes were consistently in the area of four minutes. In this short period, players had to complete several rating and tagging tasks in addition to familiarizing themselves with the source's content to assess relevance and credibility. Several students told us they skimmed sources, but very few described strategies akin to a technical reading (i.e., an efficient reading strategy that enables the reader to obtain a great amount of information in a short period). Both instructors and librarians should teach students how to perform a technical reading of a source so that they minimize time spent on nonrelevant sources and maximize contact with relevant ones.

Players averaged two hours and twenty minutes to play BiblioBouts. In focus groups, some students complained about how long it took them to play the game. They did not, however, take into account the amount of time they would have spent searching for, finding, and selecting sources for their papers, tasks they accomplished during game play, or how they benefited as a result of playing the game. With regard to the latter, students might feel differently about the time they spent playing BiblioBouts if they find themselves almost instinctively drawing upon what they learned as a result of playing BiblioBouts the next time they conduct library research.

Particularly troublesome was players' telling us their interest waned as a result of the game's fits-and-starts nature. Our response was to generate best practices #11 and #12 cautioning game designers about games that are played in fits and starts (see pages 198–200) and plans for a redesigned BiblioBouts minus the fits-and-starts aspect (see pages 229–31).

SUMMARY

This chapter surveys the BiblioBouts games students played. Overall, 70.4 percent of players were full or partial players of the BiblioBouts game, and 29.6 percent were nonplayers (table 8.1). The majority of classes (52 percent) were English and writing classes (figure 8.1). An in-depth analysis of three BiblioBouts games played by three separate classes demonstrated that full-game play styles characterized the game play of a little over one-half of player-invitees, and partial-game styles characterized the game play of a little over one-third of player-invitees; the remaining one-tenth of player-invitees failed to play due to disinterest, the extra-credit nature of the game, dropping the course, or technical difficulties (table 8.3). These three games produced lower percentages of nonplayers than BiblioBouts games overall probably due to their being played at the home institution of the BiblioBouts team, where we were on hand to assist, especially meeting one-on-one with students to solve technical problems.

Daily game play results were a mixture of game play activity occurring immediately before each bout's deadline or remaining low with two or three spikes during a bout. Suggestions were made about how games and instructors could work together to increase student participation. Estimates of how long players took to donate sources (4.9 minutes) and evaluate sources (4.1 minutes) seemed low, considering the many subtasks required to fully accomplish each task. Students complained about the T&R bout being too long and its quota too high. Although they sought shortcuts, few described strategies comparable to performing a technical reading of sources; thus, an information literacy game that teaches students how to perform a technical reading might interest game designers.

Understanding the extent to which students played each bout and how often and how long they played gives us a glimpse of how serious their game play was and how much time and effort they put into finding, evaluating, and selecting sources for their research papers. The next chapter continues the discussion of how students played BiblioBouts, focusing on credibility and relevance assessment tasks in the T&R bout.

Chapter Nine

How Students Evaluated BiblioBouts Sources

Of the game's several bouts, the Tagging & Rating (T&R) bout was the most demanding. It required players to evaluate their opponents' closed sources. How many sources they were required to evaluate depended on game play activity leading up to the T&R bout—specifically, these two values: (1) the total number of closed sources all players contributed to the game, and (2) the number of players in the game. Instructors set the third value: the number of player evaluations per source. Because most instructors accepted BiblioBouts's default of five, players usually had to meet a T&R quota of about twenty sources. Motivating players to achieve this bout's quota was the 3,040-point bonus that BiblioBouts added to the paltry sum of ten points it awarded for each source they evaluated up to reaching quota. Players also received bonus points when their relevance and credibility ratings were close to the average relevance and credibility ratings for the source and their big ideas, information formats (IFs), and publishers (PUBs) matched other players' big ideas, IFs, and PUBs. Thus, repeated practice in source evaluation, points, and bonus points were the rewards players received as a result of playing the T&R bout in its entirety.

This chapter assesses the nature and quality of student game play pertaining to credibility and relevance assessment tasks in the T&R bout. It seeks answers to these questions:

1. Do students submit relevant sources to the BiblioBouts game?
2. Do students submit scholarly sources to BiblioBouts?
3. Do students correctly identify the information formats of BiblioBouts sources?
4. What criteria do students use to assess the credibility and relevance of BiblioBouts sources?

5. Are these "seat-of-the-pants" criteria, or are they based on evidence gleaned from the sources at hand?
6. Do players' credibility ratings agree with the credibility ratings of experts?
7. Do players give higher credibility ratings to scholarly sources than to nonscholarly sources?

CLASS ASSIGNMENTS

This chapter's analysis of player-evaluated sources enlists game play data from two of the three classes that figured into chapter 8's analysis of how students played the BiblioBouts game. These were the Adaptation and Election classes at the BiblioBouts team's home institution. Although instructors assigned different broad-based topics to their respective classes, their pre-game preparation was similar. The Adaptation instructor expected students to use the sources they found online to write a paper in support of a causal argument that some particular cause A had brought about some particular effect B. Students had the freedom to specify a narrower topic as long as it fell within the broader spectrum of the Adaptation topic. With regard to citing sources in their papers, the course syllabus instructed students to cite at least five outside sources, no more than two coming from the open Web; citations to Wikipedia were not acceptable.

The Election instructor gave similar instructions to students. Student papers were expected to make an argument, take a position, and defend it. Students were graded on their ability to support their stance, provide logical and persuasive rationales, and use solid evidence. The course syllabus instructed students to provide proper citations to outside sources and cite a minimum of three sources from the university library's online or print collections.

Prior to playing BiblioBouts, librarians visited both classes, introduced students to the online library database portal, and identified relevant databases where students could find relevant information for the assigned topics. Librarians, instructors, or both talked about the characteristics of scholarly journals and how they subject manuscripts to a rigorous peer-review process. Thus, pre-game orientation events should have predisposed students to submitting scholarly sources to BiblioBouts.

DO STUDENTS SUBMIT
RELEVANT SOURCES TO BIBLIOBOUTS?

This question is a good starting point for this chapter's analyses of source evaluation data. A positive response would indicate that students took game play seriously, that they made progress on their writing assignments as a result of playing BiblioBouts, and that their submissions had the potential to help classmates who were also playing BiblioBouts to find relevant sources for the writing assignment.

Players' relevance ratings for Adaptation and Election sources averaged 72.7 and 72.3 percent, respectively. Election players rated scholarly sources (73.4 percent) a little higher than average (72.7 percent) and a little higher than nonscholarly sources (71.0 percent), but the difference between the two ratings was not significant. Although the difference between Adaptation players' relevance ratings for scholarly sources (73.1 percent) and nonscholarly sources (67.4 percent) was more pronounced, there were only eleven non-scholarly sources in the analysis, making for inconclusive results.

Adaptation players' relevance assessments ranged from 42.3 to 89.9 percent and Election players' from 12.0 to 100.0 percent. Adaptation players rated only 16.4 percent of closed sources in the eighties and gave no ratings above 89.9 percent; in contrast, Election players rated one-third of closed sources in the eighties and nineties and gave two sources perfect ratings. Here are examples of the comments players from both games made on the highest-rated sources:

- "Is specifically about the topic and has true important information."
- "I am writing about the impact of global warming and the reaction taken by countries that are economically developing. That is entirely the focus of this paper and it comes from a very credible source. Thus, it will be a great source for me to use in my paper."
- "This is a great source for this paper as it compares social media techniques to 'old' techniques."
- "Definitely g[o]od stuff, it draws interesting conclusions and gives good evidence for it. Though not perfect, it can definitely help refine one's topic and give evidence for it."
- "This article definitely contains useful information that pertains to our paper because it discusses many aspects of adaptation to climate change on an international domain. I think it also has accurate and high quality information because its authors represent a credible academic institution."
- "Outline[s] strategies for adapting to its impacts and mitigating the effects in the longer term which is exactly what [the] topic is looking for."

This analysis of players' relevance ratings, including the comments they made about their ratings, provides convincing evidence that players took game play seriously, especially with regard to submitting relevant sources about the broad-based topics in play. Whether players used their opponents' sources—citing them in their papers and using them to think through topic selection—is discussed in chapter 10 so that we can continue our focus on source evaluation here.

DO STUDENTS SUBMIT SCHOLARLY SOURCES TO BIBLIOBOUTS?

Submitting sources to BiblioBouts took place during the Closer bout. This number was capped at five for both the Adaptation and Election games; players received 10 points per submission and a 360-point bonus for meeting the cap. Instructors and librarians advised students to choose their best sources on the broad-based Adaptation and Election topics because they would "play" these sources during the game and wanted fellow students to give them high ratings and choose them for their best bibliographies, two crucial ingredients that would ensure players placed high on the leader board and, possibly, won the game.

To determine whether player-submitted sources were scholarly, we had to examine each one to identify its information format. We used the same list of information formats (IFs) that players used to evaluate sources in the T&R bout (figure 5.7). Sampled were three-quarters and two-thirds of the sources players closed in the Adaptation and Election games, respectively. We trained coders who were master's-level students in the School of Information to identify IFs, met to agree on the coding system, and mutually resolved the most difficult identifications. We instructed the coders to consult *Ulrich's Periodicals Directory* for the correct IFs that the information industry uses for serial titles.

Adaptation and Election players closed 190 sources and 328 sources in their respective games. Table 9.1 gives the number and percentage of sampled sources coders classed into scholarly and nonscholarly IFs.

Adaptation players in particular chose scholarly sources to play the game; in fact, 72.1 percent of their closed sources were scholarly journals, and 92.2 percent overall were scholarly IFs. Election players split their source selection between scholarly and nonscholarly IFs. Most scholarly sources were scholarly journals and conference proceedings (Election only), and most nonscholarly sources were consumer magazines and trade magazines. Although the encyclopedia IF was originally classed as nonscholarly, we recategorized it as scholarly because no encyclopedia articles that players closed emanated from the open Web. All were written by scholars whose academic affiliations were stated prominently in bylines, published by reputable publishers, and accessible through the library's database portal; they also all included bibliographies that cited seminal publications.

The topic that Election students researched—"Social media and the 2012 election: the effect of social media and other information technologies on the

Table 9.1. IFs of Players' Closed Sources

Coder IFs	Adaptation Sources		Election Sources	
	N	%	N	%
Scholarly IFs				
Book	3	2.1	9	4.1
Conference proceedings	2	1.4	23	10.6
Encyclopedia	10	7.2	13	6.0
Research report	9	6.4	12	5.5
Scholarly journal	101	72.2	57	26.3
Trade journal	4	2.9	6	2.8
Subtotal	129	92.2	120	55.3
Nonscholarly IFs				
Blog	0	0.0	8	3.7
Consumer magazine	3	2.1	6	2.8
Consumer newspaper	3	2.1	57	26.3
Directory	3	2.1	0	0.0
Online repository	1	0.7	0	0.0
Promotional material	0	0.0	5	2.3
Trade magazine	1	0.7	18	8.3
Trade newspaper	0	0.0	3	1.3
Subtotal	11	7.8	97	44.7
Total	140	100.0	217	100.0

2012 U.S. election"—targeted a current event of great national and international interest. Students researched it in fall 2011, a full year before the election took place, while candidates' use of social media was playing out. That Election players closed a large proportion of nonscholarly sources from Web-based consumer newspapers, trade and consumer magazines, and blogs would be expected because these modes of communication respond quickly to current events in comparison to scholarly journals, books, and dissertations, which take a long time to appear due to the rigor of the scholarly review process.

In contrast, the Adaptation topic was much more established, with many scholarly sources available. Heeding their instructor's advice about using scholarly sources in their papers, Adaptation students responded accordingly, submitting mostly scholarly sources to BiblioBouts.

DO STUDENTS CORRECTLY IDENTIFY THE INFORMATION FORMATS OF BIBLIOBOUTS SOURCES?

Because the project's instructors, librarians, and teaching assistants urged students to use scholarly sources for their BiblioBouts sources and their written papers, we were curious about whether students were able to correctly identify their closed sources' information formats. If their identifications were incorrect, then it might make sense to instruct students in identifying scholarly sources and where they would be likely to find them.

To analyze the correctness of students' IFs, we used the same sample of sources that figured into table 9.1, extracted player-assigned IFs from T&R bout logs, and compared their IFs with coders' IFs. While performing the analysis, we noticed that some nonmatching IFs were not really incorrect; instead, they were "reasonable" matches of the particular source's information format or genre. For example, the research report IF was a reasonable IF to describe a journal article that reported research. Thus, to our analysis of matching IFs we added the "reasonable" match type, but assigning it required scrutiny on the part of coders. Several more examples are given below to demonstrate the decisions coders made when choosing between reasonable and incorrect match types. Table 9.2 summarizes the results of the analysis using three match types: (1) exact matches of coders' IFs, (2) reasonable matches of coders' IFs, and (3) incorrect IFs.

On average, 7.1 players assigned IFs to each of the 140 closed sources sampled from the Adaptation game and 3.9 players assigned IFs to each of the 217 closed sources sampled from the Election game. More assignments by Adaptation players was due to this game's several above-quota players and superplayers (table 8.3).

Adaptation players fared quite well, exactly matching coders' IFs for 65.0 and 61.9 percent of scholarly and nonscholarly sources, respectively. Remember, however, that Adaptation players closed scholarly sources almost exclusively, and almost three-quarters of their sources were scholarly jour-

Table 9.2.   Players' Exact, Reasonable, and Incorrect IFs

	Adaptation Player IFs for 140 Sampled Sources		*Election Player IFs for 217 Sampled Sources*	
	N	*%*	*N*	*%*
Match types for scholarly sources				
Exact	599	65.0	185	41.7
Reasonable	236	25.6	152	34.2
Incorrect	86	9.4	107	24.1
Total	921	100.0	444	100.0
Match types for nonscholarly sources				
Exact	621	61.9	331	39.4
Reasonable	261	26.0	321	38.2
Incorrect	122	12.1	189	22.4
Total	1,004	100.0	841	100.0

nals (table 9.1); thus, the Adaptation set of closed sources had less variability than the Election set.

With respect to details for specific source types, Adaptation players performed better than average at identifying scholarly journals, exactly matching 71.6 percent of expert coders' IFs. They did almost as well with encyclopedias, exactly matching 68.4 percent of expert coders' IFs. Research reports were more difficult for them, their exact matches dipping to 40.7 percent. Adaptation players closed so few instances of the remaining IFs (e.g., books, conference proceedings, consumer newspapers) that it is difficult to detect a trend with certainty.

In contrast, Election players' IFs exactly matched coders' IFs for 41.7 percent of scholarly IFs and for 39.4 percent of nonscholarly IFs. With respect to the details for the four scholarly source types that Election players closed in moderately large numbers, their exact-match rates for these were (1) conference proceedings (18.8 percent), (2) encyclopedias (32.8 percent), (3) research reports (44.9 percent), and (4) scholarly journals (53.9 percent). Turning to nonscholarly sources, they closed moderately large numbers of three nonscholarly source types, and their exact-match rates for these were (1) blogs (33.3 percent), (2) consumer newspapers (51.3 percent), and (3) trade magazines (9.2 percent). Only for consumer newspapers did they exceed their average match rate of 39.4 percent.

Let's examine reasonable IFs for certain source types starting with scholarly journals. About one-quarter and one-third of Adaptation and Election players' nonmatching IFs were judged to be reasonable, respectively. Players from both games assigned the research report and trade journal IFs most frequently to scholarly journals. These IFs could be considered reasonable because it is likely that few students would understand the subtle distinctions between the scholarly journal, trade journal, and trade magazine IFs. Also considered reasonable for the scholarly journals was the dissertation/ thesis IF because dictionary definitions of dissertation, "a formal and lengthy discourse or treatise on some subject," and thesis, "a formal and lengthy research paper" (Neufeldt and Guralnik 1996, 397, 389), also apply to scholarly journals. The same argument could be made for the research report IF, particularly when scholarly journals report the results of research. It is unlikely that undergraduate students are familiar with "research report" as a literary genre. Instead, they might take the phrase "research report" literally and understand it to mean a report of research and, thus, applicable to the contents of most scholarly journals. Also acceptable for the scholarly journal IF was the book IF when students applied it to book reviews published in scholarly journals or to excessively lengthy (over fifty pages) journal articles.

At first glance, we were baffled by moderate numbers of Adaptation players' assigning the database IF to scholarly journals. We surmised that players were responding to an e-journal aggregator's database-search engine that displayed full-texts. For example, figure 9.1 shows an actual article from a scholarly journal displayed in an aggregator's database-search engine to which players assigned the database IF. Election players did much the same but split their selections between the database and online repository IFs.

In a way, the source in figure 9.1 is simultaneously a scholarly journal and a database. It is a scholarly journal because of Ulrich's classification of the journal *Neglected Tropical Diseases* in which this article is published. It is a database because it allows users to display the full-text and search, retrieve, and display more sources on the Adaptation topic or on other topics that this journal covers. This type of distinction may be difficult for undergraduate students to make when they have not yet been exposed to professional scholarly journals. When coders noticed full-texts embedded in a database architecture, they deemed database a reasonable IF.

Adding reasonable IFs to exact IFs boosts match rates for scholarly journals to 94.0 and 78.6 percent for Adaptation and Election players, respectively. Doing the same for the other scholarly IFs also boosts match rates into the high seventies to the low nineties.

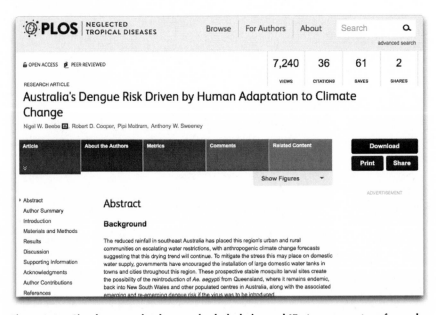

Figure 9.1. Simultaneous database and scholarly journal IFs (screen capture from plos .org, August 17, 2013).

The analysis of match rates for nonscholarly sources makes sense only for the Election class, where players closed large to moderately large numbers of consumer newspapers, blogs, and trade magazines. Their exact matches were high for consumer newspapers (51.2 percent) and much lower for blogs (33.3 percent) and trade magazines (9.2 percent). Examining each consumer newspaper to determine reasonable matches, we discovered that players split between assignments of the trade newspaper and consumer magazine IFs. Thus, they seemed to sense that these sources were newspapers in nature and targeted consumers. We deemed the public sharing site IF reasonable for consumer newspapers that allowed readers to comment on news stories, assuming that players interpreted this IF literally to mean a website where people shared their comments about published news stories. This again may be a literary category unfamiliar to students. Reasonable IFs of consumer newspapers boosted this format's match rate to 85.3 percent. Determining reasonable IFs for blogs was idiosyncratic, requiring an examination of each blog. Thus, IFs, such as promotional material, public sharing sites, and consumer newspapers, were reasonable based on an analysis of individual sources. There were several reasonable IFs for trade magazines. The trade newspaper and trade journal IFs reflected the "trade" aspect of these publications that geared them toward practitioners, the consumer magazine and consumer newspaper IFs reflected the more casual nature of their delivery, and articles embedded in a database architecture reasonably matched the database and online repository IFs. Thus, reasonable matches boosted the very low exact-match rate of 9.2 percent for trade magazines to 56.6 percent.

Applying reasonable IFs to both scholarly and nonscholarly sources revealed several instances of sources for which there was not one particular IF but several IFs that applied simultaneously. Table 9.3 gives examples of these IFs and uses italics (in the right column) for coders' IFs.

Table 9.3's numerous examples demonstrate how difficult it is to typecast sources into one IF. We suspect that new technological developments are making digital versions of traditional IFs into a moving target. There may be no general consensus about what to call them for some time to come, perhaps not until the evolution of these formats slows down long enough for names to become established and familiar to users—and once they do, we bet that technology will introduce even more change!

IF identification was one of several components of the BiblioBouts's source evaluation process. Although Adaptation players excelled at correctly matching scholarly journal IFs, they and Election players had difficulty correctly identifying IFs for other source types, even encyclopedias, a format that we might expect to be easy to identify. Perhaps having a long list of IFs from which to choose muddied the waters for students. Expecting undergraduate students to correctly identify the IFs of online sources may be too much

Table 9.3. Nonscholarly Sources That Are Simultaneously Several IFs (Coder's IF in Italics)

Nonscholarly Source Description	Why These IFs Are Reasonable
National Geographic summarizes research findings on climate change using an interactive map that reports information in a way that is easy for everyday people to understand.	*Research report* = Research is reported. Information video = This is the only available IF that implies interactive media. Consumer magazine = Information is presented to nonexperts in an understandable way. Scholarly journal = Research is summarized.
Symbols on world maps summarize climatic conditions during prehistoric periods.	*Teaching material* = The map's home page suggests that the maps be used for teaching and research. Research report = The university professor asserts that these conditions are a result of his University of Chicago dissertation research. Encyclopedia = The Climate Conditions home page bears links to maps for over two dozen prehistoric periods.
News from the government of Trinidad and Tobago (T&T) reports how small developing Caribbean states are preparing for a future international meeting on climate change.	*Public affairs information* = News posted at the website of the T&T government addresses small developing Caribbean states. Consumer newspaper = News from the T&T government is presented. Consumer magazine = News from the T&T government is easy for everyday people to understand.
A news story from NPR.com titled "How Tweet It Is" describes politicians' uses of social media and includes readers' opinions.	*Consumer newspaper* = News stories on an encyclopedic array of topics are presented. Consumer newspaper = National and international news is presented. Public sharing site = Opinions on specific news stories are posted by registered readers and listeners.
A news story from Mashable.com titled "Why Obama Needs Social Media to Win in 2012" includes readers' opinions.	*Trade newspaper* = News stories discuss how digital innovations inspire or empower people. Trade newspaper = News specific to people's use of technology is presented. Public sharing site = Opinions on specific news stories are posted by registered readers and listeners.

of a stretch in the absence of tutorials to brief players on IF identity before or while they play the game. Considerable rethinking would be necessary to make IF identification tasks a useful component of a credibility assessment module in future information literacy games.

WHAT CRITERIA DO STUDENTS
USE TO ASSESS BIBLIOBOUTS SOURCES?

After identifying a source's IF, the game's source evaluation process transitioned to credibility assessment. To assess a source's credibility, players rated the author's expertise, the source's trustworthiness, and its scholarly nature on a scale from 0 to 100 (figure 5.8). They earned bonus points for entering into the dialogue box a comment that explained their reasons for their ratings. Assessing relevance followed a similar routine, with players rating on a scale from 0 to 100 the source's usefulness, its accuracy, and whether it was good enough for their course assignments (figure 5.9). This section examines whether players' reasons for their credibility and relevance assessments were grounded in evidence or relied more on seat-of-the-pants approaches, such as intuition or projections about the source's nature.

Students' Credibility and Relevance Assessments

To perform the analysis, we used the same sample of sources used previously in this chapter. Despite BiblioBouts's prompts for players to rate credibility and relevance, they did not rate all the sources the T&R bout displayed to them for these reasons: (1) they observed no full-text attached to the source's citation, (2) they detected incorrect full-texts attached to the source's citation, that is, the citation and the attached full-text did not match, or (3) they skipped rating, perhaps being disinterested, tired, or in a rush. In response, BiblioBouts recorded zeros, or null values, to logs. Because it was not possible to determine whether null values represented players' deliberate "not credible" or "not relevant" ratings or their skipping rating tasks for the reasons cited above, we omitted null values from the calculation of credibility and relevance ratings. Table 9.4 gives the results of the analysis.

Playing the T&R bout were thirty-eight Adaptation students who rated on average almost forty sources, nearly two times their T&R bout's quota of twenty-two sources. This average was due to the large numbers of above-quota players and superplayers in the Adaptation game (table 8.3). Although many more students (seventy-three) played the Election game than the Adaptation game, they averaged only 19.4 sources, exceeding quota by three to

Table 9.4. Sample Ratings

Basic Facts about Rated Sources	Adaptation Game	Election Game
Number of sources players rated	190	328
T&R bout's quota	22	16
Number of students who played the T&R bout	38	73
Number of credibility ratings	1,517	1,415
Average number of sources students rated	39.9	19.4
Facts about Credibility Ratings		
Number (percentage) of players making no comments about credibility	5 (13.2)	15 (20.5)
Number (percentage) of ratings with comments about credibility	798 (52.6)	669 (47.3)
Average credibility (minus skipped ratings and 0 percent ratings)	79.8	71.8
Facts about Relevance Ratings		
Number (percentage) of players making no comments about relevance	7 (18.4)	18 (24.7)
Number (percentage) of ratings with comments about relevance	783 (51.6)	650 (45.9)
Average relevance (minus skipped ratings and 0 percent ratings)	72.8	72.1

four sources. Sampled Adaptation and Election sources averaged credibility scores of 79.8 and 71.8 percent, respectively. Relevance ratings were almost the same at 72.8 percent for Adaptation sources and 72.1 percent for Election sources. About half of Adaptation (52.6 and 51.6 percent) players gave reasons for their ratings. Election players were less forthcoming, giving reasons for a little under half of the sources they rated (47.3 and 45.9 percent).

We submitted players' written credibility and relevance assessments to a content analysis to determine the criteria they gave for their positive, negative, or neutral assessments. The analysis yielded these three top-level categories: (1) evidence based, (2) projection, and (3) intuition. Into the *evidence-based* category were placed reasons that cited the specific criteria students used to assess the source's credibility or relevance. Evidence that was internal to the source included references to author affiliation information, date of publication, length, format/genre, and cited references; evidence that was external to the source included references to the database or online repository where the source was retrieved or the topic that the instructor assigned students to research. Into the *projection category* were placed reasons that speculated on or imagined a source's credibility or relevance but failed to specify criteria internal or external to the source that would have been evidence for the credibility assessment. Examples are student comments such as "well written" or "not well written." Had these comments referred to aspects of the source's format or genre, such as graphs, research, tables, or statistics, then they would have qualified for the evidence-based category. A second projection instance is a comment that infers the bias of the source's author, sponsor, publisher, and so on—for example, "This person could be biased politically and may not be an expert on these issues." Had the comment cited specific evidence of bias, such as links to a particular political party's websites or the source's failure to present more than one viewpoint on issues, it would have qualified for the evidence-based category. Into the *intuition* category were placed bold or unfounded assertions about a source's credibility or relevance. Examples are "'cause I said so," "very credible source," "seems credible enough," and "appeared relevant."

The few comments that were categorized into more than one category qualified for both the projection and evidence-based categories. For example, consider the credibility comment "NPR is pretty trustworthy. Article appears well-researched." The first sentence qualifies for the evidence-based category because it cites the website's sponsor; the second qualifies for the projection category because no evidence supports its "well-researched" assertion. Had the comment referred directly to NPR or the student's previous experience with NPR as a producer of well-researched articles, then it would have qualified for the evidence-based category.

Credibility Assessments

Figure 9.2 shows the percentages of comments about credibility placed in the three top-level categories. The vast majority of players' credibility comments were evidence-based, accounting for 91 and 85 percent of player comments from Adaptation and Election classes, respectively. Intuition comments were more characteristic of Election players than Adaptation players, but overall

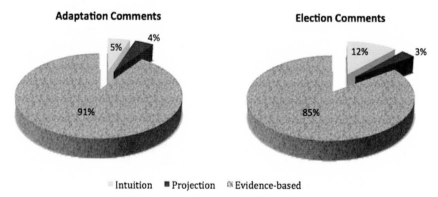

Figure 9.2. Top-level credibility comment categories.

Table 9.5. Definitions and Examples of Evidence-Based Subdivisions

Subdivision	Definition/Examples
Authorship	Criteria that refer to author credentials, reputation, affiliations with named or unnamed organizations, sponsors, publishers, and so on
Author affiliation (named)	The author's affiliation with a particular institution, sponsor, publisher, and so on "Author is affiliated with the Department of Environmental Health Sciences, Johns Hopkins Bloomberg School of Public Health." "The author works for the Institute of Political Science at the University of Zurich, and therefore one can conclude that the source is scholarly and trustworthy."
Author affiliation (unnamed)	A generic or general reference to the author's affiliation with a particular institution, sponsor, publisher, and so on "Written by a doctor, from a university, professionally done." "This article was published by a professor."
Author credentials	References to author credentials (e.g., education, academic degrees, profession, subject expertise, honors, reputation, and so on) or acknowledgment of their absence "John Farley is a professor in the Department of Physics and Astronomy at the University of Nevada, Las Vegas, where he has won several awards for distinguished teaching."
Authorship	Indeterminate remarks about a source's authorship "The article was published in a scholarly journal that is rather scholarly and trustworthy; however I'm not sure that the author is an expert. The author's name isn't even given."
Numerous authors	An acknowledgment of the responsibility of several institutions, sponsors, publishers, and so on "There were a lot of authors working on this source, so the collaboration of research and ideas help to make the article trustworthy."
Verification of the author's expertise	A description of how verification was or could be done "Google search shows no results to lead researcher Willis's credentials." "The author is the CEO of SocialVibe which indicates to me that he has a solid grasp on the topic. It is an opinion blog however. So although there are some neat ideas, there isn't much of a fact-base developed."
Content	Criteria that refers to the source's content "It was an interview with a Democratic media strategist." "Nice graphs and images to support the weight that social media has on political action."
Internal noncontent	Criteria that describe noncontent characteristics of sources that are internal to the source

Subdivision	Definition/Examples
Currency	The source's date of publication
	"This article was recently published last October so it is fairly recent."
Cited references	The source's cited references
	"This source used countless references."
	"The sources used are cited at the end."
Detail	The source's detail, depth, or exhaustiveness
	"Good brief general insight on finding solutions to climate change."
Features	The source's internal features, such as info-graphics, tables, figures, and maps; its internal formats or genres, such as interviews, case studies, research, and experiments; or substantive remarks about its internal structure, such as arguments, clarity, and articulation
	"Author seems to know what she's talking about and presents her argument in a trustworthy and scholarly manner."
	"Nice graphs and images to support the weight that social media has on political action."
Length	The source's length
	"Many in-text citations and an extensive discussion of the source topic lends to sound creditability."
External noncontent	Criteria that describe noncontent characteristics of sources that are external to the source
Format/genre	The source's information format, literary format, or genre
	"The article was published by a reputable newspaper."
	"It is from a credible and scholarly magazine."
Personal experience	The player's personal experience with the author, organization, sponsor, publisher, and so on
	"It's from a UN website that I'm not familiar with."
	"I have never heard of this organization before, but it could be trustworthy."
Recommendations	The recommendation of a person or organization, including remarks about the source's accessibility
	"Ranks higher than average because it is accessible through the Michigan Library Services."
	"It is from a scholarly journal in the MLibrary."
Review	An acknowledgment that the content has been subject to editorial or peer review
	"The site itself does not seem to be strongly edited or peer-reviewed, having more of the freely sharing atmosphere like Facebook and Twitter."
Topic	References to the instructor-assigned broad-based topic, assignment, project, or paper students will write

they accounted for small percentages of comments. Percentages of projection comments were about the same: 4 percent for Adaptation players and 3 percent for Election players. Projection comments had these three themes: (1) unfounded assertions about how well or not well the source was written, (2) the source's physical/visual design, and (3) inferences about the motivation or bias of the author, publisher, sponsor, and so on. Overall, however, there were too few projection comments to detect a trend.

To determine which criteria players cited most frequently in their credibility assessments, we subdivided the evidence-based category and named subdivisions for the evidence players used to support their credibility ratings. Table 9.5 uses the broad-based captions "Authorship," "Content," "Internal Noncontent," "External Noncontent," and "Topic" to characterize the many subdivisions, defines both captions and subdivisions, and gives one or two examples of player comments.

Table 9.6 quantifies the evidence players give for their credibility assessments. Comments could be posted into more than one subdivision. For example, the first half of the comment "Scholarly journal contains many references and is accessible through MLibrary" qualifies for the cited references subdivision and the second half for the recommendations subdivision. Overall, relevance comments were placed into 1.3 subdivisions.

When posting comments into evidence-based subdivisions, we scrutinized players' reasons to determine whether they were positive or negative about the source's credibility. Rarely were players entirely negative. Instead, they almost always hedged, giving both positive and less-than-positive reasons. Here are examples:

- "Information about the author is not clearly shown, seems scholarly due to nature of article and journal."
- "This is a book review so many of the claims are opinion-based."
- "The EPA is a very credible source, but it is presented more casually then I would have like it."

When in doubt about the positive-negative nature of comments, we checked the player's ratings. Typically comments accompanying ratings under 65 percent were less-than-positive, but not always. If we were still in doubt, we considered the comment positive. Table 9.6 also quantifies less-than-positive comments.

Almost half (48.9 percent) of Adaptation players' credibility assessments addressed authorship. The highest-posted authorship subdivisions were author affiliations and author credentials. External noncontent was a close second-place finisher, accounting for 41.7 percent of Adaptation players'

Table 9.6. Number and Nature of Subdivided Evidence-Based Comments

Subdivision	Adaptation			Election		
	N	%	N (%) Less-Than-Positive	N	%	N (%) Less-Than-Positive
Authorship						
Author affiliation (named)	107	21.0	14 (13.1)	88	17.3	9 (10.2)
Author affiliation (unnamed)	74	14.5	7 (9.5)	70	13.7	13 (18.6)
Author credentials	39	7.7	6 (15.4)	18	3.5	6 (33.3)
Authorship	8	1.6	7 (87.5)	12	2.4	5 (41.7)
Numerous authors	13	2.5	1 (7.7)	0	0.0	0 (0.0)
Verification of the author's expertise	8	1.6	5 (62.5)	18	3.5	8 (44.4)
Content	16	3.1	4 (25.0)	40	7.8	16 (40.0)
Internal Noncontent						
Currency	7	1.4	3 (42.9)	0	0.0	0
Cited references	15	2.9	0	41	8.1	9 (22.0)
Detail	2	0.4	1 (50.0)	6	1.2	0
Features	8	1.6	3 (37.5)	79	15.5	31 (39.2)
Length	0	0.0	0	9	1.8	8 (88.9)
External Noncontent						
Format/genre	98	19.2	15 (15.3)	95	18.7	30 (31.6)
Personal experience	12	2.4	8 (66.7)	10	2.0	2 (20.0)
Recommendations	81	15.9	1 (1.2)	3	0.6	2 (66.7)
Review	11	2.2	2 (18.2)	15	2.9	2 (13.3)
Topic	10	2.0	1 (10.0)	5	1.0	0
Total	509	100.0	78 (15.3)	509	100.0	141 (27.7)

comments, with format/genre and recommendations being the highest-posted external noncontent subdivisions. Internal noncontent, content, and topic were distant third-, fourth-, and fifth-place finishers.

Less-than-positive comments averaged only 15.3 percent of Adaptation players' credibility comments. Less-than-positive comments characterized none of the highly populated subdivisions. Low-posted subdivisions, such as authorship, verification of the author's expertise, currency, and personal experience, had above-average shares of less-than-positive comments. Let's examine each subdivision to see why less-than-positive comments prevailed.

The authorship subdivision was a catchall for players' comments about authors and authorship that did not qualify for other authorship subdivisions. Most of these comments addressed the absence of author names or author affiliations; examples are "Difficult to find author" and "Not sure who it's written by." Players who went to the trouble of verifying the author's expertise did so because it was suspect. Examples are "Google search show[s] no results to lead researcher Willis's credentials" and "There is no information given on the author of this source [expert], or his credits [trustworthiness], and academic affiliations. Seems to me that this source wasn't properly searched using scholarly databases." Few Adaptation players mentioned currency in their credibility comments, but when they did, they commented on older sources and expressed skepticism about them. Adaptation players making less-than-positive comments in the personal experience subdivision usually commented on their unfamiliarity with the author, publisher, sponsoring organization, and so on.

Authorship also figured prominently into Election players' comments about their credibility ratings, accounting for 40.4 percent of their comments. Not-so-distant second- and third-place finishers were the two noncontent subdivisions, each accounting for about one-quarter of comments. Features and cited references were the most popular internal noncontent subdivisions. With respect to the former, players mentioned specific literary features or devices that authors used, such as arguments, data, analyses, facts, research, statistics, complex vocabularies, graphs, and so on, to explain the credibility ratings they gave to sources. Cited references could be considered a literary feature, but because they figure so prominently in scholarly and technical literature, we chose to create a separate subdivision for them. Typical were comments that addressed both cited references and features; examples are "No specific sources given for the displayed data," "The source is well researched and cited," and "The authors . . . did a considerable amount of research/citations. They also reasonably thought out counterarguments to their point and supported the reasons the counterarguments were wrong with research."

Unlike Adaptation players, who were keen on the recommendations subdivision, only 0.6 percent of Election comments qualified for this subdivision. Curious about this phenomenon, we reviewed the Adaptation game's recommendations comments and discovered almost 90 percent of them were made by only two superplayers.

Less-than-positive comments averaged 27.7 percent of Election players' credibility comments. Such comments characterized only one highly populated subdivision: features. Players usually made features comments about nonscholarly sources from the open Web, such as blogs and magazine and newspaper articles. Here are several examples that cite both features (in bold) and format/genre (in italics) criteria:

- "The article is from *NY Times* whose employees are just reporters, not necessarily experts. The argument seems trustworthy as it's pretty much based on previous **facts** and it's rather scholarly, although no extensive **research** was completed."
- "Published on a *blog* without many **statistics**."
- "It is on online *newspaper* and *blog* site about politics, so people are intelligible about the subjects. There is a lack of **factual evidence** in the information provided."
- "No citations for **statistics** and no **error margins** = not reliable. This is very typical for a *news article* though."

The vast majority of Adaptation sources were scholarly, unlike Election sources, which were divided between scholarly and nonscholarly sources. Had they been more evenly divided, we might have seen the same phenomenon occurring with respect to the less-than-positive nature of features comments. As it stands, there were too few nonscholarly Adaptation sources to make the same observation.

Larger-than-average percentages of less-than-positive comments were characteristic of the subdivisions for authorship and verification of the author's expertise in the Election game, too. Most Election players' comments about length were less than positive due to the source's short length.

Relevance Assessments

Figure 9.3 shows the percentages of comments about relevance placed in the three top-level categories. Except for flip-flopping percentages of intuition and projection comments, the results for the two classes are the same. Ninety percent of players' comments cited evidence for their relevance assessments. Intuition comments were simple and unimaginative, asserting the source's

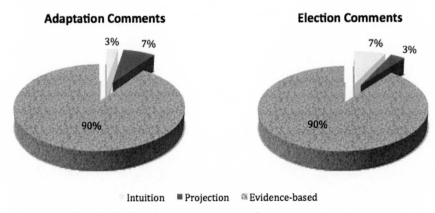

Adaptation Comments

3%   7%

90%

Election Comments

7%   3%

90%

Intuition   ■ Projection   ▨ Evidence-based

Figure 9.3.   Top-level relevance comment categories.

relevance but failing to tell how relevance was assessed. Examples are "There is relevant information," "Decent information," and "Could be better." With respect to projection, three themes were identified: (1) unfounded assertions about how well or not well the source was written, (2) unfounded assertions about the source's understandability, and (3) inferences about the motivation or bias of the author, publisher, sponsor, and so on. In the Adaptation class, instances of the first two were somewhat plentiful, but a closer analysis revealed almost all were made by only two players, one who entered "well-

Table 9.7.   Definitions and Examples of New Evidence-Based Subdivisions

Subdivision	Definition/Examples
Content	Criteria that refer to the source's content
Relevant content	A description of the source's relevant content
	"The article describes the role Twitter will have in the upcoming election, as compared to the past election in which Facebook was the main source for social media."
	"Social media is playing a huge role, but can it backfire?"
	"It describes human systems and the effect of climate change to them in general, making it useful for students to write their essays."
Nonrelevant content	A description of the source's nonrelevant content
	"After reading the abstract, I was comfortable with the material presented, however the topic of discussion is various species' vulnerability, not human adaptation."
	"The content is very interesting, analyzing the use of social media tools by the political parties and companies in Holland, but it does not pertain directly to the 2012 U.S. presidential elections."
	"The article has very little reference to campaigns and talks mostly about digital democracies."

Subdivision	Definition/Examples
Absence of content	Topics missing from the source that, had they been present, would have rendered the source relevant "Has to do more with ecology as opposed to human adaptation, our topic." "It does not talk about adapting but gives a lot of information on global warming and the effects." "The elections described are in Ireland—not the U.S."
Scope	Acknowledgment of the source's content vis-à-vis the topic of the assignment but minus a description of specific source content "General ideas are covered, but specific statistics are missing." "It is an OK article, but there isn't anything special about this one that separates it from all the others. Most of the ideas presented are pretty common." "Sections of the paper could be used to fit our specific topic, but the overall text may be slightly out of scope."
Topic	Criteria that describe noncontent characteristics of sources that are internal to the source
My interests	References to this student's essay, topic, or interests "This topic does not really pertain to my paper topic, even though the information is probably pretty accurate for the topic at hand." "Pertains a lot to what I'm interested in." "The subject of tourism seems to be a little far away from where I want to focus my paper."
Others' interests	References to the essays, topics, or interests of other students in the class "If students are writing about tropic vulnerability, it would work for them." "This is specific to Africa and malaria; therefore, this may not apply to everyone." "Might be tough for students to adapt this to some topics chosen."
This assignment	References to this particular assignment, including the paper students will write "This article can back up an argument one makes in the paper, however would not provide intense evidence making it appear a little less useful in how social media is tied to elections." "A potential reference in the course paper, but not a primary source on which to base the entire paper." "This may not be all that relevant to all of the potential topics that people have decided on for this assignment."

written" repeatedly and a second who frequently commented on the source's understandability.

The same broad-based divisions (i.e., authorship, content, internal non-content, external noncontent, and topic) that characterized the evidence that players used in their credibility assessments also characterized the evidence players used in their relevance assessments. However, because players made so many comments in the content and topic divisions, we introduced new subdivisions for these divisions to fully describe the range of relevance assessments posted under them. Table 9.7 defines these new subdivisions and gives a few examples of player comments.

Table 9.8 reports the evidence players gave for their relevance assessments. Because players made so few comments about authorship, all comments were consolidated in the authorship division. Comments could be posted into more than one subdivision, but this happened infrequently, resulting in 1.2 subdivisions per comment. Table 9.8 also reports the number and percentage of less-than-positive subdivided comments.

Table 9.8.   Number and Nature of Subdivided Evidence-Based Comments

	Adaptation			Election		
Subdivision	N	%	N (%) Less-Than-Positive	N	%	N (%) Less-Than-Positive
Authorship	18	3.4	4 (22.2)	6	1.2	2 (33.3)
Content						
Relevant content	152	29.0	29 (19.1)	129	25.5	24 (18.6)
Nonrelevant content	26	5.0	24 (92.3)	42	8.3	27 (64.3)
Absence of content	69	13.1	57 (82.6)	59	11.6	34 (57.6)
Scope	26	5.0	12 (46.2)	20	3.9	9 (45.0)
Internal Noncontent						
Currency	17	3.2	9 (52.9)	14	2.8	7 (50.0)
Cited references	3	0.6	0	20	3.9	7 (35.0)
Detail	2	0.4	0	3	0.6	2 (66.7)
Features	12	2.3	3 (25.0)	29	5.7	7 (24.1)
Length	1	0.2	0	9	1.8	8 (88.9)
External Noncontent						
Format/genre	16	3.0	12 (75.0)	20	3.9	14 (70.0)
Personal experience	0	0.0	0	3	0.6	0
Recommendations	1	0.2	0	5	1.0	5 (100.0)
Review	0	0.0	0	2	0.4	0
Topic						
My interests	35	6.7	18 (51.4)	23	4.5	6 (26.1)
Others' interests	69	13.1	28 (40.6)	12	2.4	3 (25.0)
This assignment	78	14.8	18 (23.1)	111	21.9	35 (31.5)
Total	525	100.0	214 (40.8)	507	100.0	190 (37.5)

When engaged in relevance assessment, players enlisted entirely different criteria from those they used for credibility assessment. Content was king, accounting for 52.1 percent of Adaptation comments and 49.3 percent of Election comments. Players also relied heavily on topic; 34.6 percent of Adaptation comments and 28.8 percent of Election comments addressed topic. Comments pertaining to the three remaining divisions—internal noncontent, external noncontent, and authorship—were distant third-, fourth-, and fifth-place finishers, respectively. Of the four content subdivisions, relevant content and absence of content were the favorites among players in both classes. Greater-than-average percentages of less-than-positive comments were the norm for three of the four content subdivisions. Considering that two of these three referred to nonrelevant content (i.e., nonrelevant content and absence of content), we expected less-than-positive comments to prevail, and they did. Of the three topic subdivisions, this assignment was the favorite of players in both classes. Less-than-positive comments were typical of half of Adaptation players' my interests comments. None of the other topic subdivisions were inclined toward less-than-positive comments. Other subdivisions that inclined toward less-than-positive comments in both credibility and relevance assessments were currency and length. Format/genre was given to less-than-positive comments especially for nonscholarly sources, such as newspapers, blogs, opinion pieces, and book reviews.

WHETHER PLAYERS AND EXPERTS AGREE ON THE CREDIBILITY OF ONLINE SOURCES

To determine whether players and experts agreed on the credibility of online sources, we developed a coding scheme that experts applied to assess the credibility of online sources and compared their assessments with the credibility scores players gave to sources during game play (figure 5.8). We considered other researchers' coding schemes but decided not to adopt them due to the low-quality scores that their schemes assigned to websites and online information generally. All sources in the BiblioBouts game emanated from online, Web-based sites; thus we needed a coding scheme that could distinguish sources from credible and noncredible websites, rewarding the former with high-quality scores and penalizing the latter with low-quality scores.

Our scoring scheme is a format-neutral taxonomy that can be applied to both online and offline sources. Its design was inspired partly by the quantitative rating scale of Middleton's Scholarly Index (2005) and by Crowston and Kwasnik's (2004) faceted classification system for categorizing online genres. Because the taxonomy is faceted, scoring is multidimensional, taking several factors into consideration.

The taxonomy bears five facets: (1) information format (IF), (2) literary content (LC), (3) author identity (AI), (4) editorial process (EP), and (5) publication purpose (PP). Each facet is subdivided by categories that describe attributes of sources. Academic faculty who teach undergraduate students were recruited as experts to assign numerical values to each category based on the desirability of the attribute in a source for use in a college research paper. In pre-tests of the taxonomy, scores were consistently higher for scholarly, academic, and peer-reviewed sources, while scores were consistently lower for anonymous, self-published, and nonreviewed sources. For example, taxonomy scores for scholarly journals ranged from 18.9 to 19.6, while scores for blogs ranged from 8.0 to 8.4 (Markey, Leeder, and Taylor 2012). Details on the development and pre-testing of the taxonomy are published elsewhere (Leeder, Markey, and Yakel 2012).

We recruited and trained coders, second-year master's students at the University of Michigan's School of Information, to apply the taxonomy to players' closed BiblioBouts sources. Two intercoder reliability studies were conducted because two different pairs of coders evaluated sources from the Adaptation and Election games. Reliability between coders ranged from 80.0 to 84.1 percent. Given the large number of possible codes for each facet, we felt confident about the overall level of agreement between the two sets of coders. Our next step was to apply the taxonomy to the same sample of scholarly and nonscholarly sources from the Adaptation and Election games

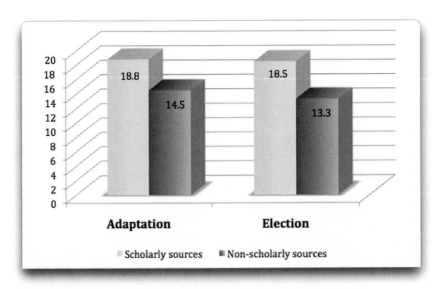

Figure 9.4.   Quality scores for sampled Adaptation and Election sources.

used previously. Coders did precisely that, and figure 9.4 gives the results. The scale for taxonomy quality scores ranged from 5 (lowest) to 20 (highest).

Coder-assigned quality scores for scholarly sources were higher (18.8 and 18.5) than their quality scores for nonscholarly sources (14.5 and 13.3). T-tests confirmed that quality scores were significantly higher for scholarly sources than for nonscholarly sources (Adaptation: $t[140] = 13.686$, $p < .001$; Election: $t[214] = 20.260$, $p < .001$).

Figure 9.5 shows players' credibility ratings for these same scholarly and nonscholarly sources. The credibility scale ranges from 0 percent (lowest) to 100 percent (highest). Both Adaptation and Election players gave significantly higher credibility ratings to scholarly sources than to nonscholarly sources (Adaptation: $t[138] = 3.662$, $p < .001$; Election: $t[215] = 8.245$, $p < .001$). Credibility ratings for scholarly sources were in the high seventies and low eighties, and such scores for nonscholarly sources dipped to the mid-seventies and sixties. Thus, we are confident about concluding that players sensed the quality of scholarly sources over nonscholarly sources and represented this in their credibility ratings.

We extended our analysis of players' credibility ratings to standard deviations, thinking that players might have been less certain about the credibility

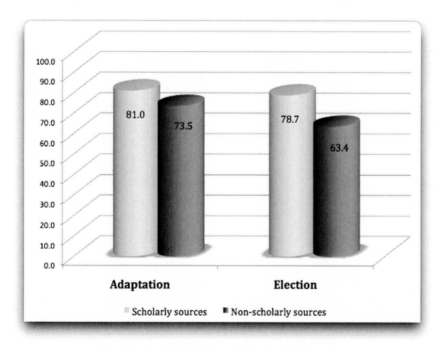

Figure 9.5.   Credibility ratings for sampled Adaptation and Election sources.

of nonscholarly sources and that their uncertainty would be reflected in greater variability between credibility scores. Standard deviations for scholarly sources were 14.6 (Adaptation) and 15.4 (Election); for nonscholarly sources, they were 17.5 (Adaptation) and 23.0 (Election). In both cases, standard deviations for nonscholarly sources exceeded those for scholarly sources; however, t-tests were mixed with significant results coming only from the analysis of Election data (Adaptation: t[138] = −1.462, p = .146; Election: t[214] = −5.256, p < .001).

DISCUSSION

Students submitted sources to BiblioBouts on the broad-based topic that their instructors set for the game. Players rated their opponents' sources and gave reasons for their ratings. On a scale of 0 (low) to 100 (high), relevance ratings averaged in the mid-seventies. About one-third of Adaptation sources and one-sixth of Election sources earned relevance ratings of 80 percent or higher. That players accompanied their highest relevance ratings with especially positive comments is also evidence that players submitted useful sources to the BiblioBouts game. Generally, players' closed BiblioBouts sources had potential for helping players get a head start on their papers, furthering their learning and thinking about the topic, and helping them decide on a topic.

Students submitted scholarly sources in BiblioBouts (table 9.1). In fact, Adaptation players submitted scholarly sources almost exclusively. Election players split between scholarly and nonscholarly sources. It was expected that Election students would find nonscholarly sources on the Election topic because it was a current event of great national and international importance, in the process of becoming while students conducted their research and thus the subject of publications oriented to the general public and available on the open Web and in general-interest databases.

Answers to the question about students' ability to correctly identify the IFs of BiblioBouts's sources are complicated (table 9.2). Players of the Adaptation game correctly identified about two-thirds of IFs, but they closed mostly scholarly sources, three-quarters of them being scholarly journals; thus, they did quite well correctly identifying scholarly journals specifically and scholarly sources generally. Players of the Election game who split on scholarly and nonscholarly sources had more difficulty, correctly identifying only two-fifths of IFs.

The analysis revealed problems with IF identification. Some players interpreted IFs literally instead of conventionally—for example, assigning the research reports IF to reports of research in scholarly journals, conference proceedings, books, and the like, instead of assigning it to sources in the research report information format. That several IFs were needed to characterize some online sources' IFs makes us skeptical about IFs generally (table 9.3). Determining IFs for print publications was a straightforward task. Now new technology is transforming longtime, familiar IFs into new modes of communication, including compounding IFs, so that no one IF is satisfactory. It is also introducing new formats for which no current IFs exist or for which there is no general consensus about the appropriateness of the various existing IFs.

Information formats are a moving target right now. Maybe the fast pace of technology and the new information formats and genres it is creating will slow down, allowing things to settle and enabling consensus and stability in IF nomenclature and imputation. Until then, expecting students to correctly identify online IFs may be a lost cause.

Thankfully, students did not use seat-of-the-pants criteria to assess the credibility and relevance of online sources (table 9.6). Only about 10 percent of their credibility and relevance assessments relied on intuition or projection. Mostly, students used evidence they gleaned from the source at hand or from external sources, including their own prior experience with authors, publishers, sponsors, and so on. When students assessed credibility, the evidence they used most frequently was authorship and internal and external noncontent source characteristics. Students rarely referred to content or topic. When students assessed relevance, the evidence they used was just the opposite (table 9.8). They used content and topic and rarely referred to authorship and internal and external noncontent source characteristics. These results confirm what other researchers have concluded—that credibility and relevance judgments are distinctive assessments (Rich 2010). For credibility, students rely on evidence that serves as "peripheral cues"; for relevance, they focus on the quality or topic of the content.

Students were seldom negative about the reasons they gave for the credibility and relevance assessments (tables 9.6 and 9.8). Their expressions of negativity or doubt were hedges in which they described both positive and less-than-positive reasons. This seemingly indecisive nature of their less-than-positive credibility and relevance assessments made it difficult for us to single out subdivisions for which less-than-positive assessments were the norm; however, two relevance subdivisions are noteworthy: nonrelevant content and absence of content. In fact, their names have negative connotations. External format/genre had its share of less-than-positive assessments, especially when the source at hand involved nonscholarly formats such as newspapers, blogs, and magazines. Players had less-than-positive assessments about sources when they were too short, outdated, or short on detail.

Requiring players to give source credibility and relevance ratings and asking them to describe the reasons for their ratings were much more effective strategies than using IFs for evaluating sources. Players primarily relied on evidence for their assessments, they were thoughtful about the evidence they reported, and they rarely dismissed sources out of hand. The much-cited Elaboration Likelihood Model (ELM) has been widely applied in studies on information evaluation. ELM presents two kinds of constructs affecting the argument: quality of content/message and peripheral cues (Petty and Cacioppo 1981, 1986). This chapter's analyses reaffirmed that there are two distinctive kinds of assessment—relevance judgment and credibility judgment. Additionally, the criteria players used—authorship and noncontent characteristics for credibility and content and topic for relevance—are also distinctive.

Here is a comment from the focus group interviews that sums up how we wanted players to benefit from T&R ratings and comments.

> I thought it was really interesting to see how I rated articles versus how other people rated articles because it gave you an idea if you're, like, on the right track when you read these things if you think they're true and other people think they're true.

Unfortunately, some players gave source evaluation short shrift, skipping rating tasks, repeatedly cutting-and-pasting comments, or entering less-than-useful comments. Serious players noticed this, and they had lots to say about it in focus groups.

- "I noticed that some people didn't actually do anything. Like, they kind of just gave you a zero just because they wanted to get it done. Like they actually didn't even read the article and, like, there was no comments, no nothing, just a flat-out zero."
- "Some [people were] going through and spreading irrelevant comments for no reason. Like it was like they were just trying so hard to get points that they weren't even [trying]."
- "I noticed during the Tagging & Rating section, a lot of students would just cut-and-paste comments to get the extra twenty points when it does clearly state, it asks for a unique comment, and I'm understanding 'unique' as in every comment is going to be somewhat different."

Players' credibility ratings agreed with the credibility ratings of experts (figures 9.4 and 9.5). The quality scores coders gave to closed scholarly sources were significantly higher than scores they gave to nonscholarly sources, and players' credibility ratings for the former were significantly higher than their ratings for the latter. Despite sensing differences in credibility, students admitted difficulties with credibility assessment tasks in focus groups.

- "I just really had no idea how to assess credibility at all. . . . Being naïve, you figure, 'If it's published, it's true.' But you don't really know. . . . I just had no idea how to actually evaluate the credibility of anything."
- "On the accuracy question, I figured a lot of times, like, I personally didn't know because I don't know if this information is accurate and that's why I'm looking it up. But at the same time, I didn't know if it was accurate or not because I'm going to them to find out the information. So I'm going to assume it's accurate, but you don't know. They could say, 'Obama used Twitter for, like, a certain percentage,' and you don't know if that's right. So you'd have to do further research to really figure out is that really accurate or not?"
- "If I saw that it was from, like, a university, I automatically gave it credibility points, however, I mean, if that's how you planned for [the] credible rating to go, then yes. But I just felt like I had no idea how credible actually that person was. That professor could have been, like, fired the year after because they were, like, giving bad information [some students are laughing]. So it was just hard for me to really, like, at least for me, like, I was trying to get really into it and it was just hard for me to tell what was credible and what wasn't."

Several reasons explain students' difficulty with credibility assessment. Students understand the importance of using credible information, but they do not have sufficient domain knowledge or expertise to filter out noncredible information (Fogg 2003; Rieh 2010). They may be concerned about information credibility and intend to find credible information but lack the knowledge and skills to judge if it is credible or not. Some students are concerned about information credibility, but they do not put effort into making credibility judgments. For example, Metzger (2007) notes that people are aware of the need to critically evaluate information credibility but rarely have the time or inclination to do it. Finally, students might have considered information credibility but been unable to articulate the specific reasons for the assessments they made.

SUMMARY

We expected players to play BiblioBouts, submitting relevant sources that addressed the broad-based topic that the instructor assigned to students and the specific topics that players were considering for their written papers. Players did just that. We were less concerned about finding significant differences in relevance ratings for scholarly and nonscholarly sources than in credibility ratings for scholarly and nonscholarly sources. Finding significant differences in the latter increases our confidence about the game's ability to increase players' consciousness about scholarly sources, searching for them online, contributing them to the game, giving them higher credibility ratings than nonscholarly sources, and using evidence-based criteria to justify their credibility ratings. That players were able to find quality sources and reflect this in their credibility assessments is evidence of their awareness of the importance of source credibility. Whether players used scholarly sources to write their papers is an important topic, which the next chapter addresses.

Chapter Ten

How BiblioBouts Influenced Students' Research Papers

BiblioBouts gave players four opportunities to scrutinize online sources before they made final decisions about the sources they would cite in their research papers. First, they searched the Web and library databases for sources on the broad-based topic and saved them to Zotero. Second, they chose a subset of their saved sources—presumably their best ones—to submit to BiblioBouts in the Closer bout. Third, they evaluated their opponents' sources in the T&R bout (and since they were making progress toward writing their papers, they might have made a mental note of sources that piqued their interest—for example, sources on aspects of the broad-based topic that interested them, that were better than the ones they found on their own, or that changed their minds about what they expected to write about). Fourth, they chose a subset of everyone's saved sources—presumably the best ones on an aspect of the broad-based topic that interested them—for their own best bibliographies in the game's Best Bibliography bout.

By the time the game ended, BiblioBouts players had been exposed to many more sources than they would have found on their own and to information literacy concepts that should have increased their awareness of the need to use quality sources in their research papers. Thus, we hypothesized that players' final papers would bear more cited sources than nonplayers' final papers and that the quality of the sources players cited in their papers would be better than that of nonplayers' final-paper sources. This chapter describes tests of these hypotheses and discusses results about the sources students cited in their research papers.

RESEARCH QUESTIONS AND METHODS

In this chapter, we sought answers to these research questions:

1. Does the quality of the sources students choose at each step of the research process steadily improve?
2. Do BiblioBouts players cite better-quality sources in their final papers than nonplayers?
3. Do BiblioBouts players cite more sources in their final-paper bibliographies than nonplayers?
4. Do BiblioBouts players cite BiblioBouts sources in their final papers?

The basis for the analysis was logged game play data from the two classes. Also available for the analysis were the sources that Adaptation and Election students cited in their final papers. To assess source quality, coders used the taxonomy to rate the quality of students' BiblioBouts sources and their cited final-paper sources (see pages 145–47).

The bibliographies of players and nonplayers were compared. Note that the definitions for player and nonplayer for the two classes varied because instructors gave their students different incentives for playing BiblioBouts. With regard to the Adaptation and Election students, game play was required for the former, and extra credit was given to the latter. Thus, Adaptation players included twenty-two students who met each bout's caps or quotas, and nonplayers included twenty-three students who failed to play one or more bouts, failed to meet all bouts' caps or quotas, or did not play BiblioBouts at all. Election players included forty-seven students who met each bout's caps or quotas and received extra credit for playing BiblioBouts; nonplayers included fifty-three students chosen randomly from the 106 students who did not play BiblioBouts and thus did not receive extra credit for game play.

DOES SOURCE QUALITY IMPROVE
AT EACH STEP OF THE RESEARCH PROCESS?

Adaptation players' closed sources were almost exclusively limited to scholarly information formats (IFs); 92.2 percent were scholarly IFs, and 7.8 percent were nonscholarly (table 9.1). They gave closed sources from scholarly IFs significantly higher credibility ratings than sources from nonscholarly IFs (figure 9.5). Coders did the same, giving closed sources from scholarly IFs significantly higher quality ratings than sources from nonscholarly IFs (figure 9.4).

Because sources from scholarly IFs predominated among closed sources in the Adaptation game, when players chose sources for their best bibliographies, they chose from a pool of mostly scholarly sources. In fact, 94.2 percent of their best bibliography sources were from scholarly IFs, and only 5.8 percent were from nonscholarly IFs. Credibility rating and quality results for best bibliography sources were similar to closed sources results. Best bibliography sources from scholarly IFs had a higher credibility rating (73.7 percent) and quality score (18.9) than best bibliography sources from nonscholarly IFs (70.9 percent credibility rating and 14.6 quality score).

Election players split their closed sources between scholarly (55.3 percent) and nonscholarly (44.7 percent) IFs, so they had large numbers of sources from both scholarly and nonscholarly IFs to choose from for their best bibliographies (table 9.1). Table 10.1 enumerates the number and percentage of sampled sources Election players chose for their best bibliographies.

Despite the availability of almost equal numbers of closed sources from scholarly and nonscholarly IFs, Adaptation players cited a slightly lower percentage of scholarly sources (51.2 percent) in their best bibliographies than they originally closed (55.3 percent; table 9.1). On one hand, our hypothesis about players' choosing better sources as they made progress in the library research process was not supported. On the other hand, Election players sensed source quality, giving significantly higher credibility ratings to best

Table 10.1.   IFs of Election Players' Best Bibliography Sources

Coder IFs	Election Sources	
	N	%
Scholarly IFs		
Book	5	4.0
Conference proceedings	14	11.2
Encyclopedia	5	4.0
Research report	9	7.2
Scholarly journal	29	23.2
Trade journal	2	1.6
Subtotal	64	51.2
Nonscholarly IFs		
Blog	5	4.0
Consumer magazine	3	2.4
Consumer newspaper	36	28.8
Promotional material	2	1.6
Trade magazine	14	11.2
Trade newspaper	1	0.8
Subtotal	61	48.8
Total	125	100.0

bibliography sources from scholarly IFs (75.4 percent) than to those from nonscholarly IFs (66.6 percent) (t[123] = 18.2, p < .001).

DO PLAYERS CITE BETTER-QUALITY
SOURCES THAN NONPLAYERS?

To answer this section's research question, all sources that Adaptation players cited in their research papers were analyzed, and samples of sources used by Adaptation nonplayers (40 percent) and Election players (30 percent) and nonplayers (30 percent) were taken; during the analysis, these sample percentages dropped by about 3 percent because of our inability to relocate full-texts for some players' and nonplayers' cited sources due to incorrect citations or sources disappearing from the open Web and online databases.

Let's start with the Adaptation class. Scholarly IFs accounted for 44.6 percent of Adaptation players' final-paper sources—nowhere near the 92.4 and 94.2 percent scholarly sources among their closed and best bibliography sources! With regard to scholarly IFs, Adaptation players cited mostly scholarly journals, research reports, and encyclopedias. Adaptation nonplayers cited an even smaller percentage of scholarly sources (35.3 percent) in their final papers, and their favorite IFs were the same as for players with the exception of research reports.

Nonscholarly IFs accounted for 55.4 percent of Adaptation players' final-paper sources. Mostly these players cited consumer magazines, consumer newspapers, policy statements, and promotional material. Nonscholarly IFs accounted for 64.8 percent of Adaptation nonplayers' final-paper sources. When citing sources, these nonplayers favored blogs, consumer newspapers, promotional material, and public affairs information.

Figure 10.1 shows the IFs of Adaptation players' and nonplayers' final-paper sources. It is limited to the IFs players and nonplayers cited most frequently (i.e., their favorite IFs). Notice how players cited higher percentages of scholarly IFs—encyclopedias, research reports, and scholarly journals—than nonplayers. While we might expect this trend to switch for nonscholarly sources—that is, for nonplayers to cite higher percentages of nonscholarly IFs than players—the results were mixed. Nonplayers cited higher percentages of blogs, consumer newspapers, promotional material, and public affairs information than players, and players cited higher percentages of consumer magazines and policy statements than nonplayers.

Coders' quality scores confirmed the distinction between scholarly and nonscholarly final-paper sources. Adaptation players' scholarly and nonscholarly final-paper sources achieved the same quality score of 17.4, and

Percentage

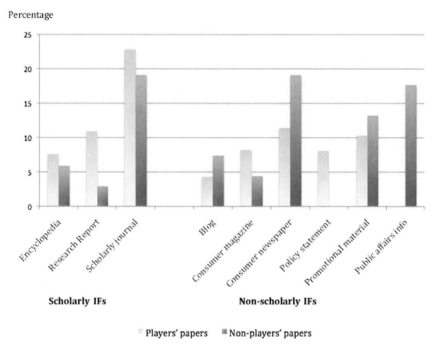

Scholarly IFs   Non-scholarly IFs

Players' papers   Non-players' papers

Figure 10.1. Favorite IFs cited in Adaptation players' and nonplayers' final papers.

nonplayers' scholarly and nonscholarly final-paper sources achieved quality scores of 14.7 and 14.4, respectively. We did not perform statistical tests to determine whether results were significant due to small frequencies (less than five) in the majority of cells.

The comparison of final-paper sources cited by Elections players and non-players is next. Scholarly IFs accounted for 47.2 percent of Election players' final-paper sources—a little less than the 55.3 and 51.2 percent of scholarly sources among their closed and best bibliography sources. We would have preferred to see these percentages reversed, but that did not happen. With regard to scholarly IFs, Election players cited mostly scholarly journals, research reports, and conference proceedings. Election nonplayers cited a somewhat smaller percentage (44.7 percent) of scholarly sources in their final papers, and their favorite IFs were the same as for players with the exception of conference proceedings.

Nonscholarly IFs accounted for 52.8 percent of Election players' final-paper sources. Players cited blogs and consumer newspapers almost exclusively. Nonscholarly IFs accounted for 55.3 percent of Election nonplayers' final-paper sources. Nonplayers favored blogs, consumer magazines, and consumer newspapers.

Figure 10.2 shows the IFs of Election players' and nonplayers' final-paper sources and is limited to the IFs players and nonplayers cited most frequently (i.e., their favorite IFs). While we hoped to distinguish trends such as players citing higher percentages of scholarly IFs and nonplayers citing higher percentages of nonscholarly IFs, this did not happen. Results were mixed, with players and nonplayers favoring this or that IF and not limiting their cited sources to scholarly or nonscholarly IFs generally.

Once again, taxonomy-based quality scores confirmed the distinction between scholarly and nonscholarly final-paper sources. Election players' scholarly and nonscholarly final-paper sources achieved taxonomy-based

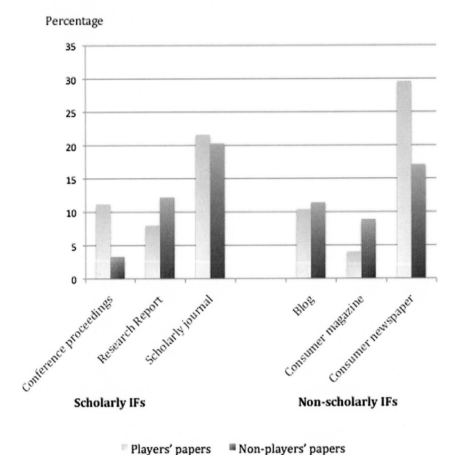

Figure 10.2.   Favorite IFs cited in Election players' and nonplayers' final papers.

quality scores of 18.8 and 13.1, respectively, and nonplayers' scholarly and nonscholarly final-paper sources achieved quality scores of 18.4 and 13.4, respectively. Statistical tests were not performed due to small frequencies (less than five) in the majority of cells.

DO PLAYERS CITE MORE SOURCES THAN NONPLAYERS?

In final-paper bibliographies, Adaptation and Election players averaged 9.0 and 9.9 cited sources, and Adaptation and Election nonplayers averaged 7.6 and 8.0 cited sources, respectively. Differences between averages were not significant for the two classes. Although the difference between the two averages was not dramatic, players generally cited more sources in their final-paper bibliographies than did nonplayers.

DO PLAYERS CITE BIBLIOBOUTS SOURCES IN THEIR RESEARCH PAPERS?

Let's determine the extent to which players cited BiblioBouts sources in their final-paper bibliographies. Checking closed BiblioBouts sources for matches among the cited sources in students' research papers was difficult due to the variability in students' citation practices and the large number of closed sources. Instead of sampling cited sources, the BiblioBouts team opted for an alternative approach: checking final-paper bibliographies for citations to the highest-cited sources in players' best bibliographies. Because highest-cited best bibliography sources were ones to which players gave high relevance and credibility ratings, presumably such sources would be great starting places for players, giving them ideas about their paper's content and how they might specialize in an aspect of the broad-based topic. Thus, players were likely to cite those sources in their final-paper bibliographies. Choosing highest-posted best bibliography sources limited the analysis to fewer sources; as a result, fewer matches would likely be overlooked, and more final papers could be included in the analysis.

To generate a list of at least two dozen high-cited best bibliography sources, BiblioBouts team members chose all Adaptation sources cited three or more times in best bibliographies, resulting in a list of thirty sources that were cited three to thirteen times in best bibliographies. This analysis calls such cited sources "popular BiblioBouts sources." We compared popular BiblioBouts sources to *all* sources cited in players' and nonplayers' final papers, searching for matches between the two. The results were disappointing.

Adaptation players cited only two popular sources in their final papers and nonplayers only one. Thus, the percentage of popular BiblioBouts sources in Adaptation students' final papers was miniscule.

We chose all Election sources that were cited six or more times in best bibliographies, resulting in a list of thirty-two sources. We compared popular BiblioBouts sources to all sources cited in players' and nonplayers' final papers, searching for matches between the two. Of the sources Election players cited in their final papers, 26.2 percent were popular BiblioBouts sources. Overall, 83.0 percent of Election players cited one or more popular BiblioBouts sources in their final papers. Players cited all but five of the thirty-two popular BiblioBouts sources in their final-paper bibliographies. Although Election nonplayers did not have access to the BiblioBouts game or Post-Game Library, 10.8 percent of their final-paper bibliographies cited popular BiblioBouts sources. Overall, 54.7 percent of nonplayers cited at least one popular BiblioBouts source in their final paper. Nonplayers cited a little over half (53.1 percent) of popular BiblioBouts sources in their final-paper bibliographies. The reason why nonplayers cited BiblioBouts sources, even though they had no access to BiblioBouts, might have been due to librarians visiting classes before game play began and recommending keywords and databases for retrieving relevant sources. Using these keywords in their searches, nonplayers retrieved many of the same sources as BiblioBouts players and cited them in their final papers.

DISCUSSION

The quality of the sources students chose at each step of the research process did not steadily improve. In both games, the percentages of scholarly sources among players' closed and best bibliography sources were about the same. Adaptation players closed scholarly sources almost exclusively, so they had only scholarly sources to choose from for their best bibliographies. Although Election players split between scholarly and nonscholarly sources in both the Closer and Best Bibliography bouts, they did sense that scholarly sources were more credible than nonscholarly sources.

The percentage of scholarly sources in Adaptation players' final-paper bibliographies plunged from in-game percentages in the nineties to the mid-forties; however, this percentage was still higher than the percentage of scholarly sources (35.2 percent) in nonplayers' final-paper bibliographies.

In the Closer bout, Election players roughly split their source selection between scholarly (55.3 percent) and nonscholarly (44.7 percent) sources. The percentage of scholarly sources dropped to 51.2 percent in their best bibliographies and dropped even more (to 44.6 percent) in their final-paper bibliographies; however, players' final-paper bibliographies cited a higher percentage (44.6 percent) of scholarly sources than did nonplayers' final-paper bibliographies (35.2 percent).

Chapter 9 (see page 148) commented on the current events nature of the Election topic. Students might have been hard-pressed to find scholarly sources on the use of social media in the 2012 presidential election because they conducted their library research a full year in advance of the election. Of scholarly IFs, conference proceedings would be the quickest to reach publication, perhaps taking researchers twelve to eighteen months to conduct their studies from start to finish. In contrast, research in scholarly journals takes about three years to reach publication, and students might not have been able to find much research published in scholarly journals yet. When students did cite scholarly journals, they cited sources that drew on the results of the 2008 election, including ones that made predictions about the 2012 election. In fact, examples of scholarly journal titles—such as "Obama: The Marketing Lesson," "Brand Obama: The Implications of a Branded President," "A Celebration That Defined a Generation: Grant Park, New Media, and Barack Obama's Historic Victory of the U.S. Presidency," and "Digital Democracy: Reimagining Pathways to Political Participation"—all published in 2010, imply that their authors looked back and ahead to the 2008 and 2012 presidential elections. Perhaps when players and nonplayers wanted direct references to the 2012 election, they were more inclined to cite nonscholarly sources, such as blogs, consumer newspapers, and consumer magazines, because these IFs could publish much more quickly on this current events topic compared to scholarly IFs.

When it came to citing sources in final papers, the Adaptation class almost totally disregarded BiblioBouts sources. The Election class was different, with at least one-quarter of their papers' bibliographies citing such sources. The disparity between the two classes in terms of citing BiblioBouts sources was probably due to the topics students researched. The instructor who assigned the Adaptation topic did not fully specify this topic. He wanted students to specialize, discussing a particular population's adaptation to global warming. Students did precisely that, limiting their sources to ones that addressed the target population. As a result, Adaptation students might have been inclined to dismiss sources that did not discuss their specific interests. Here are examples of research paper topics that focused on narrowly defined populations, suggesting that their cited sources would have been acceptable only to others writing about the exact same population:

- Bicycling in Ireland in response to global warming
- Global warming's impact on agricultural production in India
- Health effects of global warming in Los Angeles

- Responding to rising sea levels in California, New York City, and Holland
- Las Vegas's growing population and freshwater needs

In contrast, the Election topic was much more self-contained than the Adaptation topic. Students could have specialized, choosing a particular social media genre such as Twitter, Facebook, or YouTube, but most did not, preferring instead to discuss the use of social media in the presidential election or politics in ways that could be applicable to a number of their fellow students. For example, sources cited in a paper on one of these topics might have been acceptable for any or all of them:

- Social media for persuading or mobilizing voters
- How to successfully use social media in a political campaign
- Fact-based accounts of politicians' use of social media
- Benefits of social media in political campaigns
- How social media has changed politics and political campaigns

Another reason for students' failure to cite BiblioBouts sources was their in-game unpreparedness with respect to their research paper topics. Three to four weeks prior to the research paper's deadline, the game began with the Donor and Closer bouts, which required students to find and save sources on the broad-based topic and submit them to BiblioBouts. During these early bouts, students likely had a ballpark idea of their topics but had not given enough thought to their topics to submit sources to the Donor and Closer bouts on what they would eventually write about. Their donated sources on the broad-based topic might have been satisfactory for game play, but did not address their specific needs later on. After the game ended and their research paper's deadline drew closer, students had to narrow the broad-based topic, and many went back online to retrieve new sources particular to their interests. Table 10.2 features three students per class (A = Adaptation class and E = Election class), showing how their interests evolved over a three- to four-week period with (1) a description of their closed sources' subject matter, (2) their best bibliography topic from the Best Bibliography bout, and (3) their final paper's topic.

With respect to the three Adaptation players' topics, the ideas of climate change and global warming seemed to form a backdrop against which they entertained various aspects of these ideas, their interests meandering here and there until settling on something more concrete and specific for their papers. As a result, it is doubtful that they were able to draw on their closed sources to write their research papers because their topics continued to evolve until they settled on a topic due to the final paper's impending deadline. Election play-

Table 10.2. The Evolution of Students' Final-Paper Topics

Class	Closed Sources Description	Best Bibliography Topic	Final Paper Topic
A1	Developing countries' responses to climate change	Instituting pollution-abatement policies that are sensitive to the needs of developing countries	Reducing greenhouse gas emissions in China's industrial sector
A2	Human adaptation to climate change in a particular geographic area (e.g., two cities in the United Kingdom, Australia, Burkina Faso, urban areas generally, tourist sites in Mexico)	Human adaptation to climate change	How Cuba is adapting to climate change
A3	All different topics (e.g., developing countries, temperature change, habitat conservation, reducing greenhouse gases, politics of global warming)	How climate change affects the area, land, and inhabitants	How African populations are adapting to global warming
E1	New media and new forms of social interaction in politics	Effect of social media on 2012 elections	How to use social media successfully in a political campaign
E2	Effect of social media on politics and elections	Politicians' use of social media platforms to reinvigorate voters and improve the political process	Effect of social media on 2012 elections
E3	Use of social media in the U.S. presidential elections	How social media will affect the 2012 election	The use of Twitter in U.S. presidential elections

ers were different. From beginning to end, three themes—politics, the election, and social media—were always present, and their original ideas did not go far afield. Additionally, the Election topic was current and timely, hardly given to specialization because it was so new, late breaking, and in the process of becoming. Thus, Election players were able to use more BiblioBouts sources than Adaptation players to write their research papers.

Realizing players were not citing BiblioBouts sources in their final papers, we asked students to comment on this in focus group interviews. They gave several reasons for failing to cite BiblioBouts sources—wanting to browse the Post-Game Library for both ideas and sources before finalizing their topics, switching their topics, and procrastinating about topic selection. Unpreparedness was a key reason, and here is what students had to say in this regard:

- "We're supposed to concise down the topic to something we want to talk about. And that was a long time ago. When we put the sources up, people weren't really thinking about it yet, and they just kind of searched for something and put it up."
- "When I did do BiblioBouts, I didn't have my thesis, like, all the way constructed. . . . I had to do a lot of other research after the fact to find information. . . . It would be beneficial to have the class, like, decide exactly what their thesis is going to be . . . before we do BiblioBouts."

BiblioBouts game play gave students a taste of the evolving nature of serious library research. Usually students procrastinate, waiting until the last moment to conduct their research (Onwuegbuzie and Jiao 2000; Head and Eisenberg 2010). As a result, they do not experience serious library research in which their initial interaction with sources on a topic fosters greater understanding of the topic, which has the potential to scaffold them from simple to increasingly more intellectually challenging sources, change their understanding of their object of study, and shape it into a more complex synthesis. This new understanding neither mimics exactly what experts say nor is limited to unsupported opinion. In place of the one-off episodes that characterize most students' library research, BiblioBouts had the potential to expose students to serious library research, giving them repeated opportunities to interact with sources and be affected by them. Instructors were attentive to this and made these remarks:

- "[Students] have taken much more seriously the idea of really exploring and thinking about what their sources are saying about the topic, and many more of them seem to be rethinking their own ideas about the topics based on their research. And so they seem much more involved in the research process . . . [doing less] skimming and scanning [for] 'Where is the quote that I can pull?'"

- "[Students] developed better critical skills regarding other perspectives, other peoples' ideas about a subject. It forced them to really think about this other perspective, and then they had to kind of problem-solve in terms of, like, 'Okay, so how do I understand this issue now in relation to what these other folks have said?' And so they're really developing a dialogical relationship not just with their topic but with what other people are saying about it. . . . I saw some growth there."

The results of analysis have two distinct practical implications. The first pertains to the information-seeking process. Kuhlthau (2004) characterized this process in her holistic, seven-stage Information Search Process (ISP) model. ISP describes "three realms of experience: affective (feelings), cognitive (thoughts) and physical (actions) common to each stage. Central to the ISP is the notion that uncertainty, both affective and cognitive, increases and decreases in the process of information seeking" (Kuhlthau 2013). ISP includes the zone of intervention, defined as "area in which an information user can do with advice and assistance what he or she cannot do alone or can do only with great difficulty" (Kuhlthau 2004, 129). When seeking information, users' uncertainty and confusion are highest, and their confidence is lowest, when they start searching in the exploration stage; however, this stage is also a zone of intervention in which students are particularly open to advice and assistance. BiblioBouts intervened in the exploration stage of students' ISP, exactly when they were open to assistance, giving them opportunities to find, scan, read, and accept online sources and consider their fellow players' ratings and comments. These sources might not have been directly influential or become core sources when students wrote their papers, but they helped students formulate a focus and narrow down a topic. Once students had a clear sense of the topic and assignment requirements, they went back and found more sources. That students did not cite many BiblioBouts sources in their final papers does not mean that these sources were not useful for their papers. BiblioBouts sources served well during the exploration stage rather than in the information-collection or search-closure stages of the ISP. This result supports Kuhlthau's theory regarding the exploration stage being a more effective zone of intervention than any other ISP stage.

The second practical implication is related to classic and interactive information retrieval (IR) models. One of the limitations of BiblioBouts was the game's timetable, which allowed just enough time for players to find and evaluate relevant sources. Players had little time to linger, retrieve sources, read them for learning and greater understanding, and build on their knowledge in subsequent searches. Interactive IR models involve multiple information-seeking episodes (MISEs) that feature iterative and evolving searches (Bates 1989; Kuhlthau 2004; Lin and Belkin 2000; Xie 2007). Most likely Adaptation players experienced MISEs because, instead of citing BiblioBouts sources, they went back to the drawing board, searching the Web and library databases for different sources for their final papers. Of the eight MISEs that Lin and Belkin propose, BiblioBouts players from both classes were mostly likely to experience these: (1) the original problem transmuted, becoming enriched, polished, and expanded with new concepts; (2) the original problem spawned new subproblems that the player pursued; or (3) the original problem changed into an entirely new one (2000, 140). In the long run, most players' experience with the library research process was faithful to interactive IR models that are not limited to a single search for information. Game-related curriculum material should promote a debriefing session with instructors or librarians that encourages students to recall their searches for information and bring to mind the reasons why they selected some sources over others at various stages in the library research process. Students could then realize that this process is less about finding relevant sources on a topic within a single information-seeking episode and more about exploring information, formulating and narrowing topics, increasing understanding, and building knowledge.

SUMMARY

This chapter demonstrates that game play did not make players more inclined to cite scholarly sources in their final papers or restrict them to the sources they and their classmates submitted to the BiblioBouts game. Instead, when players wrote their papers, they went back to the drawing board, searched for new sources on their papers' topics, and cited many more new sources than their original BiblioBouts sources. Players did not disregard BiblioBouts sources; in fact, such sources helped them formulate a focus and narrow down a topic. This result supports Kuhlthau's theory regarding the exploration stage being the most effective zone of intervention of all the stages of the information-seeking process.

That players supplemented their BiblioBouts sources with additional ones after the game ended is also in keeping with modern information retrieval models that feature MISEs in which people search repeatedly for information. Students may benefit from instructor and librarian debriefings regarding MISEs so that they expect information seeking to involve MISEs and realize that they are benefiting from repeated exposure to sources in terms of knowledge acquisition and intellectual growth.

Chapter Eleven

How Students Benefited from Playing BiblioBouts

This chapter tells how players benefited as a result of playing BiblioBouts. Data for the analysis came from pre- and post-game questionnaires, focus groups, and follow-up online chat interviews with students and personal interviews with instructors. Students represented participating institutions only. Instructors were a half-and-half mix from participating and nonparticipating institutions. A discussion of benefits from playing the game concludes the chapter.

IMPROVED PERCEPTIONS OF THEIR INFORMATION LITERACY SKILLS

In selected classes at participating institutions, students were encouraged to complete pre- and post-game questionnaires. Three questions queried students about their self-perceptions of their information literacy skills. Pairing their pre- and post-game answers to these questions enabled the BiblioBouts team to determine whether game play had a significant effect on their self-perceptions. Despite reminders from instructors and library liaisons, too few students in each class completed both questionnaires, and so we could not pair responses for statistical tests. Instead, we pooled student responses from four classes—two information studies classes, one education class, and one English and writing class—and report totals for the self-perception questions. The four classes yielded 133 and 86 pre- and post-game questionnaires, respectively.

Self-perception questions asked students to rate how challenging they found library research tasks, how well they could perform them, and how

Table 11.1. Library Research Tasks

Task	Abbreviated Title
Adjusting my topic based on the information I find	Adjusting my topic
Choosing the best citations, full-text articles, websites, and so on, to cite in my paper	Choosing the best citations
Downloading full-text articles online for the citations I find	Downloading full-texts
Finding full-text articles online for the citations I find	Finding full-texts
Judging sources with regard to their relevance to my selected topic	Judging sources' relevance
Judging sources with regard to their scholarly nature	Judging sources' scholarly nature
Judging sources with regard to their trustworthiness for my selected topic	Judging sources' trustworthiness
Keeping track of the citations, full-text articles, websites, and so on, that I find online	Keeping track of citations
Selecting a topic to research	Selecting a topic
Using a structured/BiblioBouts structured library research process to conduct library research for my course work.	Using BB's research process
Using the databases that experts use to conduct library research	Using databases
Knowing where to find good information after I exhaust Google, Wikipedia, and the Web	Knowing where to find information

confident they were about their skills. Table 11.1 lists these twelve tasks along with abbreviated titles used in this chapter's figures.

Rating options used five-point Likert scales (i.e., 2 = very [challenging, well, confident], 1 = somewhat [challenging, well, confident], 0 = neutral, −1 [somewhat unchallenging, poorly, unconfident], −2 [very unchallenging, poorly, unconfident]). Overall, students' ratings ranged between 1 and −1. Few students chose the "very" ratings at either end of the scale.

Students' responses to the pre- and post-game questions "Rate how confident you think you would be performing these library research tasks today" and "Taking into consideration your experience playing BiblioBouts, rate how confident you think you will be the next time you have to perform these library research tasks" ranged from halfway between neutral and somewhat confident (0.50) to somewhat confident (1.05), respectively. Thus, students felt that they would be more confident performing individual tasks—all twelve of them—after playing BiblioBouts.

Figure 11.1 summarizes responses in terms of the differences between the average of students' pre- and post-game responses. For example, there was a positive half-point (0.50) difference between students' responses to the pre- and post-game questions about their confidence keeping track of citations, full-texts, and so on. Thus figure 11.1's horizontal bar for this question extends in a positive direction up to 0.50.

Playing BiblioBouts gave the greatest boost to their confidence about knowing where to find information and databases. In fact, when completing pregame questionnaires, students rated their confidence about knowing where to find information second lowest (0.32), so playing BiblioBouts was a boon to their confidence. Rated the lowest (0.20) on pre-game questionnaires was using a structured research process, which would be expected because students had not yet experienced a structured research process by playing the game. Playing BiblioBouts increased students' confidence in this regard by more than a half point. Five other tasks registered half-point or more increases in students'

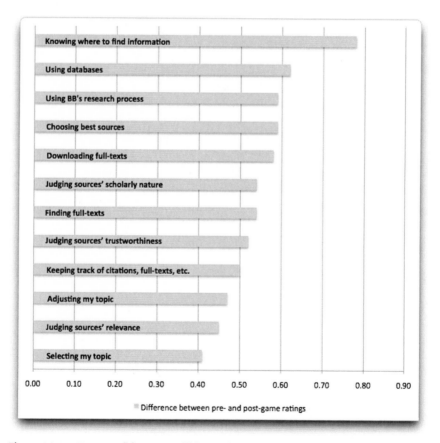

Figure 11.1. How confident you will be performing these tasks.

confidence: choosing best citations, downloading full-texts, judging sources' scholarly nature, finding full-texts, and judging sources' trustworthiness. Game play gave students repeated practice with each; for example, players chose sources to put into play and for their best bibliographies (i.e., Closer and Best Bibliography bouts). However, despite players' practice time on two topic tasks (i.e., choosing my topic and adjusting my topic) and one rating task (judging sources' relevance), the increase in their confidence was a little less than a half point. Students apparently needed more instruction and practice to raise their confidence in performing these tasks.

Students' responses to the pre- and post-game questions "Rate how well you think you would perform these library research tasks today" and "Taking into consideration your experience playing BiblioBouts, the next time you perform these research tasks, rate how well you think you will perform them" also ranged from halfway between neutral and somewhat confident (0.52) to somewhat confident (1.05), respectively. Thus, students felt that they would perform individual tasks—all twelve of them—somewhat well after playing BiblioBouts.

Figure 11.2 summarizes responses in terms of the differences between the average of students' pre- and post-game responses. For example, there was a positive four-tenths of a point (0.40) difference between students' responses to the pre- and post-game questions about their confidence judging sources' relevance. Thus figure 11.2's horizontal bar for this question extends in a positive direction up to 0.40.

Again, the two finding tasks (i.e., knowing where to find information and using databases) were high on the list. Half-point or more boosts were registered for six library research tasks. For a second time, selecting a topic, judging sources' relevance, and keeping track of citations, full-texts, and so on, were at the bottom of the tasks list (cf. figures 11.1 and 11.2). Choosing best sources might be a difficult task for players to perform because they reported a large increase in their confidence (0.59), but their assessment of their ability to perform the task well was somewhat lackluster (0.45).

Students' responses to the pre- and post-game questions "Rate how challenging you think it would be to perform these library research tasks today" and "Taking into consideration your experience playing BiblioBouts, rate how challenging you think it will be the next time you have to perform these library research tasks" ranged from the positive side of neutral (0.13) to between neutral and somewhat unchallenging (−0.34), respectively. Thus, students felt individual tasks—all twelve of them—would be less challenging after playing BiblioBouts.

Figure 11.3 summarizes responses in terms of the difference between the average of students' pre- and post-game responses. For example, there was a negative half-point (−0.50) difference between students' responses to the pre- and post-game questions about the challenge of judging sources' trust-

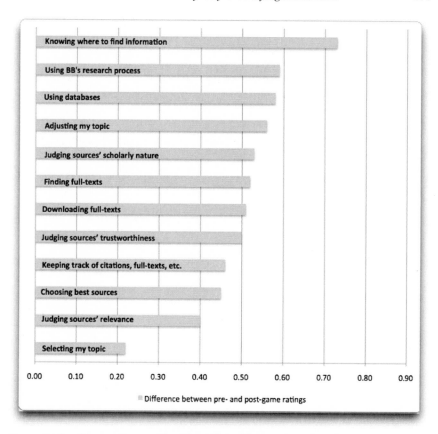

Figure 11.2.   How well you will perform these library research tasks.

worthiness. Thus, figure 11.3's horizontal bar for this question extends in a negative direction down to –0.50.

Especially less challenging would be the two finding tasks (i.e., using databases and knowing where to find information), two credibility assessment tasks (i.e., judging sources' trustworthiness and scholarly nature), and one searching task (i.e., finding full-texts). Students' low ratings for four tasks—selecting my topic, adjusting my topic, choosing best sources, and judging sources' relevance—was in keeping with previous low ratings for one or more of these tasks (cf. figures 11.1 and 11.2).

GREATER FAMILIARITY WITH LIBRARY DATABASES

The analysis of questionnaire responses gave a first glimpse of the game's benefits with respect to familiarizing players with the library databases for

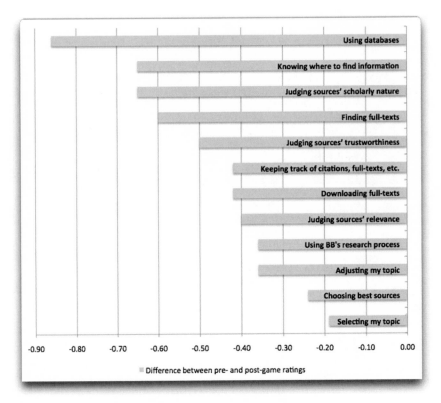

Figure 11.3.   How challenging these library research tasks will be.

quality sources. Focus group interview participants cited library databases repeatedly, telling us how they produced quality sources for their research papers. In the following comments, players tell how playing BiblioBouts introduced them to library databases for the first time:

- "The best part about BiblioBouts is I learned about different databases and different ways of searching for articles for papers. Because, like, in high school, I never really wrote research papers or anything, so I didn't have to cite [sources because] my papers were opinion papers or persuasive papers. So, like, I learned a lot doing BiblioBouts."
- "For me, it was the first time I have ever used the library system, and so it was a really interesting experience for me just because I have searched Google, Google Scholar, and other things like that, but I have never used [library] databases before. And so I think it really helped me, and I have

been using it for other classes too. So just as a learning experience for me, it was really helpful."

- "I had no idea before my class taught me about it. It was like, wow! Everyone said that the [university library] had so many resources but you are never shown what they are."

Even more important was players' realization that library databases yielded sources that were qualitatively better than Google, Wikipedia, and the Web. Here is what they had to say about this:

- "At the beginning, I feel like all that I would do is [go] straight into Google. Now I know about library databases and that kind of thing, and now I definitely go straight to [the databases]."
- "I mean I just think that, like, usually I use Google just, you know, and, like, comparing the results I would get from Google to these databases is a huge difference and, like, I really realize that now, that the material that I was getting was not that reliable and not that scholarly and to be writing research papers and stuff, I need to be using, like, databases and stuff like that."
- "I was really able to see a difference between the academic quality of sources from a database and from Google. Nowadays, we don't really go to the library and get a hard copy of a book. So the electronic equivalent of that kind of quality could be found in a database rather than on Google."

Players were unanimous in their praise for library databases. Should they need quality sources in the future, they will know that they reside in library databases.

EXPOSURE TO MORE AND VARIED SOURCES

Students praised BiblioBouts for its emphasis on sources. Players benefited from experiencing these different aspects of sources: (1) getting exposure to many more sources than they would have found on their own, (2) accumulating sources and winnowing them down to the most relevant ones, (3) reading more sources than they would have read on their own, (4) finding relevant sources among other players' contributed sources, (5) using sources for the paper's content, (6) thinking about sources for more than just quotes, (7) using sources to narrow or adjust the topic, (8) increasing their attention to cited sources in the paper's bibliography, and (9) having full-texts available in BiblioBouts. Table 11.2 lists these benefits alongside one or two sample comments from focus group interviews.

Table 11.2. The Game's Benefits Pertaining to More Sources

Better Sources Aspect	Focus Group Interview Comment
Getting exposure to more sources	"It was just nice to have a stockpile of sources you can look through. I know of the five that I initially chose, I think maybe I selected one or two in my bibliography. But it was just nice having a bunch of other ones that you're like, 'Oh, I didn't see this. This is interesting and this actually suits my topic really well.' And so I think, like, just having additional perspectives of sources . . . [is] always nice."
Accumulating and winnowing sources	"I used to find however many citations needed or however many the professor had required for the particular assignment. After the game, I now get a huge amount of research done, then . . . narrow it down, much in the same way that we did in the game. We started off by looking and researching and seeing as much as we can find and then we donated our top however many. That's the one thing that's stuck with me after the game finished."
Reading more sources	"It was really beneficial to just read a lot of the articles . . . It was just like having, like, basically an overload of sources and just reading through like seventeen or eighteen. That's way more than I probably would have read through if I hadn't [played BiblioBouts]. Especially on the diverse topics as you got to choose randomly what you read about."
	"One thing that I did find is that since I had so many relevant articles to the election, that I did a lot more reading about different topics than what I would have done on my own."
Finding relevant sources among other players' contributed sources	"I actually ended up finding a couple of articles that I ended up using for the last paper that was due in here that I hadn't found before, and I thought that I had searched exhaustively for this topic. But it ended up that I found this article that someone had put in BiblioBouts, and it was really good and useful for me. And so that was just another way to get that information that I hadn't found before."
	"There are some different sources that you might not necessarily come across yourself."
Using sources for the paper's content	"I think that just the fact that I got to see all other articles, it helped me kind of think of new things that I never thought of. I read an article, it was, like, Voters from 18–25 or something, and it was like, 'Oh, I never thought that, like, just that factor could [be] really interesting.'"

Better Sources Aspect	Focus Group Interview Comment
Thinking about sources for more than just quotes	"I think it was helpful to me because sometimes I just know I need, like, a quote for this or that, and I look for something to support what I am saying. But with this, I was able to actually, like, see the process I should go through and be able to get more information to back up my research and make sure it was credible information instead of just, like, grabbing something that looked [like] it went along with what I was trying to say. . . . It made my papers stronger in that aspect."
Using sources to narrow or adjust the topic	"I read articles that [gave me] ideas I didn't even think of and changed the direction of my paper. . . . I was like, 'I never even thought of that.' And it kind of made me want to change my paper a lot because I was kind of focused on, like, one thing, and it kind of brought it into a more interesting and different direction."
	"You learn to be rather adaptable at your topics because if you find something that's not adequate to your topic, then you see what you do have out there and adjust to what you find out there. And you can change your topic . . . so you can get more sources."
Increasing attention to cited sources	"Being forced to read through the sources much earlier, it kind of like puts it in the back of your head, even if you're not actually doing the assignment right away. So it kind of makes you think about it and kind of gets absorbed a little bit."
	"I feel like the bibliography in a paper is something that is the most rushed and least cared about thing. When someone writes a paper, it will be due in a few days and they're like, 'Oh, well, I'll just do the bibliography the day before and I'll just put it together and I don't care about the format.' And I thought that having this game even before the paper was due kind of, like, helped you pay more attention to it and kind of would make you have a better bibliography because you would pay more attention to it and kind of give it the attention that it deserves before you even start the paper."
Having full-texts available	"One thing that I liked about it is once you were on there and you had to look at other people's sources and stuff, you could actually get the full-text for it. It was just like going to an online database."

PRACTICE EVALUATING SOURCES

Students benefited from evaluating sources during the Tagging & Rating (T&R) bout. Reaching this bout's quota of twenty or so evaluations gave students repeated exposure to the questions they needed to answer to rate a source's credibility and relevance and practice defending their ratings with explanatory comments. Both ratings and evaluations were available to them when making decisions about the sources to cite in their best bibliographies and final-paper bibliographies. That the vast majority (about 90 percent) of their comments cited evidence for their credibility and relevance assessments demonstrated the game's ability to elicit source evaluations (tables 9.6 and 9.8). Players acknowledged the usefulness of both ratings and comments, and when the latter were inadequate, they wanted a "thumbs-up/thumbs-down" feature that enabled them to rate their opponents' comments. If BiblioBouts were enhanced with such a capability, it might also make sense to program the game to take back bonus points from players whose comments received more "thumbs-down" than "thumbs-up" evaluations.

Focus group interviews revealed the different aspects of source evaluation that players said they benefited from: (1) evaluating sources generally, (2) knowing what questions to ask and answer to evaluate sources, (3) practicing source evaluation generally, (4) practicing source evaluation (credibility), (5) practicing source evaluation (relevance), (6) having available everyone's evaluations to check one's own evaluation, and (7) learning a structured library research process. Table 11.3 lists these benefits alongside one or two sample comments from focus group interviews.

Table 11.3. The Game's Benefits Pertaining to Evaluations of Sources

Evaluating Sources Aspect	*Focus Group Interview Comment*
Evaluating sources generally	"I think the process of source evaluation was kind of cool. It's not something necessarily everyone always does all the time, but if you're forced to do it, it's not bad for you [some laugh]. I mean it's good. I think it's a good thing."
	"So I think actually analyzing each source and examining the criteria that you would specify like credibility, where it's from, how scholarly is it, and how relevant is it and stuff like that. I felt like that was a lot more important than just finding the source."
Knowing what questions to ask and answer	"I think those questions that [the T&R bout] asked you were questions that I really felt that I never ask myself about sources. . . . So I think what really helped was those questions. I would apply them . . . even if I just printed out the questions . . . to apply to evaluating a source."

Evaluating Sources Aspect	Focus Group Interview Comment
Practicing source evaluation generally	"[BiblioBouts] definitely helped me reevaluate what sources I want to use and at a university level rather than just what I've been doing thus far. So it did change my mentality on what a good source is and what isn't and a lot of it was the repetition of constant tagging and looking at different sources and being able to evaluate them in those terms."
Practicing source evaluation (credibility)	"What I liked about it is, like, I obviously picked sources that I thought had value, but until I was actually shown or asked how credible is this, how trustworthy is this, I didn't realize what it is that gives something value and what it is I should be looking for."
	"For me it made me realize that you can't just pick any kind of article written by anybody because you've got to be able to make sure that it's a credible source because you just don't want to pick an article that somebody [wrote] and they don't know anything about what they're talking about."
Practicing source evaluation (relevance)	"I learned how to analyze which ones are relevant, just because there are so many in the game."
Having available everyone's evaluations to check	"It was really interesting to see the articles that other people chose. . . . I still used some of my sources, but it was kind of, you know, reassuring just to see, 'Oh, people are using some of the same journals that I am using,' or 'Oh, I never thought to look at this journal.' Like, it . . . reassured me, the fact that I was doing okay on it and everything. So I thought that was helpful. That was really helpful."
	"[BiblioBouts] showed me what [sources] people think . . . are credible. Because it's not just what sources are credible, it's what people think is a trustworthy source and what [is]n't because there are actually a decent amount of *New York Times* [articles] that were up there [rated] in the eighties and nineties . . . which is not like a scholarly journal, but it's a highly respected, like, newspaper. And the journals, like, from the [library] website were [rated] really high up there too, and, like, the ACL, like, database and stuff like that. So it was interesting just to see how those lined up with the credibility ratings and stuff like that."
Learning a structured library research process	"[BiblioBouts] gave me a more unified method of getting sources, so previously maybe I would have just gone ad hoc and tried to get sources, looked at the best ones from one database, then gone back. This sort of helped me learn that maybe I should just go holistically and get as many sources as I can, weed through those sources, and really narrow it down, and then take notes after that. So it gave me a better approach, I think, to finding sources."

All players participating in follow-up online chat interviews several months after the game ended had no trouble describing the game's structured research process without prompts from the interviewer. Asked whether they would use this process in the future, they responded positively, but most qualified their responses, saying that they would not be as diligent about evaluating sources. Here is what they said in this regard:

- "Rather than literally rating every source I come across, I would just mentally judge whether or not it would be a credible one to use."
- "I wouldn't say all the exact same steps, but for future research I would apply most of what I learned. For example, I don't know if I could be able to do the peer review all of the time."
- "I probably won't be as systematic with actually rating the articles, but I would use pretty much the same criteria."

LEARNING HOW TO USE THE ZOTERO CITATION MANAGEMENT TOOL

Despite players' difficulties using Zotero (see pages 99–102), many became enthusiastic Zotero users as a result of playing BiblioBouts. Their comments about Zotero's benefits underlined its capabilities for saving sources, organizing them, making them accessible through a single interface, and creating bibliographies. These comments revealed students' facility with Zotero:

- "I'll definitely try to use Zotero more. . . . You just click a little button, and all of the information is already saved, and you don't have to worry about writing it down or keeping some window open while you're writing your paper or anything like that. So that was definitely helpful."
- "It's nice that I can use Zotero and that's where all of my sources are instead of, like, you're weeding through all the Web pages [some laughing]. [Using Zotero] . . . you can make your own folder, and it's just easy, and when you save it, it just makes it a lot simpler. And it also, like, splits up the information so you can see, like, who's the author, where is it from, the year, and then it also helps you create a bibliography."

Of the praise students heaped on Zotero, most convincing were students who described how they had used Zotero since playing BiblioBouts or vowed to do so:

- "I thought Zotero was really useful. Like, I even told some of my room-mates about it."
- "I have used Zotero regularly when doing research."
- "I do a lot of research. . . . Zotero would definitely help me just organize articles and topics and, like, scientific journals and just kind of [a] better organization so I can look at 'em more efficiently."
- "Zotero . . . I've been using that for my papers now. That's, like, totally awesome. It helps keep everything organized."

CONDUCTING LIBRARY RESEARCH COLLABORATIVELY

Collaborating on the building of a database of sources on the assigned broad-based topic benefited players. Not only did they find relevant sources that they had not found on their own, but having to rate and tag so many sources introduced them to new ideas. This influence was minimal for some, limited to keeping the research assignment task salient in their minds, and major for others, impacting their paper's topic, argument, and overall content. Players acknowledged the impact of BiblioBouts's collaborative influence on their papers:

- "Just the sheer fact that so many people uploaded different sources, it just promotes collaborative learning basically, so we have more information."
- "Where everyone can input their sources on the same topic and everyone can look at each other's sources, it makes it a lot easier in finding quality sources."
- "I was able to go on and then put that on BiblioBouts, save that as a source online and later on basically just mind-share with other individuals to see where they got their information from. . . . It was the sharing [that helped me]."

Students suggested that the library research for papers need not be a solitary process. Instead, it could become a collaborative process, just like Bib-lioBouts, where everyone chips in, sharing sources and evaluating their usefulness. From the several students who imagined how this could happen, these comments were especially illustrative:

- "I think that this is definitely something that could be applicable in other classes but in small groups—you get five people from your study group or ten and all of you [are] just sharing the sources. I mean . . . you wouldn't have a rating system and everything, but you can just talk about it. Because

I really think that sharing sources is something that saves you a lot of time, and it gives you better sources."
- "I think [the game] could be targeted towards any subject and let [you do] anything you want. Maybe football. And if you want to make a game about that, have people find articles about it or anything useful so individuals who have an interest in that field who want to learn more about it, even more academic, let's say like finance, if you don't know much about the markets and you [have] a group of people playing a game to find sources about markets where you can just read articles to learn about it without having to take a class, that could be something that could be done. To get people with similar interests to collaborate together to find material that they can all benefit from."

PLAYING A GAME WHILE CONDUCTING LIBRARY RESEARCH

Other benefits that players mentioned were less procrastination, learning about library research while playing a game, and BiblioBouts's game format for learning about library research. With regard to procrastination, players recognized that BiblioBouts gave them a huge head start on their assignment so that they did not have to cram at the last moment. At the very least, game play enabled them to give some thought to their research paper's title, content, and cited sources, and they could search the Post-Game Library for more sources. Here is what players had to say about procrastination:

- "[Because of BiblioBouts,] kids don't end up pulling consecutive all-nighters. You have to do the first step before you can get to the second, because if you want to do the second and you didn't do the first, sorry, you're out of luck. You can't do it. I thought that was good incentive too to kind of motivate you to get going."
- "Another thing that BiblioBouts did well was making you take some time to do this. It gave you an incentive to start early and to pace yourself out and take your time instead of what a lot of people do is do everything at the last minute [some laughing]."
- "I am, like, a sucker for procrastinating and writing my paper and finding all of my sources one or two days before it's due and everything like that. So this BiblioBouts, it forced me to start thinking about the paper and start finding sources weeks ahead of the due date."

Learning about library research intrigued a few students. Perhaps they sensed that library research would contribute to their academic success; however, with no institutional incentives in place to encourage students to improve their library research skills, students would not make the effort to do so on their own. Here is what they said about BiblioBouts as an opportunity to hone their library research skills:

- "I would have never, like, been as likely to just on my own see if I can better my research, and this game really kind of attracted me, and it made it somewhat fun and definitely not as annoying as I thought it would be [many laughing]. And it's good because in the process I learned something, and I think for students like us, if you can find a way to address something that's continuously a problem, and research is continuously a problem with students, this game did it in a great way."
- "Basically [I learned] how to do [library research] better and faster and more efficiently just from the process of having to do it a lot for the game. I think it gave me a lot of practice that I otherwise hadn't had in using the library as a resource."
- "At first, like, when the whole idea of BiblioBouts was brought up in class, I thought it was going to be a little bit gimmicky. I didn't really think there was a point to it. I figured, 'Hey, I'm in college. I think I already know, like, how to research things and put together a bibliography.' But during the process of playing the game and after, you then begin to realize that there is a lot to the process of writing a paper that many of us even at this age still didn't know. [Playing BiblioBouts] reinforced some thoughts and helped create new ways to look at things. So it was definitely a plus."

Players acknowledged that playing a game to learn about library research added fun, friendly competition, and a sense of urgency to a task that they would otherwise consider boring and tedious:

- "I think the competition adds a motivating factor. If you see other people are scoring higher, then you kind of want to score higher just 'cuz—I don't know—maybe that's just my nature playing high school sports. But I think having the deadlines and having that competition really kind of just provides a motivation to kind of get things done and to do 'em well."
- "I feel like if there wasn't a game . . . it wouldn't be so fun or interesting. And so I probably wouldn't have gone out with any enthusiasm, where, at least with BiblioBouts, we had incentives, including the points. So if you're a competitive person, you have an incentive to beat a friend or to be in the top five or whatever your desire was. So it was something we had to do regardless because it was a research paper that we were assigned. So I think BiblioBouts made it at least more interesting than if we had just gone about it by ourselves."

As a result of playing BiblioBouts, students gained valuable hands-on experience conducting library research and made progress on their research papers.

- "I thought [playing BiblioBouts] was helpful because you actually have to do it, do the research, while you're kind of playing the game instead of just having someone come in and stand up in front of the class and tell you, 'Now you click on this, and now you click on that,' because it's hard to follow what someone else is doing on the computer if you're not doing it yourself."
- "If it wasn't for this game, [we] wouldn't know where to find research in the beginning, [we] did find research through playing this game, [and we] . . . have [a] bibliography to finish the paper. This is a great source for people that just need to get by for class or for people that are serious and need to do research and have a better bibliography or better-organized resources. So I think it's definitely a great source to help out anybody that needs better research."
- "I think [the game] is good because you're not realizing at the time that you're learning about research. Like, you might not want to think, 'Oh, I want to go learn about library research today.' You're playing the game, and you're learning about it without doing that."

BENEFITS FROM THE INSTRUCTORS' VIEWPOINT

Instructors seconded what students had to say about the benefits of playing BiblioBouts. They underlined the game's ability to give students greater familiarity with library databases, introduce them to and give them practice using Zotero, require students to evaluate sources, encourage them to use quality sources, and transform library research from a solitary into a collaborative endeavor. Telling us how their students were more attentive to the sources they cited, instructors expressed this in one of two ways, scrutinizing sources with respect to their standing among their peers and in the academic community. Here are instructor comments regarding the former:

- "[BiblioBouts] really made [students] . . . think about what makes a good source, in part by making them look at other people's sources. That idea that, 'Here is somebody else who is working with the same kind of questions. What do you think of this?' That comparative element I think was really useful."
- "I think they developed better critical skills regarding other perspectives, other peoples' ideas about a subject. It forced them to really think about

this other perspective, and then they had to kind of problem-solve in terms of, like, 'Okay, so how do I understand this issue now in relation to what these other folks have said?' And so they're really developing a dialogical relationship not just with their topic but with what other people are saying about it. And I thought I saw some growth there, which I hadn't really looked for before or thought about very concretely as I did this term."

Here is an instructor's comment regarding the latter:

> I think that what they learned as a result of playing BiblioBouts was it helped them become more proficient in assessing what is a good source. What is a viable source, not just relevant to me, but actually [one that] would be recognized by a larger academic community.

A few instructors mentioned that students' research brought new sources to their attention on topics that overlapped with their academic expertise and research interests. One instructor suggested that BiblioBouts need not be limited to undergraduates. It would appeal to instructors who could challenge their graduate students to find the best sources on a research topic they were exploring together so that everyone benefited as a result.

STUDENTS WHO DID NOT BENEFIT FROM GAME PLAY

Not everyone was positive about playing BiblioBouts or reaping benefits as a result of playing the game. Chapters 7 and 8 have already discussed technical difficulties that marred the start of the game, described the nature of these technical difficulties, and estimated the number of students affected. Technical difficulties were an important reason why some students failed to receive benefits from game play.

Focus group interviews yielded additional reasons why students who successfully registered and played BiblioBouts failed to receive benefits from game play. Some had difficulties expressing their displeasure in words; they just did not like the BiblioBouts experience and did not mention specifics. Others were more articulate and cited these reasons: (1) they preferred their makeshift source management methods over Zotero, (2) they did not have tolerance for so many nonrelevant sources from others, (3) playing BiblioBouts was too time-consuming, (4) game play felt like course work, (5) game play was not fun, and (6) they already knew how to conduct library research.

Using Zotero was burdensome to some players. They found it complicated and preferred their makeshift source management methods over Zotero (see page 100). They blamed Zotero for their failure to benefit from game play.

Despite exposure to Zotero, these players described how they would continue to use their makeshift source management methods:

- "I typically [use] Delicious and then will tag it for a certain class or with a certain tag so then I can just search for it and they're all right there. I feel like with the extra step of saving it locally and having to figure out how to save it correctly in Zotero, it just seemed more complicated to me. I thought [Zotero] was going to be the new optimal, like, bookmarking site. I was disappointed."
- "I just make a folder, I drag [sources] into the folder. I . . . start with finding as many articles as I can that are relevant. I'll read through them, I'll take out pieces that would match my paper, and if I happen to, while I'm writing my paper, realize, 'This doesn't really fit,' then the article is out of my folder."
- "I just kind of find the articles, save my PDFs, and then if an article ends up not fitting my criteria, I just toss it out. Maybe I should change my ways, but I'm probably not going to, honestly."

Some players accrued no benefits as a result of their exposure to other players' sources. They felt that exposure to so many sources was a burden and preferred limiting their efforts to their own work. Here are sample comments:

- "I didn't find any help at all from people's sources. I found them more a chore to read and rate than actually benefiting my own study."
- "What I am writing about might be different than what anyone else is writing about, so, like, the sources they find might not help me, and so it's just kind of like another, like, thing that you have to [do]."

Other students resented the time that they devoted to game play. Some felt that conducting their own research would have taken a fraction of the time it took to play BiblioBouts:

- "I'm not going to lie. I don't really think I learned that much because I just know that I enjoy writing research papers. I take classes where I have to do that . . . so I have been able to figure out on my own how to find articles. I feel that I can [spend] ten to fifteen minutes [and] find four sufficient articles that will help my paper, and then I'm done. This has, like, been going on for, like, weeks."
- "I wasted too much time on BiblioBouts when I would have been much better off using that time to actually work on *my* paper, not rate other people's sources that have nothing to do with my particular argument."

Some players viewed BiblioBouts as course work or yet another assignment to complete for a class. Their comments were troublesome because they appear dismissive of games generally that are academic in nature.

- "I understand, like, that's what we had to do for the assignment, but I just don't really see it as, like, a game per se because it just wasn't something that I would want to do in my free time [laughs]. It got boring after a while."
- "It's a part of our grade, so that's why I saw it as an assignment. And finding sources [in the game], it was helpful definitely, but it was another assignment."
- "It didn't really feel like a game. . . . Games are supposed to be really fun, and the only really fun thing about that was the challenge. It wasn't really something that I would, like, sit down and do on my own time. My own fun time. It's a class, so I don't think anything [would make it fun]."

Criticism came from players who were not convinced that BiblioBouts was a game or that conducting research could be conceived as a game. Here is what they had to say:

- "I don't think they should call it a game. . . . I think they should call it BiblioBouts, period. Because people said we were coming to play a game, and I was like, 'Oh, a game!' And it wasn't a game."
- "In the classroom, we were really expecting a game, and then we sat down at the computer and got this. 'Game' need[s] to be taken out. Just call it something else because we were under the impression that we were going to do something fun. . . . Then when we got this, it was the total opposite. . . . Yeah, I was kind of looking for some Pac-Man or Mario or something."
- "I think the word 'game' threw off a lot of people. Everyone's like, 'Okay, a game.' You know, it's something enjoyable . . . [but] it was more research."

A minority of students dismissed BiblioBouts because they felt they already knew how to conduct library research. They had received information literacy training in high school or freshman orientation or picked it up on their own.

DISCUSSION

After playing BiblioBouts, most students felt that they would do well performing the same library research tasks that they had encountered during game play, that their confidence performing these tasks had increased, and that these tasks would present less of a challenge the next time they had to perform them. Always at the top of the results were using databases and knowing where to find information tasks, providing strong evidence of the gains players experienced in this regard as a result of playing BiblioBouts.

At the bottom of the results were selecting a topic and adjusting my topic tasks. Game play gave BiblioBouts players several opportunities to deliberate on their paper's topic—when they searched for sources, when they selected sources to submit to the game, when they selected a topic for their best bibliographies, and when they wrote their final papers. Although table 10.2 presents evidence of players' evolving topics, their questionnaire responses demonstrate their need for additional practice and experience in this regard.

Also at the bottom of the results were judging sources' relevance and choosing best sources tasks. These two tasks have a certain amount of overlap—that is, a writer's best sources are usually ones that are relevant and that he or she cites. The T&R bout gave students plenty of practice with the former task. In fact, the former was especially salient to players who complained in focus groups that they had to evaluate too many sources to reach quota. Both Closer and Best Bibliography bouts gave students practice with the latter task. We suggest that the codependencies among all four lowest-rated tasks were much more about writing the research paper than about conducting the library research for the paper.

For some players, playing BiblioBouts introduced them for the first time to the library's database portal, library databases, and Zotero. For all, game play gave them hands-on practice using these tools. Players voiced concerns about Zotero's complexity, but using Zotero helped them understand how it could help them manage their online sources, and a fair number of players planned to use Zotero in the future. Not only were players enthusiastic about library databases, but they realized sources from library databases were qualitatively better than sources they found on the open Web. Such a realization may be enough to win students over, making them less dependent on the open Web for information for both academic pursuits and personal interests. The latter is especially important because, all too soon, today's students will enter the workforce, start families, and find themselves making important decisions about health care, financial planning, employment, voting, elder care, their children's education, and much more. They need to become knowledgeable consumers of information because of the importance of their decisions for themselves and their families, now and in the future.

The analysis of players' source evaluations demonstrated the game's ability to elicit substantive source evaluations from players (chapter 9). Whether players make a habit of evaluating the sources they use for their course work is in their hands. Comments like the following make us skeptical about this:

> BiblioBouts forced me to be more meticulous because it seemed to draw out the steps of researching, which wasn't my favorite. When researching and not using BiblioBouts, sometimes I am in a hurry. . . . BiblioBouts helped me while I was playing it, but if I am not forced to play, then I tend to revert back to my own research habits.

Game play increased players' awareness of the importance of source evaluation, ushered them through a step-by-step process of evaluating sources, and put them into situations where good and bad source evaluations were available to them so that they could determine for themselves whether evaluating sources was worth practicing on one's own, minus prompting from BiblioBouts.

Players cited many aspects of the game's emphasis on sources that benefited them (tables 11.2 and 11.3). Because players said that skimming sources helped them assess their relevance, we could have added "technical reading" to the list; however, players' descriptions of skimming sources did not indicate that they were practicing technical reading. One instructor in particular advocates technical reading as a strategy that would benefit her international students, whose seriousness about their studies compels them to read sources from beginning to end. Here is what she said in this regard:

> My students who are new to campus and international . . . read everything. My other students who have had more experience don't read everything that they are assigned, or they skim. In casual interactions, I'll say, you know, "What did you do this weekend?" And some students will say, "Oh, I was up until 4 am every night reading my assignments." And other students will be like, "What?!? That's ridiculous! You just skim it!" or like, "Read the first page. Read the first and last paragraph." And the new students are like, "How could you do that? How can you just skim? Don't you take your studies seriously?"

Additionally, instructors and librarians should reassure their students that technical reading is not cheating or cutting corners but a well-regarded, time-saving approach that experts use to winnow high-posted search results to the most relevant sources.

BiblioBouts players were positive about the game's ability to transform library research from a solitary activity into a collaborative venture. Most of the technology for enabling collaborative research is already in place through online citation management systems. Needed enhancements to these systems would be rating and tagging capabilities not unlike

BiblioBouts's. Thus, only a few tweaks here and there would be necessary to turn this vision into a reality.

SUMMARY

Students received these important benefits as a result of playing BiblioBouts:

- Developed more positive perceptions of their information literacy skills
- Played a game that introduced them to library databases, where they found sources that were qualitatively better than open-Web sources
- Found sources—were exposed to more sources than students would find on their own, found relevant sources among the sources fellow players submitted to the game, enlisted available sources to make adjustments to research paper topics, and much more
- Learned exactly what questions to ask and answer to evaluate sources
- Practiced answering evaluation questions with evidence to support one's relevance and credibility ratings
- Had everyone's source evaluations available to check against one's own evaluation
- Was exposed to a structured library research process that students remembered after the game ended
- Practiced using Zotero for source management, which convinced a fair number of students to use it in the future
- Collaborated on the building of a database of tagged and rated sources on an assigned broad-based topic
- Made progress on an assigned research paper while playing a game that taught players how to conduct library research
- Procrastinated less on research paper assignments
- Enjoyed the fun, competition, and urgency of the game format to learn about conducting library research

Instructors seconded what students had to say about the benefits of playing BiblioBouts. If they were to rank the above list, they would put learning about library databases, Zotero, evaluating sources, and library research collaboration at the top. Players who responded negatively to BiblioBouts regarding benefits gave these reasons:

- Technical difficulties, especially at the start of the game, that soured them on BiblioBouts or prevented them from playing altogether
- Zotero's complicated nature

- A preference for their makeshift source management methods over Zotero
- BiblioBouts's time-consuming nature
- BiblioBouts being just another academic assignment
- BiblioBouts not being fun
- Already knowing how to conduct library research

Chapter Twelve

Best Practices for Building Information Literacy Games

This chapter embodies advice on the design of future information literacy in the form of best practices that were the result of our experience designing, developing, deploying, and evaluating both the Defense of Hidgeon and the BiblioBouts information literacy games. We are the first to admit that these games were far from perfect; however, we learned from their limitations and share our experience here, especially suggesting how the best practices would impact BiblioBouts's design. We urge aspiring designers to heed this chapter's best practices so that they design information literacy games that students want to play.

REVISITING THE NEEDS ASSESSMENT

The game design effort dovetails with the results of the needs assessment (chapter 2). If your interpretation of the needs assessment convinces you and others that an online game is the solution to the problem, your next step is game design. However, before you proceed, make sure you have explored all other avenues, including an analog game and solutions that do not involve games. Share needs assessment results with others, and talk things through before initiating game design.

Game design comes before seeking funding, because whoever supports your project financially will want to know how your game works, and you will have to estimate game design and development costs in a proposal. By the way, your original design and your game's beta version will not be the same, because you will incorporate into the game what you learn from your design efforts, pre-tests, and usability assessments with prospective users. You will also encounter difficulties along the way to which you will apply solutions that alter your original design plans. Eventually you will need institutional or external funding for the game enterprise in support of game design, development, deployment, evaluation, enhancement, operation, user support, and long-term maintenance.

GETTING STARTED ON GAME DESIGN

This section's six best practices may be likened to the backdrop of a stage set or the setting of a historical event. They set the stage for the main event, which *is* your information literacy game.

Best Practice 1

Game play must contribute in a useful way to the course work students are already doing. This first best practice is the most important one. We generated it from our earliest game design experience when we learned that students did not want to play information literacy games that failed to contribute in a useful way to the course work they were already doing (Markey et al. 2008b). Students do not necessarily see a cause-and-effect relationship between their course grades and information literacy expertise. Institutions without required information literacy components in the curriculum reinforce students' notions about the less-than-important nature of information literacy skills. Do not expect your information literacy game to stand on its own. To be successful, it must align with academic course work.

When we designed BiblioBouts, we envisioned a game that students played while they wrote a research paper or worked on a project with a research component. Writing a research paper or working on a project with a research component maps directly onto assignments that instructors give to undergraduate students. When you design your game, you need to pair your game's objectives with a typical academic assignment.

Best Practice 2

Game play must yield artifacts that students can apply directly to their course work. Design a game that produces artifacts that *are* students' course work. For example, as a result of playing BiblioBouts, students had at hand two artifacts: a prospectus bearing their research paper's topic, argument, and sources they planned to use to write the paper (figure 5.14) and the Post-Game Library bearing the sources all players contributed to the game (figure 5.15). Students could share their prospectus with instructors or librarians to get their advice on the paper's content, including finding better sources. If the instructor advised the student to find more sources on this or that aspect of a paper's topic, the student could search BiblioBouts's Post-Game Library for more sources. The Post-Game Library contained all sources (i.e., citations and full-texts) that students submitted to the game and game play data (i.e., tags and evaluations) that the game added to sources from players' evaluations. An improvement to the prospectus could have been a list of the most popular databases in which players found the sources they submitted to BiblioBouts so that the player could build on what he or she found in the Post-Game Library. In fact, after BiblioBouts ended, most players conducted follow-up searches to reseed their best bibliographies with additional relevant sources on their paper's topic (see page 164).

Best Practice 3

Game play that gives players mastery over one key concept, task, effort, or procedure is preferable to comprehensive game play. Limiting the game to *one* key concept, task, effort, or process may be hard. For example, BiblioBouts focused on the process of conducting library research, and its bouts divided this process into finding sources, evaluating them, and choosing the best ones, resulting in a rather complex game. Despite our efforts to simplify BiblioBouts, eliminating two bouts (i.e., Policing and Sorter bouts) and delegating a third (i.e., Donor bout) to Zotero, BiblioBouts players experienced the full range of the information-seeking process. Some complained that the game was too long (see page 118), whereas others wanted the game to pay more attention to finding sources (see page 232).

Keeping a game simple and focused may come down to designing it to fit within certain time constraints. For example, an information literacy game played in middle and high school classes might entail a work effort that respects fifty-minute class periods, and a game played in college classes might take into account sixty-minute college classes over ten- to fifteen-week terms. The time it takes students to play the game may be the tipping point for instructors in either deciding to adopt it or dismissing it out of hand. If your game is meant for middle or high schools, we suggest planning on one class period for game setup/preparation, a second period for game play, and a third for instructors to debrief students. In colleges, plan on one class period being devoted to game setup/preparation, on game play being conducted outside class, and on a second class period being devoted to the debriefing. Pre-game preparation that involves librarians visiting classes to demonstrate the library's database portal and selected databases will likely consume most of the one class period devoted to game setup/preparation, so plan wisely right from the start.

Best Practice 4

Your game should have goals/objectives, rules, moves/actions, outcomes/ feedback, competition, interaction, duration, and representation. Prensky (2001a, 119) proposed these six structural elements of games:

1. Goals/objectives
2. Rules
3. Outcomes/feedback
4. Conflict/competition/challenge/opposition (hereafter named competition)
5. Interaction
6. Representation/story (hereafter named representation)

To this list we have added two more items:

7. Moves/actions
8. Duration

The design of your information literacy game breathes life into each of these elements, and they are anything but independent—they are all related to one another. In fact, that is why game design is so difficult: while you are thinking through one element, others intervene.

The information literacy skills and concepts students learn as a result of playing the game grow out of its goals/objectives. The constraints that the game places on moves/actions are the rules. The moves/actions that players take to achieve the game's goals/objectives result in the outcomes. The guidance that the game gives players regarding their moves/actions, so that their future actions will be skillful, helps them reap the game's rewards, and bringing them ever closer to overall game goals/objectives is the feedback. While engaging in moves/actions to achieve the game's goals/objectives, players engage in competition. "Conflict/competition/challenge/opposition is what gets your adrenaline and creative juices flowing, and what makes you excited about playing the game" (Prensky 2001a, 122). The interactions that players experience—playing in real time on a computer and playing with fellow students—intensify the competition. Representation refers to the game's narrative or story. It "means that the game is *about* something . . . abstract or concrete, direct or indirect" (Prensky 2001a, 123). The player's activities in the pursuit of goals/objectives are the moves/actions. Duration is the amount of time it takes to play the game, including all pre- and post-game debriefing.

Six of these elements—goals/objectives, rules, outcomes/feedback, representation, moves/actions, and duration—are very real in the sense that they can be instantiated in the form of game play and game artifacts. That is, the game's instructions declare the game's goals/objectives and enumerate the rules, the game responds to players' moves/actions with feedback, the overarching narrative or story framing the game is its representation, game play takes place through players' moves/actions and results in duration, and all six elements make it possible for players to make progress on their assignments.

The two remaining game elements, competition and interactions, do involve instantiation but take place mostly in the minds of game players. Thus, they may be the hardest for game designers to conceive. For the most part, designers are responsible for putting in place the *conditions* for competition and interactions to take place. Conditions that hook players into the game so that they play above and beyond their instructor's minimal-level expectations are the ones game designers want to put into place. Minimal-level expectations will be different for every game; in terms of BiblioBouts, instructors set these expectations in the form of the game's caps and quotas (see page 52).

Because information literacy games and academic games generally involve grades, interactions might have to involve aliases that enable players to keep their identities a secret. Revealing one's true identity would be a personal decision on the part of each and every player.

These eight structural elements were integrated into the design of BiblioBouts. The game's instructions stated its goals/objectives and enumerated its rules. BiblioBouts responded to students' game play with feedback about how they earned points, how their source evaluations compared with opponents' evaluations, and where they ranked on the leader board vis-à-vis other players. Interaction and competition also focused on the leader board—players wanting to be ranked first or ahead of their friends and fellow classmates. Initially, representation in BiblioBouts referred to the "bouts" portion of the game's name, and on the banner of the alpha version of BiblioBouts, it took the form of a boxer posed in a fighting stance and outfitted with gloves and trunks. In the banner of the beta versions of BiblioBouts, representation took the form of an archery bulls-eye motif to indicate to players the importance of targeting the most relevant and credible sources for their papers (figure 5.2). Players making progress on their assigned papers—finding sources, evaluating them, commenting on their opponents' ratings and comments, formulating their paper's topic, and selecting the most relevant sources to cite in their papers—were the game's moves/actions. Duration involved both the time periods instructors set for the game's three bouts and the amount of time players devoted to playing each of them.

These focus group interview comments demonstrate how players' thoughts about interaction and competition manifested themselves in more game play to earn more points and move up on or remain at the top of the leader board:

- "I would always get really, like, upset in the last, like, few hours of the game because I thought, like, I had a head start, like I had a pretty good lead, and then either [Joe] or I think her name was [Joan], they'd, like, surpass me by just a minimum amount just so I'd have to start playing again, and obviously there's a big jump in points between certain groups. There'd be, like, three or four that are the very top, and then there'd be, like, a huge section in the middle, and so on. So I think for those individual groups, it was a stiff competition. . . . And I mean, for myself, I know that I'd play to the very end."

- "The leader board part—to know, like, who was on and who was behind and, like, how far you were, like, from being, like, the top five or whatever, like, that was—I liked that because it pushed you, and it gave you, like, the motivation to be, like, 'Oh, I'll, like, do more.'"

Best Practice 5

Formalize your game's design in the game design document. Once your team reaches a general level of understanding and agreement on your game's eight structural elements (i.e., game's goals/objectives, rules, moves/actions, outcomes/feedback, competition, interaction, duration, and representation), it is time to formalize the design in the form of a written game design document. This document ensures that the fruits of your labor—the many hours your team spent discussing, brainstorming, and debating the game's design—do not get lost or forgotten or morph into something else over time. Do not feel locked into the specifics of the game design document—it is a living document that will undergo considerable change during the course of the project.

There are no hard-and-fast rules about the format, length, or contents of the game design document. Our advice is to take a break from brainstorming, sit down, and write; in the course of writing, the game design document will take shape. Our game design document was a single-spaced, eight-page document describing each bout's game goal, pedagogical goal, game play, and scoring (Markey et al. 2009, 13–20). The game's design changed considerably between that original document and the beta 2.0 version of BiblioBouts.

We shared our game design document with early prospective instructor-users of BiblioBouts to get their reactions and to convince them to test the game in their classes (see page 39). We also used it as a springboard to generate shorter versions, especially in the form of PowerPoint slides that we and library liaisons used to recruit prospective instructor-users and to brief anyone else interested in the game. Before we had a working prototype of BiblioBouts, the game design document was the primary artifact that we could share with others to convey our vision of the game. For more details about the game design document, check out Scott Rogers's (2010, 57–82) advice.

Best Practice 6

Game play that fosters a community of learners is a win-win for everyone. More than any other best practice, this statement sums up what students should experience as a result of playing your game. They share the burden of the academic enterprise and perform actions that benefit others—they no longer have to go it alone. BiblioBouts demonstrated that everyone in a class could work together to build a database of sources on a topic and learn how to evaluate sources by studying how students rated them during the game. How can your game stack up to this best practice?

DEVELOPING THE SCORING SYSTEM AND HOW TO WIN

Best Practice 7

Implement a straightforward scoring algorithm that places players who achieve the game's objectives at the top of the leader board. Scoring is important to students because they know that their grades depend on it. They constantly monitor their score. They will not tolerate games that update their scores too long after their game play activity. They want instant scoring updates that tell them how many points they have earned and why. They are always on the lookout for loopholes to "game the game," that is, to reap scoring rewards for effortless activity. When they find loopholes or game play activity that awards gratuitous points, they take advantage of them, and their respect for the game plummets.

Your game's scoring algorithm should be straightforward, rewarding players who achieve and exceed the game's objectives. Scoring should not give some players a lead that seems insurmountable, because other students will get discouraged, will not play, or will meet minimum-level expectations for a passing grade or an extra-credit boost.

BiblioBouts's scoring algorithm was complicated. The game awarded in-bout points based on player actions as well as post-bout points based on multiple-player interactions. BiblioBouts did not report the latter until after a bout ended because it needed to calculate average ratings per source to award points, and it added post-bout points onto in-bout points, making it impossible for players to distinguish between the two. Thus, players were unsure which actions resulted in points and how many. We added a scoring log (figure 5.17) so that players could distinguish between in- and post-game points, but it did not grab players' attention. Giving feedback to players about post-game points was a problem that a redesign of BiblioBouts would have to address.

Because of players' obsession with points and scoring, game designers should take advantage of opportunities not only to inform players of their score but to include feedback so that they can check their performance vis-à-vis opponents and make needed adjustments.

Best Practice 8

Game-winning accomplishments must be directly related to the game's overarching objective. Ultimately, game designers must decide what specific game play accomplishments will be game winning. We urge game designers to build scoring algorithms that reward players whose game play actions reflect the desired behaviors with placement at the top of the game's scoreboard. For example, BiblioBouts's winners were players who met and exceeded work-effort expectations and submitted the most popular sources in the game. To make sure BiblioBouts rewarded such players with placement at the top of the leader board, we built Excel-based scoring models, assessed the impact of increasing and decreasing scores for various actions, and altered BiblioBouts's scoring algorithm accordingly. We strongly urge game designers to do the same so that their games produce deserving winners.

Best Practice 9

Players expect "just right" rewards for skillful play that are neither gratuitous nor stingy. The points players earn for their actions should be congruous with the amount of effort they put into the action, the relative difficulty of the action, and its importance to the game's overarching objective. We learned this lesson firsthand. The scoring algorithm for BiblioBouts's alpha version was tiered, awarding few points for player actions in the initial bouts and more points for player actions in later bouts. We thought this approach would reduce player dropouts. We did not expect players to skip early bouts entirely and join the game midstream to reap later-bout point bonanzas! In fact, our approach encouraged dropouts among the students who were the most serious players because they were demoralized by newbie players cashing in on the points giveaways at the end of the game.

Our response was to completely overhaul BiblioBouts's scoring algorithm, awarding points based on the amount of effort players put into the action, the relative difficulty of the action, and its importance to the game's overarching objective of producing credible and relevant sources for student papers. For your game, rank various user actions in terms of effort and difficulty, assign points accordingly, avoid scoring that unfairly gives too many rewards to players who exceed work-effort expectations, and reward players who are especially skillful in achieving the game's overarching objective so that they are among the top finishers in the game.

Best Practice 10

Be prepared for players to "game" the game; make sure all loopholes have been plugged and scoring is foolproof. To avoid loopholes and scoring gaffes that result in students gaming your game, challenge prospective game players to find ways to reap scoring rewards for effortless activity and receive gratuitous points. We did exactly this, inviting a class of students enrolled in a "Serious Games" course in the School of Education to play BiblioBouts. They were quick to find most of the loopholes, and in response, we completely overhauled BiblioBouts's scoring algorithm using Excel-based scoring models. Our efforts were successful, save for certain students who asked their instructors to remove them from an ongoing game and let them start the game anew because they were dissatisfied with their submitted sources. We recommend that future game designers perfect their game's scoring algorithm with Excel-based scoring models, then invite enterprising students to "game" the game and respond accordingly with improvements to the game's scoring algorithm.

IMPLEMENTING THE GAME IN COURSE CONTEXTS

Best Practice 11

Game design must acknowledge students' predilection to wait until the last minute to play.

Best Practice 12

Sustained, nonstop game play is preferable to a fits-and-starts approach. Because best practices #11 and #12 introduce a chicken-or-egg scenario, we present them together here. Best practice #11 is easy to understand. Students wait until the last minute to register and play the game. Why they wait until the last minute may be linked to their viewpoint that academic course work, including playing a game, is just that, academic course work, and they would rather occupy themselves with their favorite pastimes (see page 85).

If your game depends on players' responding to the actions of one or more other players, then students' procrastination will have an adverse affect on the flow of the game. That is, early birds will get their work done, but they will have to wait for procrastinating players to get their work done.

Let's use an example from BiblioBouts to clarify this point. BiblioBouts required each player to submit five sources to the game for opponents to evaluate. The game did not allow players to evaluate their own sources because of the likelihood that they would overrate them to earn more points. Thus, early birds had to wait until their fellow players submitted their sources so that they had sources to evaluate. The longer their fellow players procrastinated, the longer early birds had to wait. Our solution to this problem was to divide BiblioBouts into separate bouts, each with its own work-effort expectations and deadline. The Closer bout focused players on submitting sources, and when its deadline drew near, we expected players to finish their source-submitting activity, resulting in a smooth transition to the Tagging & Rating bout, where there would be enough sources for players to evaluate, and the game could continue uninterrupted. However, designing BiblioBouts as a series of self-contained bouts or mini-games meant that students played BiblioBouts in fits and starts—they never experienced sustained, nonstop game play.

Evaluation results revealed that dividing BiblioBouts into bouts spoiled the flow of the game, especially for enthusiastic players who got hooked on watching their scores increase. Meeting a particular bout's work-effort expectations long before its deadline occurred meant that there was no more game to play, and players had to wait until the next bout began to pick up where they left off. Quick starters told us that their enthusiasm waned, especially when they had to wait for half a week or more. Thus, we do not recommend segmenting games into bouts or mini-games. Instead, games should feature sustained, nonstop game play.

To remain faithful to best practice #12, game designers could individualize game play so that it does not depend on other players. Other than playing the game to meet an academic requirement, individualized game play might mean beating someone else's high score, like the old-fashioned Pac-Man or Space Invaders. Alternatively, we would advise game designers to take advantage of the social situation that is inherent to the classroom setting, letting the game spark interpersonal competition between friends and fellow classmates. Chapter 11 (see pages 179–80) features several comments from both students and instructors that underline the importance of game play that is fun and stirs up students' competitive spirit.

If your game involves a chicken-or-egg scenario, then the burden falls on game designers to build incentives into the game that encourage students to play often and early. Ideally, game play sets up mini-competitions between friends so that they talk informally about beating each other, topping each other on the leader board, collecting more game assets, and so on, and they follow up with game play that beats minimal-level expectations. Players respond to incentives connected with scoring, grading, and public recognition. Consider also enlisting strategies that keep the game salient in students' minds. Here are some ideas:

- Scoring that rewards early birds
- Online reminders (e.g., texts, e-mail messages, Tweets) that inform players of lead changes, trophy holders, impending deadlines for early-bird scoring bonuses, game deadlines, post-bout scoring bonuses, immediate availability of special bonus-point opportunities, and so on.
- Public trophy cases with names of trophy holders prominently displayed
- In-class playing time to get students started
- Games that students play for a short period—for example, between Tuesday/Thursday or Monday/Wednesday classes

Best Practice 13

Design games that require no intervention or input from instructors during game play. Because they have so many details to balance during the course of a busy semester, your game cannot rely on instructors for intervention or input during the game. Except for game administration tasks such as creating games and grading student game play, do not expect instructors to play or pay attention to ongoing games. In fact, instructors might see any game functionality that requires their input as a burden (see pages 43–44). Because some instructors will want to delegate game administration to teaching assistants or librarians, we recommend that game designers add functionality for proxy game administration so that game owners can authorize others to administer games.

Aside from librarians who adopt the game in information literacy classes, most instructors will be experts in their academic disciplines. They will not necessarily be experts at information literacy; nor will they know what information literacy content to teach or how. Most instructors will take a hands-off approach to the game, counting on it to teach students about information literacy and develop students' skills in this regard and expecting to see improvements in students' assignments as a result of game play.

Best Practice 14

Design discipline-neutral games. Ideally, information literacy games should be discipline neutral so that they can be adopted in any class in any academic unit. This will broaden their appeal and not restrict them to one particular discipline. This practice goes hand in hand with the type of academic assignment that the game is built around. If the type of assignment is limited to a specific academic discipline, such as the history of art, mathematics, accounting, or biology, then there is a good chance that the game will not be generalizable beyond that discipline.

When designing BiblioBouts, this best practice was very important to us. We wanted to design an information literacy game that had broad appeal, so we brainstormed on what types of academic assignments were characteristic of college classes generally. We seized upon the research paper assignment because of its generalizability across a wide range of humanities and social science disciplines. The one stipulation we added to the research paper assignment was that instructors had to assign one broad-based topic for all students to research. This did not sit well with instructors who wanted to give their students the freedom to choose topics that interested them and/or did not want to grade dozens of papers on the same topic; however, we had to enforce this stipulation so that players contributed sources that everyone playing the game could evaluate against other comparable sources. In response, some instructors hosted multiple, smaller games on different topics in one class; others chose not to adopt BiblioBouts in their classes.

This best practice is not a hard-and-fast rule, but do keep it in mind. Online games require continual maintenance and update, user support, and enhancement; thus, designing and developing a game with broad appeal increases the likelihood that instructors will adopt the game, make it a staple in their classes, and support it over the long term.

Best Practice 15

Every game play action must place the player closer to or farther from the final outcome. The impetus for this best practice is maintaining players' attention to and interest in the game. Players want evidence that their actions win points or desirable game assets or make a positive contribution toward achieving the game's overarching goal. They quickly catch on to unimportant or routine game play actions for which they receive no points or game assets or that do not contribute to the game later. In response, they lose interest in or respect for the game.

In BiblioBouts's alpha version, the Sorter bout required players to sort donated sources into thematic categories that described their subject contents. Although players received points for every source they sorted and bonus points when their categories for a source matched their opponents' categories for the same source, BiblioBouts never used the agreed-on categories later in the game. It could have, for example, amended source citations with these agreed-on categories—like a list of keywords or tags that described the source's content. Such keywords could have provided useful information for players during the concluding Best Bibliography bout in which players scanned source citations to choose relevant sources for their best bibliographies. Although players welcomed the points they earned for their Sorter bout activity, they did not understand the purpose of the bout because BiblioBouts failed to use its results later in the game. They also found the bout's sorting task itself repetitive and boring. Our response was to eliminate the Sorter bout from BiblioBouts and distribute its keyword/tagging function in the Tagging & Rating (T&R) and Best Bibliography bouts. The T&R bout required players to enter keywords in the form of three big ideas that the source covered. In the Best Bibliography bout that followed, players encountered big ideas several times: (1) they entered three big ideas that characterized their paper's topic (figure 5.12), (2) they could search the bout's Source Library using big ideas to retrieve sources that had been amended with agreed-on big ideas (figure 5.13), and (3) they received bonus points when their paper topic's big ideas matched agreed-on big ideas in the sources they chose for their best bibliographies. This redesign meant that players' tagging efforts were integrated and developed even further later in the game.

Best Practice 16

Players want immediate positive and negative feedback from games to improve their performance. We know this firsthand as a result of evaluating both Hidgeon and BiblioBouts. With respect to Hidgeon, our decision to give feedback to players for correct answers and omit it for incorrect answers was ill-advised—players wanted to know why their answers were incorrect. With respect to BiblioBouts, we released the alpha version before developing the source feedback pages (figures 5.10 and 5.11), so players had no idea how their opponents evaluated the sources they contributed to the game or how their evaluations stacked up next to opponents' evaluations for the same sources. In focus groups, players demanded evaluation feedback, and it was one of the team's three development priorities in the transition from alpha to beta version 1.0 (Markey et al. 2010). Here are several more examples of feedback BiblioBouts could have provided players:

- Thumbs-up/-down ratings on comments: Such comments would also figure into scoring, that is, eliminating bonus points BiblioBouts awarded to players for making comments to which two-thirds or more players gave thumbs-down ratings and adding more bonus points to player scores for comments to which two-thirds or more players gave thumbs-up ratings.

- Source popularity ratings, that is, the number of times players cited donated sources in their best bibliographies: Ratings could include a link to the donor's trophy case so players could learn the donor's alias and scrutinize his or her other accomplishments.
- Post-bout scoring details on source feedback pages: Such details would enable players to learn when their ratings were sufficiently close to fellow players' ratings and thus merited bonus points.
- Trophy citations: Citations would bear trophy names, trophy qualification information, and what player action(s) resulted in the game awarding the trophy to a player so that players know why they received the trophy.

Best Practice 17

Game play must enable players to model what experts do. Designing a game that fulfills this best practice is tough. Consider how we human beings learn how to do things. Someone tells or shows us how to do something or we observe someone doing it. We then try to do it on our own or with the assistance of an expert or someone with more experience. If the "something" is physical, like skateboarding, riding a bike, or roller blading, we can see for ourselves how experts position their body vis-à-vis the instrument we want to master, and we model their physical behavior. The difficulty with learning something physical is that it is hard to judge how to synchronize our body with the instrument's functionality, such as balancing our body, applying or lessening pressure, and resting in place. Knowing that we have failed is easy: we fail to propel our bodies using the instrument or fall and hurt ourselves—or our pride!

Learning something that is not physical involves fewer senses. Mostly we are connecting prior knowledge with new, incoming information and combining the two into something related to, but somewhat different from, each. Because this happens in our heads, we have no physical, outward, or observable cues to help us. At first, we may flounder, but eventually we achieve a passing level of understanding, and with enough practice, reinforcement, and experience, we achieve mastery and can build upon our new level of knowledge in this regard by taking in new, incoming information.

Games are fantastic for learning because game play involves practice, reinforcement, and experience. In the case of information literacy games, the new, incoming information may arrive in the form of an online tutorial, an instructor's oral presentation, or a librarian's demonstration of a professional online resource discovery tool. Playing the game gives students practice, reinforcement, and experience putting the new, incoming information to work. Initially, players may flounder at making relevance and credibility assessments. Because BiblioBouts displayed other players' relevance and credibility assessments for the same source, players could—and did—learn how to conduct such assessments from each other. From our vantage point as domain experts in source assessment, students' attempts were rudimentary and their comments barely articulate, but it was clear that they drew on evidence internal or external to the source at hand to make such assessments (chapter 9). Playing BiblioBouts, students got plenty of practice conducting source assessments, and they can draw on their experience in the future.

When we formulated this best practice, we worded it carefully, limiting our expectations to *players modeling what experts do*. In the case of BiblioBouts, we wanted students to conduct relevance and credibility assessments for the sources they might use for their academic work, but we could not expect their assessments to match exactly or even approximate the assessments of domain experts. While in college, students are just beginning to master disciplinary knowledge. Their assessments for sources may be totally different from experts' assessments because, for much disciplinary scholarship, they do not have sufficient knowledge to understand it or talk about it like experts do. For example, domain experts might give the highest credibility and relevance ratings to a source that an undergraduate student rates very low because it is beyond his level of understanding. Thus, we cannot expect domain experts and students to agree on a source's credibility or relevance. Domain experts have advanced knowledge of their chosen discipline: they know the names of the discipline's movers and shakers, think tanks, and research centers and can recognize these authors as credible sources. Gaining more knowledge in a discipline, students will begin to recognize such names so that performing credibility assessments will be less mechanical and based on prior experience with experts writing in the discipline. Maybe students will never deliberately perform credibility assessments for their academic work, but someday, when it really matters, particularly when their well-being is at stake, the appropriate behavior will kick in. If students have forgotten how to perform the desired behavior, searching the Internet should yield online tutorials to refresh their memories.

One more point applies to this best practice about games enabling players to model expert behavior. Games create an environment that allows players to apply their new knowledge. Games transform new information and the ideas, thoughts, and conceptions that arise from it (i.e., the stuff that goes on in our heads) into something concrete, observable, and measurable. Players can see for themselves how applying new information in the context of the game leaves a trail of "doing it" behind and enables them to compare how well they are "doing it" vis-à-vis other students with the same level of understanding and expertise. Naysayers may be inclined to dismiss BiblioBouts and comparable information literacy games because students' output (e.g., relevance assessments, credibility assessments, comments) does not match the output of domain experts. Our response is that we cannot realistically expect it to do so until students' domain knowledge approximates that of domain experts. Furthermore, most academics are domain novices except in a handful of topics in their chosen discipline, and everyday people are domain novices with regard to just about everything under the sun. Our objective as game designers should be to raise students' consciousness with respect to the importance of information literacy concepts, skills, and knowledge so that the next time they search for information, retrieving it elicits the desired behavior that is the purpose of the information literacy game; in the case of BiblioBouts, it was for players to evaluate sources using evidence-based criteria to justify their source evaluations.

Best Practice 18

Make sure your game is not a tutorial or quiz all dressed up. As a result of playing your information literacy game, students must be able to exercise a new information literacy skill, concept, or knowledge. Game play should give them practice, reinforcement, and experience so that they deliberately perform the desired behavior on their own; at the very least, they should know that they should be doing it or be able to recognize the right situations for performing the desired behavior.

Our literature reviews have found information literacy games that are tutorials or quizzes "all dressed up" as games; these games merely drill students on what they already know or let them guess in advance of receiving feedback regarding the correct answer. Students will quickly realize that this type of "game" is merely a dressed-up assignment and find it unsatisfactory. Games have internal structures and design principles that cannot be simulated by adding a thin veneer of "gamification." Building an effective learning game requires a commitment to designing it from the ground up.

Best Practice 19

Although students want to be in control during game play, they will collaborate with their peers when the collaboration furthers what they want to accomplish. This best practice predates BiblioBouts, coming from our experience with Hidgeon. Some students wanted to play Hidgeon on their own. To facilitate game play by student teams, Hidgeon needed a sign-on capability for multiple team members that allowed players to pass control to teammates.

BiblioBouts pooled the work efforts of all players into one database, which they consulted to write their papers. For a twenty-five-person class, players could search at least one hundred sources on the broad-based topic and retrieve citations, abstracts, and full-texts for most sources, plus everyone's source evaluations and ratings. BiblioBouts is a model for how library research could be transformed from a solitary endeavor into a collaborative enterprise. We have already made recommendations regarding the enhancement of citation management systems with competitive collaborative research capabilities (see page 187). Such capabilities would distribute library research to student working groups, encourage everyone to evaluate sources, and expose group members to more sources than they could discover on their own.

Best Practice 20

Design games that introduce students to virtual librarian reference services so that they gain confidence in librarian input and become less hesitant about approaching librarians virtually or in person in the future. Because students were introduced to librarians during pre-game preparation activities, we did not expect library anxiety to emerge as a theme in the analysis of focus group interviews (see page 97). To reduce students' reluctance to approach librarians, we challenge designers of future information literacy games to incorporate virtual librarian reference services into them. Even if done in passing, as in BiblioBouts, where game invitations included suggested databases, sample keywords, and a link to virtual librarian reference services, using information technology to ask librarians questions and receiving answers that solve their problems may undermine students' resistance to approaching a librarian in person.

Best Practice 21

Students must have concrete evidence that leaving their computer to do research will have a payoff in terms of improving their research or affecting their grades. This best practice also predates BiblioBouts, coming from our experience with Hidgeon, which students played mostly online, with occasional trips to the university library's reading room to check noncirculating reference sources. Students told us that going to the library was disruptive. They wanted game play that was entirely online and viewed any deviation from an online administration as bothersome. Some students assumed a cavalier attitude about whether the items in the library's physical collections should figure into their research because of publication dates that reached back to the days when these students were in junior or senior high school. For students in college, their high school days may seem a long time past, but they could benefit from the major monographs that detail the state of the art on a particular topic or area of inquiry, particularly in the humanities. Games that involve venturing into other-than-online territory must convince students of the value of in-library resources and provide incentives for students to leave their machine. If they do not, be prepared for students to use guesswork in, skip sections of, or disregard altogether game play that is not online.

MANAGING THE DESIGN TEAM

Here is a handful of best practices that design teams should keep in mind throughout the game design, development, deployment, and maintenance phases.

Best Practice 22

Pre-test your game design using an analog version. Before embarking on the long, arduous game design phase, consider devising an analog version of your information literacy game. If you are successful in doing so, ask yourselves whether the online version is necessary or the analog version will achieve your objectives. Building an online game is a huge undertaking that requires a long-term commitment to user support, so if you can achieve your objectives manually, without programming and software development, go for it!

An anonymous designer posted an analog version of BiblioBouts to the Web ("Bibliography-Building Game Exercise" 2011). Like BiblioBouts, it has gathering (Donor bout), self-selecting (Closer bout), rating (the "R" component of the T&R bout), and choosing-the-best (Best Bibliography bout) phases. Playing the analog version of BiblioBouts would involve lots of paper pushing, sorting, and manual scoring. To facilitate game administration, the self-selecting phase could be expanded to include citation-and-abstract activity so that students could rate sources using either or both abstracts and full-texts. Scoring especially would be a challenge, but instructors with good organizational skills could distribute various administrative tasks among students. Because the analog version would involve students in every aspect of the game, it might boost their participation, as well as encourage them to ask questions and work together to find solutions.

Pre-testing is also critical to understanding the actual experience of game play and will give designers insight into what actually works in practice and what does not. Before committing to building a game, designers should fully test it as a prototype and make any needed modifications to the design. Using a simple paper mock-up of the game is sufficient for initial pre-testing, but eventually the design team will want to migrate to pre-testing online prototypes.

Best Practice 23

Be prepared for redesign efforts to spawn entirely new problems. When re-
designing any aspect of your game to solve a particular problem, always be
prepared for the solution to introduce entirely new problems. For example,
we eliminated the Donor bout from BiblioBouts to simplify students' find-
ing-sources activity, that is, by allowing them to first focus on saving what
they found to Zotero instead of dividing their attention between Zotero and
BiblioBouts. After finding the requisite number of sources, students rushed
to start playing BiblioBouts, thinking that they could go back and find more
sources later on. Despite BiblioBouts's written warnings (in bold letters) that
they could not go back once sources were donated to the game (figure 5.3),
students were quick on the draw and pressed the red "here" button to start
play. Then, after realizing they could not go back and change or add sources,
they complained to their instructors. A shortcut solution was for the instructor to remove the complaining player from the game and reinvite him or her;
however, technical problems ensued in an ongoing game when one instructor
removed and reinvited *all* students.

Thus, we found that by solving one problem—students having difficulty
using both Zotero and BiblioBouts at the same time—the solution of removing the Donor bout in turn caused more problems (students were frustrated
and wanted to go back for better sources). It is important to be prepared for
unexpected consequences of design changes.

Best Practice 24

Be prepared for conflicting feedback from different users. Although user testing and feedback are very important for developing an effective game, game
designers must be prepared for situations in which they receive conflicting
feedback on the same issue. For instance, best practice #23 describes how
the BiblioBouts team responded to players' confusion over using Zotero and
playing the Donor bout at the same time. The team's response was to eliminate the Donor bout and rely exclusively on Zotero for Donor bout activity
(i.e., submitting sources to the game). Subsequently, the design team received
feedback that students were frustrated that they could not go back and change
their sources once they had started the game. Game designers must exercise
judgment in resolving issues, relying on their knowledge of the overall goals
of the game, and balancing diverse and sometimes conflicting feedback.

Best Practice 25

*Expect instructors and players to do something with your game that no one
on the design team ever expected.* Best practice #23 describes how an instruc-

tor used BiblioBouts in a way that was totally unexpected (i.e., removing and reinviting all players during an ongoing game). The technical problems that resulted from this user's action had to be tracked down and fixed one by one. (We should have told the instructor to create an entirely new game.) Because BiblioBouts was a research project, we did not have unlimited resources for user support and struggled to keep up with technical problems, like this one, that followed on the heels of unanticipated uses of BiblioBouts. Plan now for how your design and development team will respond in comparable situations.

Best Practice 26

Beware of third-party software—when you least expect it, vendors will make a change that affects game functionality. If your game relies on third-party software, your design team must monitor design forums that announce and document changes. BiblioBouts relied on Zotero to build a database of sources with citations and full-texts. Changes to Zotero by its creators meant changes had to be made to BiblioBouts to keep up. Make sure your design team is on top of things so that game play proceeds without interruption.

Best Practice 27

Add a graphic designer to the game design team right from the start to translate team members' ideas into visual terms. Designing an information literacy game is difficult and complex. Design team members probably all have a vision of how game play will transpire. Then they must make the leap from this vision to a verbal description of game play. Charge the on-staff graphic designer with translating the vision into prototype interfaces and game-system functionality. That is how we got started (see page 44). Our designer was a good listener who transformed brainstorming and team discussions into paper or online mock-ups, shared the mock-ups in subsequent meetings, and responded to team members' reactions with changes. Slowly but surely, progress was made. By the way, choose graphic designers who are unperturbed by criticism and can adapt to constant changes due to the iterative nature of game design and development.

Best Practice 28

Supplement our game design experience with that of other game design professionals. We neither expect nor want you to rely solely on our game design experience. Plenty of books address game design generally, and you should consult them to supplement our advice and get a well-rounded view of the game enterprise. For learning how to design games, our favorites are *Level*

Up: The Guide to Great Video Game Design (Rogers 2010), *Game Design Workshop: A Playcentric Approach to Creating Innovative Games* (Fullerton 2008), and *The Art of Game Design: A Book of Lenses* (Schell 2008). For inspiration, consider *A Theory of Fun for Game Design* (Koster 2005) and *Challenges for Game Designers* (Brathwaite and Schreiber 2009); the former will help you gain a better understanding of what it means to develop a fun-filled experience for game players, and the latter gives you exercises to develop your game design skills and flex your creative muscles.

Best Practice 29

For game designers, the job never ends because of demands from game-system users. Online games require continual maintenance, user support, improvement, and enhancement. Problem fixes, improvements, and new features often snowball into more problems to fix, improvements, and enhancements. User support services must always be available to players because their grades are at stake. If the game is a research initiative like BiblioBouts, researchers know exactly when the game development will end due to formal project deadlines, spending all available funding, and finding answers to their research questions. To ensure their game's future, researchers must seek a permanent home for it. Thus, consider the game's long-term sustainability right from the start.

GAME DESIGN EXERCISE

Let's design your information literacy game. What is your overarching objective? If you are having difficulty, complete this sentence: As a result of playing our game, students should be able to ____. Fill in the blank line with the information literacy concept, skill, or knowledge you want students to learn. For example, they should be able to conduct library research, evaluate sources, distinguish between scholarly and nonscholarly sources, perform a technical reading of a source, cite sources in papers, select the right databases, conduct a Boolean search, choose the right keywords, find a topic to research, and much more.

Next, enlist this book's top-first then bottom-up approach to designing your game's structural elements (best practice #4). While you draft your game's goals/objectives, rules, moves/actions, outcomes/feedback, competition, interaction, duration, and representation, heed this chapter's best practices, especially the "backdrop" practices—making sure game play contributes to the course work students are already doing (1), produces artifacts that further their course work (2), focuses on one key concept (3), and creates a community of learners (6).

Next, break down your game's overarching objective into specific learning objectives. Ask yourself what specific components of the overarching objective students will learn as a result of playing the game. We can break down BiblioBouts's overarching objective into these four: (1) using professional tools to find and save promising sources on the broad-based topic in play, (2) evaluating fellow players' submitted sources, (3) formulating a paper topic, and (4) selecting relevant sources for writing a paper on the selected topic.

Next, envision how players will achieve these objectives in the form of a player's moves or actions and the game's responses to them. Because the game will place restraints on player actions/moves, rules should emerge as the result of desired actions/moves. If you can clearly envision various moves/actions, consider the feedback/outcomes that the game could provide players so that their subsequent moves/actions are more skillful, efficient, and on target.

Feedback/outcomes include the game's scoring. The game's scoring and peer-review actions add competition and interaction into the mix. Player moves/actions have to translate into something quantifiable. Let's use "big ideas" in BiblioBouts's Best Bibliography bout as an example. Players entered their research paper's topic, three big ideas that they expected their paper to discuss, and ten BiblioBouts sources that they expected to cite in their papers (figures 5.12 and 5.13). BiblioBouts awarded the players bonus points for adding to their best bibliographies sources to which a consensus of players had assigned the same big idea in the T&R bout as the player expected to discuss in her paper. Feedback/outcomes are imperative because players want to know whether their efforts are in sync with what the game expects, receive the game's maximum award, and make progress in the game. Involve opponents in feedback opportunities because players are likely to shape up and embrace the desired behavior when their peers criticize them.

SUMMARY

The game design effort dovetails with the results of the needs assessment that demonstrates the need for a game to deliver information literacy instruction to students. This chapter tells game designers how to design an information literacy game using best practices that came out of our experience designing, developing, deploying, and evaluating the Defense of Hidgeon and BiblioBouts information literacy games. A top-first, bottom-up approach to game design is recommended, using this chapter's first six best practices as broad-based starting points and the next fifteen best practices to fill in the details. Best practices also involve managing the game design team. Some best practices will resonate more than others, depending on your game's overarching objective, project resources, design and development timeline, and so on.

Chapter 13 picks up with best practices for user support, game deployment, and game-system evaluation. Please resist the temptation to finalize the design of your information literacy game before you consider those as well.

Chapter Thirteen

Best Practices for Administrator, Instructional, and User Support Services

Just as important as the game interface are its administrator interfaces and instructional and user support services. This chapter covers best practices for these aspects of the information literacy game enterprise.

DESIGNING THE SUPER ADMINISTRATOR INTERFACE

Best Practice A

Online information literacy games must have a "super administrator" interface that enables the game development team to conduct game administration. At a minimum, super game administration involves user accounts, game administration, and troubleshooting and fixing technical problems. Team members whose user accounts have super administrator status should have access to a suite of tools pertaining to user accounts, technical troubleshooting, and games. Here are examples of super administrator actions:

- Logging onto user accounts to monitor ongoing games, performing actions that players or game administrators are unable to perform on their own, confirming issues that players or game administrators report, and identifying the exact nature of technical problems using super administrator diagnostic tools
- Upgrading player accounts to game administrator accounts and downgrading game administrator accounts to player accounts
- Reassigning games to different game administrators
- Deleting games and user accounts

Super administrator interfaces should be restricted to trained staff on the game development and user support teams. Such interfaces will be unique to each and every game. Chapter 4 describes BiblioBouts's super administrator interface.

DESIGNING THE GAME ADMINISTRATOR INTERFACE

Best Practice B

The game administrator interface gives authorized players tools to create and edit games, monitor each player's game play progress, and view summary game play data to assess each player's game play performance and the group's overall game play progress. The game's administrator interface is available to game players who have requested game administrator status from super administrators. This interface gives game owners tools to administer games—at the very least, to create games, monitor player participation, and grade participation.

Note that best practice B refers to *game administrators* instead of instructors. This is due to our experience with instructors who wanted to delegate game administration to proxies, such as librarians, graduate student teaching assistants, and teaching aides.

A game administrator can create a game by entering the game's name, invited players, and start and end dates and times into a form. BiblioBouts's game creation form (figures 4.3 and 4.5) requested these data and more. Expect game administrators to make changes to ongoing games, such as adding and removing players, changing start and end dates, and so on. For example, BiblioBouts had separate forms for changes, one for adding and removing players and another for changing the game's start and end dates and the parameters for each of the three bouts.

Expect a wide range of game administrator involvement levels. Some administrators will monitor students' game play very closely, checking student names on the leader board and ascertaining who has or has not registered, started playing, achieved the game's important milestones, and finished playing. Others will be less concerned or delegate player monitoring to one or more proxies (see best practice C). The information literacy game needs tools to make game play monitoring data available to game administrators. The game play data that the administrator interface serves to game administrators and their proxies will vary from game to game because of each game's unique nature.

BiblioBouts's administrator interface provided instructors with a lengthy evaluation report tool that reported on player progress and accomplishments and color-coded them so instructors could quickly eyeball the report to identify nonperforming, underperforming, average, and overperforming players (figures 4.6 to 4.9). Because instructors will vary in their knowledge of the game, instructions should accompany player performance reports, explaining the displayed data and suggesting how instructors can use it to grade students. BiblioBouts's administrator interface used game play logs as the base for its evaluation report, supplemented with a FAQ that described how instructors could copy-and-paste data from the report into a Google spreadsheet and analyze the data to generate grades.

Best Practice C

Allow multiple proxies to sign onto game administrator accounts or onto selected games as game administrators. Game administrators could also be the instructor's proxy, for example, a graduate teaching assistant, a librarian, a teacher's aide, or even a technologically astute student whom the instructor has designated to act in his or her stead. Because instructors might not always be interested in the daily administration of their games, we recommend your game administrator interface include an account permissions setup capability so that game owners can authorize multiple proxies to sign onto their accounts or onto selected games as game administrators.

Best Practice D

Games that are integrated into course management systems (CMSs) are likely to simplify game administration and facilitate instructor adoption and deployment in the classroom. Integrating information literacy games generally into a CMS could simplify game administration, delegating certain functions to the CMS and completely eliminating them from the game administrator interface. For example, all students enrolled in a CMS course site could be automatically registered into the game. Game account setup could be a one-click launch involving no separate accounts or new passwords. CMS integration would simplify grading student performance, issuing game invitations to students, and publishing reminders and news items. Instructors may be more positively inclined to adopt games with CMS integration because it lessens the burden of game administration.

ESTABLISHING INSTRUCTIONAL SUPPORT SERVICES

No information literacy game can function without instructional services. Game designers cannot guarantee that the instructors who deploy the game in their classes will give pre-game instruction to students or delegate it to librarians, instructional technology staff, or graduate student teaching assistants. Instructors who do not feel sufficiently competent to advise students on information literacy matters, but who embrace your game because they want their students to improve their information literacy skills and knowledge, will benefit from instructional support services. Some students might want to review instructional material prior to or during game play. These are just a few of the many reasons to provide instructional services for your game. This section's best practices for instructional support services begin with four best practices directed at the people most likely to embrace the game—librarians who teach information literacy classes and instructors who teach academic subjects—then focus more directly on the game's instructional services.

Best Practice E

Librarians want demo games that they can show to instructors, and both librarians and instructors want demo games that they can play to decide whether the game meets their course's learning objectives. Demo games that simulate game play are a must! You want instructors who are teaching academic subjects or information literacy to incorporate your information literacy game into their classes. Librarians and academic instructors want to know whether the game meets their course's learning objectives, and one of the best ways for them to determine whether your game is appropriate for their classes is to offer a free demo. BiblioBouts provided a demo game, and we encouraged all prospective instructor-users who contacted us about BiblioBouts to play it to familiarize themselves with the game.

Best Practice F

Make instructions available at various levels of granularity that tell instructors how to create games and monitor and grade students' game play performance. The need for instructions is not limited to student game players but includes instructors who will use game functionality to create games and monitor and grade their students' game play. We suggest that such instructions be made available at various levels of granularity so that instructors can choose how much they want to involve themselves in the game's detail. Our observations confirm the popularity of videos for giving instructions because they show and tell, and viewers are in control, deciding when to play, stop, pause, or replay.

Best Practice G

Prospective instructor-users want convincing evidence of the benefits their students will receive as a result of playing your game. How game play benefits students is important to prospective instructor-users because they want to be assured of these same benefits for their students. To convince them of your game's benefits, evaluate your game and publish the findings. Doing so is not easy. Not only does an evaluation divert resources from the design and development effort, but you must recruit instructors and their classes to the evaluation, assist instructors in securing approval from their institution's human subjects review board, draft and pre-test data-collection instruments, execute the evaluation, and analyze the results. In the event of less-than-convincing evaluation results, the game design and development effort might have to return to the drawing board, so to speak, to make improvements to the game, then follow up with another evaluation.

The BiblioBouts team conducted three evaluations of the game, one for each version (i.e., alpha, beta 1.0, and beta 2.0). Originally, we planned for a baseline study, collecting papers from students before the game was developed so that we could compare them to papers from students who had played the game, but we were unable to identify instructors who would commit to incorporating the game into their classes until they fully understood how to play the game and how it worked. We opted instead for another approach to evaluation: determining whether (1) players cited increasingly greater numbers of scholarly sources as they progressed from finding sources (i.e., in the Closer bout) to choosing sources (i.e., in their best bibliographies and final papers) (see pages 154–56), (2) players cited more sources in their final papers than nonplayers (see page 159), (3) players cited BiblioBouts sources in their final papers (see pages 159–60 and 164–65), and (4) players' perceptions of their information literacy skills improved as a result of playing the game (see pages 167–72). We urge you to conduct experiments comparing player and nonplayer performances so that you can document learning gains and publish the results.

Best Practice H

Put the most enthusiastic instructor-users to work for you. Some instructor-users are so enthusiastic about your game that they are willing to assist in your efforts. You know they are enthusiastic because they host games in successive terms, ask lots of questions, share their game deployment experiences, suggest improvements to existing functionality, and ask for new features. In fact, the design of BiblioBouts's evaluation report tool (figures 4.6 to 4.9) was largely based on the input of one particular instructor-user from a nonparticipating institution who wanted to know how her students were playing the game each step of the way. This included adding links on the evaluation report to bout-specific logs (figure 4.9). Clicking on these links downloaded the logs so she could analyze them in Excel to help her students find the best information for their papers (appendix F).

In addition to game design, enthusiastic instructor-users can assist you with publicity, spreading the word among their colleagues, blogging and Tweeting about the game, offering testimonials that you can post on your game's website, and volunteering to participate in the evaluation. If you establish user support forums, invite instructor-users to monitor them, respond to inquiries from prospective instructor-users, and share their game-deployment experiences. Hearing from satisfied instructor-users reassures prospective instructors that game play will achieve their course's learning objectives and reap benefits for their students. Some instructor-users will volunteer their support, for example, offering to write a testimonial or correspond with a prospective instructor-user. Other instructor-users may respond positively to your direct requests for assistance. It does not hurt to ask.

We encountered enthusiastic player-users in focus group interviews. That they were less forthcoming about their enthusiasm than instructor-users might have been due to the "cool factor" players felt around peers. We would not hesitate to host a player-user online forum where veteran game players shared their game play experiences with newbies; however, monitoring the forum to keep posts focused on substantive matters connected with the game would be a challenge.

The remaining best practices focus directly on instructional support services.

Best Practice I

A curriculum guide is an indispensable component of the game enterprise, especially to advise academic instructors who are going it alone without librarian assistance. A curriculum guide details how your information literacy game can be integrated into an instructor's course and meet its learning objectives. The curriculum guide's level of detail may vary based on prospective instructor-users. In the case of information literacy games, some academic instructors will want to expose their students to information literacy skills and concepts that they feel will improve students' academic work but that they do not feel entirely competent to teach on their own. In some K–12 settings, where there is no school librarian, instructors may have to go it alone. This means your game's curriculum guide will have to be extensive and detailed, perhaps including textbook-like treatments of the subject for instructors to read, as well as detailed lesson plans, lecture notes, and supplementary materials for students, such as worksheets, sample assignments, outlines, and agendas. Because each educational institution's library collection will be unique, instructions to instructors should advise them to pre-test instructional materials and revise them to fit their particular situation.

Unfortunately, we did not have a curriculum guide for BiblioBouts—we did not even think of it until we were about to deploy the game in college classes. The closest we came to drafting a curriculum guide was an Instructor FAQ with answers to these questions:

- What happens during game play?
- Is BiblioBouts right for your course?
- How should the instructor prepare classes prior to game play?
- In what class discussions should instructors engage students while and after they play the game?

We received inquiries from prospective instructor-users who would have incorporated the game into their classes had there been a curriculum guide.

Please learn from our mistake. Make the curriculum guide an indispensable component of your game and start working on it during the game design phase. Consider adding a master teacher to your game design team who knows about curriculum development and put him or her in charge of the curriculum guide and instructional support services generally.

Best Practice J

Pre-game player instruction is essential. Instructing students in the information literacy skills and concepts they will encounter during game play is essential. Otherwise, the game will merely drill students on what they know. If some students are already knowledgeable, there is a chance that novice students will learn from them through the game's feedback; however, this is unlikely because students will have to be sufficiently savvy to distinguish between skillful and nonskillful game play. Do not leave pre-game instruction to chance. At the very least, add an online tutorial to the game that gives instruction and program the game to give players bonus points every time they watch the tutorial. Librarians may be able to lead instruction sessions, introducing students to the game as well as to the university library's online portal and scholarly databases. Alternatively, charge instructors with pre-game instruction. Because some academic instructors might not feel entirely comfortable teaching students about information literacy, make sure the curriculum guide spells everything out for them.

Best Practice K

Instruction includes stating your game's overarching objective. The instructions should be frank and straightforward, telling students exactly what they will learn as a result of playing. Put this message into the game's "about" page, online instructions, introductory videos, pre-game instruction, and all other instructional materials. We know how important this best practice is from our earlier game—Hidgeon's overarching objective was never stated in the game's online documentation, leaving the majority of students in the dark about what it was all about (Markey et al. 2008b). BiblioBouts was much more forthcoming in this regard, and as a result players were able to describe the game's overarching objective in post-game chats conducted several months after they played it.

Best Practice L

Player instruction includes how to make judgments for the game's rating, assessing, and comparison tasks. Students' focus group comments were the impetus for this best practice. On one hand, they criticized the hundred-point rating scale and wanted it replaced with a five-star system. On the other hand, they wanted to know how to make rating judgments, for example, what indicators would warrant ratings of 0 percent, 37 percent, 72 percent, 95 percent, and so on. Although their comments sold us on the idea of five-star rating systems, students still need to know, for example, what distinguishes a two- from a four-star rating or a three- from a five-star rating. Not only could rating scales be the subject of class discussions, but scales could be accompanied by in-game info buttons (i) giving tips about how to judge the scale vis-à-vis the rating, assessing, or comparing tasks at hand. Consider your game's rating, assessing, and/or comparing tasks and the most appropriate pre- and in-game approaches for instructing players on how to make judgments.

Best Practice M

Not only must game play count toward students' grades in the course, but it should be announced in the course syllabus along with the maximum points allocated to game play and the related writing assignment. This best practice harks back to our earlier game design experience with Hidgeon. Students wanted to know up front what course assignments they could expect, how each related to course content, and the maximum number of points they could expect to receive for each assignment. Although no one likes to admit it, many students are motivated primarily by their grades. Thus, students will not play games minus incentives that impact their final grade in the class.

Best Practice N

Game play must foster opportunities for students to reflect on their own research habits and what they are learning. Students are ensconced in a culture in which every minute is filled with activity, and electronic devices vie for their attention. Thus, getting students to reflect on their game play may be a tall order. One suggestion is taking an instant poll that students complete after game play ends, followed by an in-class discussion of the responses. Using BiblioBouts as an example, instructors could get the online discussion started by asking students to rate their agreement with these questions:

- The sources I cited in my written paper were better than the ones I usually find.
- The next time I write a paper, I will feel more confident about finding credible sources to cite in it.
- I will always check library databases for sources for my academic course work.
- I played BiblioBouts to the best of my ability.
- As a result of playing BiblioBouts, I am more inclined to ask a librarian for assistance.

Alternatively, instructors could get the in-class discussion started by staging a *Family Feud*–style game, giving the entire class fill-in-the-blank questions such as these:

- _____ is the first place where I will search for information for my academic papers.
- My initial impression of Zotero was _____.
- The likelihood that I will use Zotero in the future is _____ percent.
- I will always check on the credibility of the sources I find online when I search for information about _____.
- When I assess a source's credibility, the first thing I will do is _____.

PUTTING USER SUPPORT SERVICES IN PLACE

Best Practice O

If the game begins with technology problems, it is doomed, especially in the court of public opinion. Players, instructors, and librarians expect online information literacy games to work perfectly from the get-go because of the flawless performance of the computer programs they have become accustomed to using on their desktops, laptops, and mobile devices. Of course, both computers and programs crash on occasion, but relaunching them is usually all that is needed to get everything working again. Thus, no one expects or wants to experience technology problems. Chapter 7 described in detail the technology problems that plagued BiblioBouts users. That both instructors and players encountered these problems at the start of the game was especially unfortunate because the problems adversely affected their attitudes toward and interest in the game. In hindsight, we should have cautioned everyone about BiblioBouts, no matter what version of the game they played, because it really was a work in progress throughout the research project.

Before game play begins, we encourage you to submit your game to a thorough pre-testing with prospective players. When you are confident that everything is in working order, challenge a corps of volunteer players to "break" the game. Alternatively, if you are unsure about your game's technical stability, tell instructors, players, and librarians that the game is still in development and to expect technical difficulties; in fact, challenge them to find bugs so that your team can continue to perfect the program. Make them feel a welcome component of your research endeavor. In fact, when we did describe their participation in BiblioBouts as research, students especially responded positively, glad to be part of the project and observe firsthand how research is done (see page 103).

Best Practice P

Players, instructors, and librarians assume on-demand user support 24/7/365. Our experience supporting BiblioBouts impressed on us that everyone involved in game play expected on-demand, individualized, instantaneous user support. To them, user support meant that a knowledgeable and experienced user support professional (i.e., a human being) would respond immediately to their inquiries 24/7/365. In anticipation of the demand for user support services, we put in place an e-mail help line, videos for registering and playing BiblioBouts, and FAQs for playing BiblioBouts and troubleshooting technical difficulties. We did not have the resources to support round-the-clock instant messaging or phone support.

User support services are an indispensable component of the game enterprise. If you expect instructors outside your time zone, country, or hemisphere to adopt your game, support extends to users around the world. Please plan accordingly.

Best Practice Q

Establish an online forum where the game's novice users can get support from more experienced users. An alternative to supporting instant messaging, phone, and e-mail helplines 24/7/365 is establishing a user forum where users (i.e., instructors, librarians, players, and technology troubleshooters) can get support from more experienced users. Forums should shoulder some of the user support responsibility so that game development and user support teams do not have to assume 100 percent of the burden. The game's user support staff should be tasked with monitoring forums, responding to unresolved problems, and referring recurring problems to development staff. Because user forums presuppose experienced users, your game enterprise might support user services 24/7/365 for a limited period as players gain experience, followed by a gradual transition to user forums.

Best Practice R

If the game is time based, synchronize the clock for each game according to the time zone in which the game is played (and do not forget to factor in daylight savings time). This best practice occurred to us as a result of students who played BiblioBouts in time zones west of the United States' eastern time zone, which BiblioBouts used to schedule bouts. When such students waited until the last minute to play a bout, they signed onto the game after BiblioBouts had switched to the new bout. It would have been complicated to program BiblioBouts to synchronize the clock for each game according to the time zone in which the game was played and to take daylight savings time into consideration. If the clock is a factor in your game, consider how to handle the clock in games played in different time zones.

Best Practice S

The game's technology must be easy to use and scaffold students from easier to more difficult technologies. Contrary to popular belief about young people's expertise with technology, our experience with BiblioBouts's deployment demonstrated that young people "are keen on technologies that entertain them and expand their social network . . . [and] eschew technologies connected with academic pursuits" (Markey, Leeder, and Rieh 2012). Six technologies greeted BiblioBouts players at the start of the game (see pages 99–100). Although conducting library research generally puts four of the six technologies on students' computer screens, the addition of two more technologies—the difficult-to-use Zotero and the never-before-seen BiblioBouts—was overwhelming to some student game players. If your game requires students to use one or more entirely new information technologies, it needs to support their learning how to use them.

There are no easy solutions to the technology maze that characterizes library research. Focusing your game on one information literacy concept or skill is a possibility. Tutorials that engage students in activities that they eventually conduct during game play is another. When you design your game, take into consideration how the game's various technologies present themselves to students so that game play does not stymie them.

DISCUSSION

When we designed the BiblioBouts information literacy game, super administrator and game administrator interfaces and instructional and user support services took a back seat to the development of the game interface. Ensconced in game deployment, we quickly learned that administrator interfaces and support services were indispensable components of the game enterprise and ramped up their development. No game can be without them. Learn from our experience and heed this chapter's best practices.

SUMMARY

The game's administrator, instructional, and user support services are indispensable components of the game enterprise. The super administrator interface is reserved for the game development team only and involves user accounts, game administration, troubleshooting, and fixing technical problems. Game administrator functionality is for game owners, and at the very least, it enables them to create and edit games, monitor their students' progress, and view summary game play data for grading students' performance. Put instructional support services in place so that game players develop the requisite technical skills and content knowledge to engage in game play at a reasonably competitive level. Offering user support services ensures that everyone involved in game play—students, instructors, librarians, teaching assistants, and technology troubleshooters—has the resources needed to solve problems encountered before, during, and after the game.

Chapter Fourteen

The Future of
Information Literacy Games

This final chapter focuses on the future of information literacy games. It examines the game enterprise, emphasizing the most salient aspects of game design, development, deployment, evaluation, and maintenance that are likely to occupy game production teams from start to finish, as well as areas where such teams can make the greatest contributions to increase our knowledge of games and learning. It describes how we would redesign the BiblioBouts information literacy game to increase its faithfulness to this book's best practices. The chapter concludes with suggestions for future information literacy games.

THE FUTURE OF INFORMATION LITERACY GAMES

As researchers, our focus on information literacy games is on proof of concept, that is, building and demonstrating games and investigating their usefulness. Fully operational games have a much more extensive production cycle that includes long-term system maintenance and enhancement. Let us walk through the complete game production cycle, emphasizing key aspects that game production teams must consider from start to finish to ensure their game's success.

The cycle starts with generating ideas for new online information literacy games. Brainstorming and envisioning games is fun; plus, there are no strings attached. Our brainstorming efforts in this regard end this chapter. Some of our new game ideas would fill gaps in BiblioBouts's coverage of the library research process, and others are on the periphery of this process. New game ideas include suggestions from both us and BiblioBouts game players.

Brainstorming on the game's overarching objective, rules, actions, feedback, and interaction then transitions to game design. The task gets harder; plus, there are all those best practices to keep in mind, especially the top three—making sure that the game contributes in a useful way to the academic course work students are already doing, yields artifacts that students can directly apply to their course work, and gives them mastery over one key concept. Before making much more headway, it is time for game designers to think about securing financial support, not just for the game's initial design, development, deployment, and evaluation but for long-term online game maintenance, enhancement, and instructional and user support.

The impetus for the information literacy game is important. If it comes from librarians who are teaching information literacy content specific to their institution and expect to deploy the game only in the information literacy classes they teach, then the challenge may be convincing local administrators to fund their efforts. Add academic instructors to the mix, and your game will have to help achieve their course's learning objectives or add a new dimension to their course, perhaps something that instructors have always wanted to do. Aligning games with entire programs—for example, English writing programs, English-as-a-second-language writing programs, or humanities programs for science majors—may require significant changes to an entire curriculum, so plan ahead, because such changes take time. Enlisting faculty support, particularly entire programs, in the search for financial assistance may just be the tipping point to convince potential funders. Eventually, pretesting the game in a few classes that are characteristic of the program as a whole may be necessary to convince program instructors and departmental chairs of wholesale adoption.

If the game's content is specific to one particular institution, then sources of local support may be tapped. For example, the impetus for the Head Hunt game at Ohio State University (OSU) came not from grassroots efforts on the part of librarians and faculty but from the highest level, the vice provost's office, where there was interest in supporting the six thousand incoming freshmen who participate in summer orientation activities (O'Hanlon, Diaz, and Roecker 2009, 106). Chock-full of content specific to OSU library collections and services, Head Hunt was funded by OSU's director of libraries beginning in 2006. More than a half decade later, the game is now an ongoing program supported by the libraries' infrastructure. For the most part, Head Hunt's framework is set. Each year, OSU librarians perform a content review and make minor updates; thus, ongoing technical support is minimal and performed by a programmer from the Libraries' Information Technology Division who supports Head Hunt and several other ongoing Web-based programs (Karen Diaz, pers. comm.).

Grants from the Institute of Museum and Library Services (IMLS) supported the design, development, and evaluation of the BiblioBouts, Citation Tic Tac Toe, and Magnetic Keyword games (Markey et al. 2012; McCabe and Wise 2009, 7). When grant funds are expended, additional financial support must be obtained to ensure, at the very least, game-system maintenance, user support, and troubleshooting. For these, game developers, working with their universities' technology transfer offices to identify vendors interested in licensing these games, may put the games back into circulation. Future game developers should consider partnering with vendors in advance so that game research initiatives have a smooth transition to routine operation.

Chapter 12's best practice #14 recommends that the design of information literacy games cut across disciplinary and institutional boundaries to maximize the game's user base and make it more appealing to vendors. Game research initiatives should not be limited to one institution. They should demonstrate widespread adoption to convince vendors—especially those who may be reluctant to engage in the library marketplace because they perceive it as too small to generate much of a profit—that game play is generalizable beyond a handful of implementations.

Online information literacy games are complicated enterprises. They have at least three interfaces: (1) a game interface where students play the game, (2) a game administrator interface where game owners set up games, invite players, monitor game play progress, and grade players, and (3) super administrator interfaces where user support staff manage authorized users and troubleshoot problems. During the game design phase, integration with course management systems (CMSs) should be considered to simplify adding and removing players from the game, publishing tips, news, and reminders, and grading student performance. Additionally, instructors may be more positively inclined to adopt games with CMS integration because it would lessen the burden of game administration.

Providing user support services is imperative. It starts with getting librarians on the bandwagon because they will eventually work with instructors to incorporate the game into course syllabi and schedule game play that syncs with related assignments, visit classes to deliver pre-game information literacy instruction, and respond to players' inquiries via in-person and virtual reference services. To get a sense of game play, everyone—potential funders, librarians, instructors, and students—wants to play a demo game.

Plan to incorporate a wide range of user support services. A curriculum guide advises librarians and instructors on every aspect of game deployment and will be a boon to instructors who go it alone without librarian assistance. Players like videos because they are in control of play, pause, and replay. Make sure pre-game instruction is straightforward, telling students exactly what they can expect to learn as a result of playing the game. Also add the game's overarching objective to videos and online tutorials. Instructors can always supplement the tutorial with additional instruction as they see fit. When seeking support for your game research and development efforts, build on-demand 24/7/365 user support into your plans because players, instructors, teaching assistants, and librarians will want it, and you will want to provide it so that your evaluation results are not marred by technological difficulties that go unresolved due to its absence.

Game-system usability testing is essential. Its initial forms may be walk-throughs with prospective game players that become increasingly intensive, involving several different research methods and ultimately extending to detailed analyses of the game's scoring algorithm. Invite game studies classes to "game the game" so that you can close all loopholes in advance of unrestricted game play.

Game deployment must involve evaluation to determine whether game play improves student performance on academic assignments, contributes to academic achievement generally, increases students' knowledge of information literacy concepts, and improves their information literacy skills. Games that can provide evidence of improvements in student performance are much more likely to be adopted by librarians and academic instructors. However, we do not think such research findings are the one and only determinant of instructors' adoption. Instructors will take other factors into consideration, such as the amount of time and effort it takes to set up and monitor the game; how long it takes students to play the game; the extent to which the game matches their course's learning objectives, content, and activities; whether students voice approval in teaching evaluations; and the amount of support instructors need to provide above and beyond the game's user support services.

Evaluations of online information literacy games do not yet provide convincing evidence of their effectiveness. When the analysis is broadened to include serious games, five of six state-of-the-art literature reviews report convincing evidence of the effectiveness of educational games for cognitive learning and three of the six, for affective learning. More research that tests motivation must be done. However, information literacy researchers need to step up their efforts on all three fronts.

We are concerned about librarians who may feel threatened by information literacy games, fearing they will take over their instructional role in both academic and information literacy classrooms. Our experience is that librarians are the linchpin in the information literacy game enterprise, helping set the game's instructional content, sparking the interest of academic instructors and helping them to synchronize the game with their course syllabi and activities, supplementing the game's tutorial with additional information literacy instruction, and helping to conduct the evaluation. For example, later in this chapter we suggest the development of an "ISP game" that would give students experience mapping their feelings and thinking to the Information Search Process (ISP) model. Librarians are especially knowledgeable about this model and would be able to engage students in a post-game interpretation of game results that helped students understand their feelings and thinking vis-à-vis the information-seeking process.

We are cautiously optimistic about what the future holds for information literacy games. Although designing and developing such games requires a huge amount of work and dedication, what makes us circumspect is the open-ended nature of the game enterprise. Online games require continual maintenance, user support, improvement, and enhancement. Problem fixes, improvements, and new features snowball into more problems, improvements, and enhancements. In the words of best practice #29, for game designers, the job *never ends* because of demands from game-system users. Ultimately, game designers must yield to big-pocket vendors who can provide professional customer support for games and give them the administration and maintenance attention that they need to thrive and succeed over the long term.

LESSONS LEARNED FROM BIBLIOBOUTS

For BiblioBouts's design to be faithful to the best practices described in chapters 12 and 13, a redesign effort would be necessary. Most redesign work would focus on these four premises: pre-game player instruction is essential (J); sustained, nonstop game play is preferable to a fits-and-starts approach (12); game play must enable players to model what experts do (17); and a curriculum guide is an indispensable component of the game enterprise (I).

A redesigned BiblioBouts would feature an online tutorial that instructs players about the information literacy concepts they will encounter during game play, such as credibility and relevance assessment, identifying sources' major themes and representing them in the form of big ideas, and formulating term-paper topics. It would also advise them on how to judge their responses to the game's rating, assessing, and comparison tasks so that their responses matched their opponents' responses and earned them more points. Students could play and replay the tutorial at their convenience, and it would simplify game deployment for instructors reluctant to devote class time to instruction or to ask librarians to give their students instruction tailored to game play. Thus, to satisfy best practices K and L, the online tutorial would be up-front about telling students the game's overarching objective and detail how to judge their responses to the game's rating, assessing, and comparison tasks.

Transforming BiblioBouts from its current fits-and-starts approach into nonstop, sustained game play would require a considerable redesign effort because information literacy games involve written sources that take time for people to process. They are not like games that entail tagging visual images in which "comprehension" involves a split second of direct perception and translating the perception into a written description (Flanagan and Carini 2012). "Comprehension" of written sources requires much more time, and time is limited in high school and college classes. A possible solution is breaking the game in half, scheduling it on successive days or class meetings, so that the fits-and-starts nature of game play would not be as apparent to students as it was to BiblioBouts players.

Here is what we would do with BiblioBouts. To create an incentive for students to play the redesigned BiblioBouts early instead of waiting until the last minute, the game would award early birds more points than procrastinators for every action. The redesigned BiblioBouts would have six levels instead of bouts. Levels would present themselves as increasingly higher levels of attainment, just like in traditional video games. Transitioning to a higher level in the redesigned game would be akin to playing the next bout in the original game, and each higher level would begin with a video or online tutorial explaining game play at this level so that game players would learn what the higher level expected from them. Level names would also match the game's visual theme of a marksman's arrow hitting a bull's-eye.

Let's walk through this redesigned BiblioBouts. Instructors would set the game's start and end dates only. Game play would begin at "novice" level one (i.e., the original Donor bout), where players would find and save sources. Choosing the best sources (i.e., the original Closer bout) would be "apprentice" level two. Evaluating sources before reaching quota would be "archer" level three (i.e., pre-quota activity in the original Tagging & Rating [T&R] bout), and evaluating sources after reaching quota would be "marksman" level four (i.e., post-quota activity in the original T&R bout). To reach "master marksman" level five, players would browse the game's library of everyone's closed sources and choose sources for their best bibliographies (i.e., the original Best Bibliography bout). Game play need not end at best bibliography activity. Players could parlay their sources after reaching level three. Finally, the game's winner would be the only player to reach the sixth and final level of "grand master marksman."

The problem of the game's failing to have closed sources available to fast-starting players would be solved by the game's awarding bonus points to players who asked for sources when none were available, putting them on a waiting list, texting them when sources became available, and tacking on a deadline for a response, after which time the source and bonus points would be withdrawn and offered to the next player on the waiting list. At any time during the game, players could gamble, in a sense, testing the waters with their closed sources, swapping new sources for original sources that got low ratings (up to level two's closed-source cap, just like in poker). They would lose points for every swapped source, but their opponents would not lose points as they put effort into evaluating them; plus, swapped sources would remain in the evaluation and best bibliography selection pools. A player could make ill-fated decisions about swapping sources that dropped him or her from the top of the leader board. Making claimed sources off-limits to the original closer and letting other players claim swapped sources in place of their own closed sources is another possibility. Perhaps procrastinators might be inclined to forego donating sources to the redesigned BiblioBouts, preferring instead to claim other players' swapped sources.

The levels approach would eliminate BiblioBouts's reliance on the mini-games, or bouts, approach that resulted in the original game's fits-and-starts nature. Additionally it would support the true nature of library research in which people learn from sources, promote and demote sources' importance based on what they learn, seek new sources with greater depth and granularity, and even redefine their original research topics.

A redesigned BiblioBouts game would acknowledge as domain experts players whose opponents consistently rated their evaluations highest. So that players could review ratings to see what the best, worst, and middling ones were like, a new display module would need to provide on-demand displays of best, worst, and in-between ratings. Bonus points and trophies would be added to boost participation. Maybe it would make sense to have multiple winners: the player whose closed sources were chosen most frequently for best bibliographies, the player who rated the most sources, the player whose evaluations were rated the highest by opponents, the player who rated the most evaluations, and the player who did all four consistently well.

Adding a curriculum guide to the redesigned game's administrative interface is a no-brainer. Academic instructors could forward it to librarians to inform the pre-game instruction they prepare for students or they could go it alone, minus librarian assistance, and consult the guide as needed.

IDEAS FOR FUTURE ONLINE
INFORMATION LITERACY GAMES

Several aspects of the research process may be suited to online information literacy games:

- Identifying relevant databases
- Distinguishing between scholarly and nonscholarly sources

- Performing a facet analysis of one's search query
- Conducting Boolean searches that feature Boolean logic and operators, controlled vocabularies, proximity operators, and truncation
- Searching with keywords and controlled vocabulary terms
- Conducting credibility and relevance assessments
- Formulating the paper's topic
- Performing a technical reading of retrieved sources
- Citing sources in papers
- Choosing a style manual and using it to formulate citations
- Understanding and avoiding plagiarism

A game that covers the research process is likely to specialize in one or two aspects and touch upon others. In fact, BiblioBouts did just that, giving students considerable practice making credibility and relevance assessments while expecting them to identify relevant databases, retrieve sources, and formulate their paper's topic. Surely we would have liked BiblioBouts to specialize in all the above-listed aspects, but we learned early on that information literacy games cannot be overly complex without running the risk of failing to accomplish their objectives (best practice #3).

Of all the new game suggestions that focus group participants made, first and foremost on their list was a game that ushered them through the online searching process, familiarizing them with databases and giving them practice generating keywords that described their paper's topic. They were especially keen on this because they noticed that BiblioBouts required them to search for and donate sources to the game but did not explicitly give them instruction or practice in this regard. Here is what focus group participants said:

- "We didn't necessarily learn how to use the database from BiblioBouts. So if you were going to be teaching how to do research, that's definitely a big component, using the database and that's not really a step in BiblioBouts so much as it's of the Donor round. . . . Databases can get really confusing. Like there's a lot of tips that you don't know."
- "[I want to play] a mini-game before you have to donate [to BiblioBouts] about how you find [sources]. Like what keywords to search for and things like that, what subjects you need to search for."
- "I think BiblioBouts was a lot about getting [sources] and, like, reading over different ones and learning how to evaluate the sources. . . . If it was [about] where to get information and how to search in the different databases, I think that would have helped more."

To respond to these focus group participants' suggestions, build a game that teaches students how to become effective online searchers. Focus it on facet analysis, identifying relevant databases, relevance feedback, and/or generating keywords. Touching upon Boolean operators, controlled vocabulary, proximity operators, and truncation might add too much depth. A game tailored to generating keywords that retrieve relevant sources may be especially of interest to students because this appears to be a particularly vexing task for them in view of several comments from focus group participants, including these:

- "I would definitely say how to form a search query. Like choosing keywords. I have talked to . . . mostly my little brothers, and the one thing that they consistently mention is, 'I always have to go talk to the librarian because I can never think of anything.'"
- "Well, maybe it could be, like, a site, like, if you have a research topic, like, you type in your research topic and then, like, on the site it could take you, like, step-by-step [through] the most effective way to get the best answer."

That students are searching for information means that they are looking for something they do not know; thus, having to put what they do not know into words compounds the difficulties students experience during the information-seeking process (Belkin 1980). A game that teaches search strategies to retrieve information while not relying on verbal expressions of a paper's topic may pique students' interest. For the sake of brevity, we will call this "nontopic" searching. Domain experts search nontopically all the time (Bates 1989; Ellis 1989); in fact, they rarely use keywords to retrieve relevant information. They ask their colleagues for the names of researchers, research centers, or laboratories, then search these names and scan retrievals for relevant information. If their colleagues give them a relevant source on the topic, they check the source's bibliography for relevant sources (also known as backward chaining or footnote chasing) and search a citation index for sources that cite the original source (also known as forward chaining). With a critical mass of sources in hand, domain experts check to see if certain journals appear repeatedly, and if they do, they peruse all the articles published in recent issues of those journals for relevant ones (also known as the journal run). Seldom do domain experts use keywords to find relevant sources. Instead, they search databases using very concrete search criteria, such as names of authors, think tanks, research centers, laboratories, and journals, and citation indexes using titles of relevant articles in hand.

Getting nontopic searches started is easy. They start with one relevant scholarly source that can be mined for author names, journal titles, and cited sources to find more like the one in hand. Some search engines feature new tools to facilitate nontopical searching, such as "find like" searches (also known as relevance feedback) and non-Boolean searching. When search engines display sources, they accompany them with a "Find Like" link on which searchers click to retrieve additional retrievals that use words in the original source to find ones like it. Non-Boolean retrieval works much the same way. The searcher merely has to find a relevant passage in a source, cut-and-paste the passage into the engine's search dialogue box, and click the "Search" button to retrieve more like it. A game could usher players through each nontopical search type, then challenge them to use each type to find retrievals that their opponents would rate as relevant to the topic in play. Players at the top of the game's scoreboard would be those who retrieved relevant sources from a variety of search types and contributed the most relevant sources.

Also mentioned repeatedly by focus group participants were games on how to find a book in the library, taking a library tour, and understanding what a call number is all about. That students do not know how to find a book in the library is not surprising because they are Millennials who have grown up with the Internet. Consider this focus group interviewee's comment about checking out books from the library:

> You mean, like, finding a book in the library? I don't know how to find a book in the library. Like, I would definitely just go straight to a librarian and, like, wouldn't even waste my time. Because I have absolutely no idea. I just use electronic resources. I can't remember the last time I had to actually check out a physical book. Everything's online. Especially here [at the university].

Ideas such as finding books in the library or taking a library tour may be so specific to individual libraries that online tutorials and reference services might be more appropriate instructional approaches. Other suggestions mentioned once or twice included distinguishing between primary and secondary sources, formulating paper topics that are just right in terms of scope and depth, citing sources, and footnote chasing.

Another idea is a game that helps students write their papers. It would give them practice with choosing a topic for the paper, performing a technical reading of retrieved sources, identifying statements that require citations to sources, and avoiding plagiarism. Consider teaming up with writing professionals who can contribute their expertise to the game's discussion of thesis statements, arguments, claims, and citations.

Brainstorm on how the Information Search Process (ISP) could be presented in a game or experiential tutorial (Kuhlthau 2004). Increasing students' metacognition about the stages of the library research process would be an ISP game objective. Another would be to demonstrate to students that they are not alone with respect to their feelings and thinking about ISP stages—that everyone who engages in the research process experiences the same ups and downs. Starting with a tutorial that teaches students about the ISP model's stages and the activities that characterize them, the game would require students to play it each time they worked on the assignment that accompanied the game. Students would checkmark the activities on which they had worked, and the game would use their checkmarked activities to select an ISP stage and query players about the nature of their feelings and thinking during this stage. When the game ended, it would present a tally of players' responses to feeling and thinking questions per stage and depict the research process visually, using stage-sequencing and iteration data collected during game play. Such a game would definitely require both instructors and librarians to debrief students to engage them in a discussion about how to cope with uncomfortable feelings that arise during the research process.

Several sources are available for generating new ideas for information literacy games. The Project LOEX website features an "Information Resources" database that you can search to link to resources that librarians have made available for the asking and to determine what information literacy concepts and skills are receiving the most attention (LOEX 2013). Book-length treatments by Jenny Levine (2006b, 2008) and Theresa McDevitt (2011) describe mostly offline information literacy games. Although the offline format may be perfectly conducive to such games, consider how interactivity, social media, and feedback might make them more compelling and attractive to students. Alternatively, learn from the experience of the game designers who built the online information literacy games cited in table 1.1.

CONCLUSION

Dear reader, the ball is now in your court. How will you get involved with information literacy games? Do you want to design and develop games? Are you a librarian who has a great idea for a game and wants to lead a grassroots effort to integrate the game into your institution's information literacy initiatives? Do you want to test games to prove that game play improves student performance on academic assignments and contributes to academic achievement generally?

Promise us that, whatever your involvement in the information literacy game enterprise, you will heed this book's best practices, particularly the first three—building games that contribute in a useful way to the academic course work students are already doing, yield artifacts that they can directly apply to their course work, and give them mastery over one key concept—so that students acknowledge your efforts with feedback like this comment, which describes the benefits of information literacy games in a nutshell:

> I think [the game] is good because you're not realizing at the time that you're learning about research. Like, you might not want to think, "Oh, I want to go learn about library research today." You're playing the game and you're learning about it without doing that.

Appendix A

Game Diary Form for Students

Game diary forms were voluntarily completed by college students in selected classes from participating institutions during the evaluation of the alpha version of BiblioBouts. Under closed-ended questions are possible answers; after open-ended questions are lines indicating spaces where students entered their answers.

1. My BiblioBouts game alias is: _____
2. Which BiblioBouts mini-game did you play today (choose 1 only)?
   - ☐ Donor
   - ☐ Closer
   - ☐ Policing
   - ☐ Rating & Tagging
   - ☐ Sorter
   - ☐ Best Bibliography
   - ☐ None of the above
3. How much time did you spend playing the game today? _____
4. Rate your motivation for playing BiblioBouts today. (Rate by choosing one answer on this scale: Very high, Somewhat high, Neutral, Somewhat low, Very low.)
5. Which statement best describes the amount of game play progress you made today (choose 1 only)?
   - ☐ I failed to make progress on meeting this mini-game's quota of N citations.
   - ☐ I made slight progress on meeting this mini-game's quota of N citations.
   - ☐ I met this mini-game's quota of exactly N citations.
   - ☐ I slightly exceeded this mini-game's quota of N citations.
   - ☐ I exceeded this mini-game's quota of N citations.
   - ☐ I exceeded much more this mini-game's quota of N citations.

6. Rate your satisfaction with your game play progress today. (Rate by choosing one answer on this scale: Very high, Somewhat high, Neutral, Somewhat low, Very low.)
7. What went well with the game today? _____
8. What did not go well with the game today? _____
9. With regard to what did not go well, how did you go about solving the problem? _____
10. Describe any other experiences, feelings, and ideas about BiblioBouts that occurred to you today. _____

Appendix B

Pre-Game Questionnaire for Students

Pre-game questionnaires were voluntarily completed by college students in selected classes from participating institutions during the evaluation of the alpha and beta versions of BiblioBouts. All questions were closed ended.

1. My BiblioBouts game alias is: _____
2. I am (choose 1 only):
   ☐ Male
   ☐ Female
3. I am a (choose 1 only):
   ☐ Freshman
   ☐ Sophomore
   ☐ Junior
   ☐ Senior
   ☐ Graduate student
4. Your library research knowledge and skills come from:
   ☐ High school teachers
   ☐ High school librarians
   ☐ Librarians at the public library
   ☐ College instructors
   ☐ College teaching assistants
   ☐ College librarians
   ☐ College peer advisors
   ☐ Parents
   ☐ Other members of your family
   ☐ Friends
   ☐ Figuring it out on your own

5. When you have difficulties conducting library research, how likely are you to: (Rate by choosing one answer on this scale: Very likely, Somewhat likely, Neutral, Somewhat unlikely, Very unlikely.)
   - ☐ Figure it out yourself
   - ☐ Ask your college instructor
   - ☐ Ask your teaching assistant
   - ☐ Ask a librarian at the college library
   - ☐ Ask a college peer advisor
   - ☐ Ask a parent
   - ☐ Ask other members of your family
   - ☐ Ask a friend
   - ☐ Ask a librarian at the public library
   - ☐ Ask your former high school teacher
   - ☐ Ask your former high school librarian
   - ☐ Search Google and the Web
   - ☐ Consult Wikipedia
   - ☐ Search the databases that the experts use

6. Rate how challenging you think it would be to perform these library research tasks today: (Rate by choosing one answer on this scale: Very challenging, Somewhat challenging, Neutral, Somewhat unchallenging, Very unchallenging.)
   - ☐ Using the databases that experts use to conduct library research
   - ☐ Thinking of keywords that will retrieve relevant information on my topic
   - ☐ Finding digital full-texts for the relevant citations I find
   - ☐ Downloading and saving relevant digital full-texts for my paper
   - ☐ Keeping track of all the citations, articles, websites, and so on, that I find online
   - ☐ Knowing where to find good information after I exhaust Google, Wikipedia, and the Web
   - ☐ Judging the information I find online with regard to its relevance to my selected topic
   - ☐ Judging the information I find online with regard to its scholarly nature
   - ☐ Judging the information I find online with regard to its trustworthiness
   - ☐ Choosing a particular topic for my paper
   - ☐ Choosing the best sources on my topic for my paper
   - ☐ Conducting library research in a structured, step-by-step approach

7. Rate how well you think you would perform these library research tasks today: (The same scale and answers as for question #6 are used here.)

8. Rate how confident you think you would be performing these library research tasks today: (The same scale and answers as for question #6 are used here.)

9. Rate yourself with respect to playing an online game to learn about conducting library research at the college level: (Rate by choosing one answer on this scale: Very high, Somewhat high, Neutral, Somewhat low, Very low.)
   - ☐ Your interest
   - ☐ Your curiosity
   - ☐ Your motivation
   - ☐ Your perseverance
   - ☐ Your desire to receive the highest grades on assignments requiring library research
   - ☐ Your desire to be the best at everything in college

Appendix C

Post-Game Questionnaire for Students

Post-game questionnaires were voluntarily completed by college students in selected classes from participating institutions during the evaluation of the alpha and beta versions of BiblioBouts. Under closed-ended questions are possible answers; after open-ended questions are lines indicating spaces where students entered their answers.

1. My BiblioBouts game alias is: _____
2. I am (choose 1 only):
   ☐ Male
   ☐ Female
3. I am a (choose 1 only):
   ☐ Freshman
   ☐ Sophomore
   ☐ Junior
   ☐ Senior
   ☐ Graduate student
4. When you answer this question, take into consideration your experience playing BiblioBouts. The next time you have difficulties conducting library research, how likely are you to: (Rate by choosing one answer on this scale: Very likely, Somewhat likely, Neutral, Somewhat unlikely, Very unlikely.)
   ☐ Figure it out yourself
   ☐ Ask your college instructor
   ☐ Ask your teaching assistant
   ☐ Ask a librarian at the college library
   ☐ Ask a college peer advisor
   ☐ Ask a parent

☐ Ask other members of your family
☐ Ask a friend
☐ Ask a librarian at the public library
☐ Ask your former high school teacher
☐ Ask your former high school librarian
☐ Search Google and the Web
☐ Consult Wikipedia
☐ Search the databases that the experts use

5. Taking into consideration your experience playing BiblioBouts, rate how challenging you think it would be to perform these library research tasks today: (The same scale and answers as for question #6 in the pre-game questionnaire are used here.)

6. Taking into consideration your experience playing BiblioBouts, rate how confident you think you would be performing these library research tasks today: (The same scale and answers as for question #6 in the pre-game questionnaire are used here.)

7. Taking into consideration your experience playing BiblioBouts, rate how confident you think you would be performing these library research tasks today: (The same scale and answers as for question #6 in the pre-game questionnaire are used here.)

8. With the experience of playing BiblioBouts to learn about library research in mind, rate yourself with respect to learning more about conducting library research at the college level: (The same scale and answers as for question #9 in the pre-game questionnaire are used here.)

9. Rate yourself with respect to playing BiblioBouts to learn about conducting library research at the college level: (The same scale and answers as for question #9 in the pre-game questionnaire are used here.)

10. The one major improvement to BiblioBouts that I would make is:

Appendix D

Focus Group Interview Questions for Students

College students in selected classes from participating institutions volunteered to participate in focus group interviews. The questions that focus group interview participants answered differed depending on which version of BiblioBouts players used—alpha or beta versions. The former questions (left column of table D.1) were oriented toward improving BiblioBouts because it was still under development. The latter questions (right column of table D.1) were oriented toward the benefits of playing the BiblioBouts game. All focus group interview questions were open ended, and most included probes to elicit details from participants.

Table D.1. Focus Group Questions

Focus Group Questions (Alpha Version)	Focus Group Questions (Beta Versions)
How adequately did we (instructor, librarians, researchers) prepare you for playing BiblioBouts?	Not used.
What did you learn from playing BiblioBouts?	What do you think BiblioBouts is all about?
Not used.	Do you think you completed your assignment differently as a result of playing BiblioBouts? Tell us what you did differently and did the same.
What did you learn from playing BiblioBouts that you will apply to your course work in the future or to your own personal research?	Tell us something you learned as a result of playing BiblioBouts that you did not know before.
Would you rather research a course assignment on your own or play BiblioBouts while researching the assignment? Why?	Not used.
Not used.	Which part of the game do you think you will have a chance to apply to your future class assignments? How do you think you will apply it?
Not used.	If we were to rewind the clock so that you could play BiblioBouts again, what would you do differently? Why?
BiblioBouts is made up of several mini-games. Put these mini-games together and the result is a step-by-step approach to conducting library research. Do you think that playing BiblioBouts was an effective way to learn about this step-by-step approach? Why or why not?	How would you describe BiblioBouts to another student? What are some adjectives that you would use to describe BiblioBouts?
How would you improve BiblioBouts?	What would you change about BiblioBouts? How and why would you change it?
Are online games like BiblioBouts the best way to learn about doing library research? Why or why not?	Not used.
What other library-based tasks do you think would be appropriate to learn by playing games?	What other aspects about using the library and its resources would you like to know more about? Would you like to play a game to learn about this? Why or why not?
Is there anything you would like to add?	Is there anything you would like to add?

Appendix E
Follow-Up Interview Questions for Students

Four or more months after University of Michigan students from selected classes played BiblioBouts, the BiblioBouts team contacted them via e-mail and invited them to follow-up interviews. Interviews were conducted via on-line chat; all questions were open ended, and most included probes to elicit details from participants.

1. Currently, when you do a research assignment, where do you start?
2. When you look at search results, how do you decide which are the best ones?
3. For scholarly sources, what library databases do you use? How did you learn about [insert database name(s)]?
4. Since playing BiblioBouts, have you had an assignment that required you to write a bibliography? Tell me about it.
5. When you did the assignment, what did you remember about playing BiblioBouts?
6. Was using Zotero helpful? Why or why not?
7. Tell me what you remember about the steps of the process of playing BiblioBouts. What do you remember about the criteria used in the Rating bout?
8. Can you tell me about any other things you learned from BiblioBouts?
9. Do you feel that you use the step-by-step process for conducting library research that was used in BiblioBouts?
10. When you're researching now, do you think back to one or more BiblioBouts mini-games? What reminds you of BiblioBouts? Why?
11. Do you think you do a better job researching now than you would have done without playing BiblioBouts? Why or why not?
12. Are there any ways that BiblioBouts could have been more helpful?

13. Since playing BiblioBouts, have you sought out any additional guidance about conducting library research? Tell me about it.
14. Is there any aspect of research you would like to get better at?
15. Looking back, did playing BiblioBouts change the way you search for information? How has it changed?

Appendix F

Game Logs

BiblioBouts recorded game play activity to logs in .csv-formatted data files that display in Microsoft Excel for export into Excel and other spreadsheet formats. Logs were available only to the instructor who created the game and to the BiblioBouts team. This appendix contains five tables that name and describe data elements in the Donor bout, Closer bout, T&R bout, Best Bibliography bout, and Best Bibliography citation logs.

Table F.1.   Donor Bout Log (Alpha and Beta 1.0 BiblioBouts Only)

Data Element	Description
Date/time	When the player donated this source
User name	The name of the player who donated this source
Donation ID	The unique number that BiblioBouts has assigned to this donated source
Citation	Zotero-supplied citation data for this donated source, including the player's manual edits to Zotero's automatically generated citations
Repository	The repository from which this donated source came; blank when Zotero cannot automatically generate the repository
URL	Zotero-supplied URL for this source; blank when Zotero cannot automatically detect the URL

Table F.2.   Closer Bout Log

Data Element	Description
Date/time	When the player closed this source
User name	The name of the player who closed this source
Donation ID	The unique number that BiblioBouts originally assigned to this donated source
Citation	Zotero-supplied citation data for this closed source, including the player's manual edits to Zotero's automatically generated citations
Repository	The repository from which this donated source came; blank when Zotero cannot automatically generate the repository
URL	Zotero-supplied URL for this source; blank when Zotero cannot automatically detect the URL

Table F.3. T&R Bout Log

Data Element	Description
Date/time	When the player evaluated this source
User name	The name of the player who evaluated this source
Donation ID	The unique number that BiblioBouts originally assigned to this donated source
Citation	Zotero-supplied citation data for this donated source, including the player's manual edits to Zotero's automatically generated citations
URL	Zotero-supplied URL for this source; blank when Zotero cannot automatically detect the URL
Full-text check	A yes or no value, depending on whether the player determined a full-text was available for the closed source
User continued?	A yes or no value, depending on whether the player decided to continue evaluating the source after conducting the full-text check (If the player did not continue, there are no values in the remaining cells for this source's T&R bout log entry.)
Source type	The player's "what is this source?" selection based on a pull-down menu bearing selections such as blog, book, conference proceedings
Publisher type	The player's "who published it?" selection based on a pull-down menu bearing selections such as individual person, commercial business, nonprofit organization
Big ideas	The big ideas the player assigned to the closed source
Citation	The player's yes, no, or maybe response to BiblioBouts' question about the completeness of this source's citation
Credibility: expert	The credibility rating from 0 to 100 percent that the player gave to this source in response to BiblioBouts' question about the author's expertise
Credibility: trustworthiness	The credibility rating from 0 to 100 percent that the player gave to this source in response to BiblioBouts' question about the source's trustworthiness
Credibility: scholarliness	The credibility rating from 0 to 100 percent that the player gave to this source in response to BiblioBouts' question about the source's scholarly nature
Credibility explanation	A yes or no value, depending on whether the player gave a reason for his/her credibility ratings
Credibility explanation	The reason the player gave for his/her credibility ratings
Relevance: usefulness	The relevance rating from 0 to 100 percent that the player gave to this source in response to BiblioBouts' question about the source's usefulness
Relevance: accuracy	The relevance rating from 0 to 100 percent that the player gave to this source in response to BiblioBouts' question about the source's accuracy
Relevance: good enough	The relevance rating from 0 to 100 percent that the player gave to this source in response to BiblioBouts' question about whether the source is good enough for course work
Relevance explanation	A yes or no value, depending on whether the player gave a reason for his/her relevance ratings
Relevance explanation	The reason the player gave for his/her relevance ratings

Table F.4. Best Bibliography Bout Log

Data Element	Description
Date/time	When the player chose this source for his/her best bibliography
User name	The name of the player who chose this source for his/her best bibliography
Topic	The topic of this player's final paper
Topic description	More description on the topic of this player's final paper
Donation ID	The unique number that BiblioBouts originally assigned to this donated source
Citation	Zotero-supplied citation data for this donated source, including the player's manual edits to Zotero's automatically generated citations
URL	Zotero-supplied URL for this source; blank when Zotero cannot automatically detect the URL
Topic big ideas	Three big ideas this player's paper will discuss
Source big ideas	Big ideas that the majority of players assigned to this source in the T&R bout
Average credibility: expertise	The average credibility rating from 0 to 100 percent that players gave to this source in the T&R bout in response to its question about the author's expertise
Average credibility: trustworthiness	The average credibility rating from 0 to 100 percent that players gave to this source in the T&R bout in response to its question about the source's trustworthiness
Average credibility: scholarliness	The average credibility rating from 0 to 100 percent that players gave to this source in the T&R bout in response to its question about the source's scholarly nature
Average credibility	The average of all three credibility ratings (expertise, trustworthiness, scholarliness)
Average relevance: usefulness	The average relevance rating from 0 to 100 percent that players gave to this source in the T&R bout in response to its question about the source's usefulness
Average relevance: accuracy	The average relevance rating from 0 to 100 percent that players gave to this source in the T&R bout in response to its question about the source's accuracy
Average relevance: good enough	The average relevance rating from 0 to 100 percent that players gave to this source in the T&R bout in response to its question about whether the source is good enough for course work

Table F.5. Best Bibliography Citations Log

Data Element	Description
User name	The name of the player whose citation record is documented in the subsequent cells of this row
Alias	The player's alias
Paper topic	The topic of the player's final paper
Donor	The number of sources the player saved to Zotero
Closer	The number of sources the player closed in the Closer bout
T&R	The number of sources the player evaluated in the T&R bout
Best bib	The number of sources the player chose for his/her best bibliography in the Best Bibliography bout
Source #1 cited	The number of times opponents chose this player's first-closed source in their best bibliographies
Source #1 URL	Zotero-supplied URL; blank when Zotero cannot automatically detect the URL
Citation #1	Zotero-supplied citation data for this player's first-closed source, including the player's manual edits to Zotero's automatically generated citations
Donation ID #1	The unique number that BiblioBouts assigned to this closed source in the Closer bout
Credibility #1	The average of all players' credibility ratings for this source
Relevance #1	The average of all players' relevance ratings for this source
Source #N cited	(The log repeats the previous six elements for the player's subsequent closed sources)

Appendix G

Personal Interview Questions for Instructors

Instructors from all participating and selected nonparticipating institutions volunteered to participate in post-game personal interviews that were conducted in person or over the phone by BiblioBouts team members. All questions were open ended, and most included probes to elicit details from interviewees.

1. After incorporating the BiblioBouts game into [insert name of course], did you change the course's learning objectives? What changed and why?
2. When you graded students' assignments, how important were their cited sources? How did you evaluate these sources, and what impact did your evaluation have on their grade?
3. What do you think students learned as a result of playing BiblioBouts?
4. How you think students' assignments changed as a result of playing BiblioBouts? What impact do you think BiblioBouts had on their completed assignments?
5. What other changes would you like to see in students' assignments? (These do not have to be changes related to playing BiblioBouts.)
6. How did you get involved in BiblioBouts game play?
7. Are you interested in incorporating BiblioBouts into future courses? Why or why not? If you decide to incorporate BiblioBouts into a future course, will you change anything about the course, the assignment, or your grading of the assignment?
8. Would you recommend BiblioBouts to other instructors? When you make such a recommendation, how will you describe BiblioBouts to other instructors?
9. Is there anything you would like to add?

Appendix H

Personal Interview Questions for Library Liaisons

Library liaisons from participating institutions volunteered to participate in post-game personal interviews that were conducted over the phone by BiblioBouts team members. All questions were open ended, and most included probes to elicit details from interviewees.

1. Before your involvement with BiblioBouts, what were your expectations about teaching students information literacy skills and concepts? How have your expectations changed as a result of your experience with BiblioBouts?
2. What do you think students learned as a result of playing BiblioBouts?
3. What other information literacy skills and concepts do you think students want or need to learn about?
4. Describe the support you gave instructors before, during, and after the BiblioBouts game play started. What worked well, and what didn't? In the future, what would you do differently and why?
5. Describe the instruction and support you gave students before, during, and after the BiblioBouts game play started. What worked well, and what didn't? In the future, what would you do differently and why?
6. Describe how you prepared your librarian colleagues to help students playing BiblioBouts. What worked well, and what didn't? In the future, what would you do differently and why?
7. What would you change about BiblioBouts? How and why would you change it?
8. Would you recommend BiblioBouts to librarians at other institutions? If so, how would you describe BiblioBouts to them?
9. Is there anything you would like to add?

Bibliography

Allen, Maryellen. 2008. "Promoting Critical Thinking Skills in Online Information Literacy Instruction Using a Constructivist Approach." *College and Undergraduate Libraries* 15, nos. 1/2: 21–38.

American Association of School Librarians (AASL). 2007. *Standards for the 21st-Century Learner.* Chicago: AASL. Available at http://www.ala.org/aasl/sites/ala.org.aasl/files/content/guidelinesandstandards/learningstandards/AASL_Learning Standards.pdf.

American Association of School Librarians (AASL) and Association for Educational Communications and Technology (AECT). 1998. *Information Power: Building Partnerships for Learning.* Chicago: American Library Association.

American Library Association (ALA). 1989. *Presidential Committee on Information Literacy: Final Report.* Washington, DC: ALA. Available at www.ala.org/ala/mgrps/divs/acrl/publications/whitepapers/presidential.cfm.

———. 2000. *Information Literacy Competency Standards for Higher Education.* Washington, DC: ALA. Available at http://www.ala.org/acrl/standards/information literacycompetency.

Anderson, Karen, and Frances A. May. 2010. "Does the Method of Instruction Matter? An Experimental Examination of Information Literacy Instruction in the Online, Blended, and Face-to-Face Classrooms." *Journal of Academic Librarianship* 36, no. 6: 495–500.

Association of College and Research Libraries (ACRL). 2000. *Information Literacy Competency Standards for Higher Education.* San Antonio, TX: ACRL. Available at www.ala.org/ala/mgrps/divs/acrl/standards/informationliteracycompetency.cfm.

Armstrong, Annie R. 2009. "Student Perceptions of Federated Searching vs. Single Database Searching." *Reference Services Review* 37, no. 3: 291–303.

Armstrong, Annie R., and Helen Georgas. 2006. "Using Interactive Technology to Teach Information Literacy Concepts to Undergraduate Students." *Reference Services Review* 34, no. 4: 491–97.

Badke, William. 2008. "Ten Reasons to Teach Information Literacy for Credit." *Online* 32, no. 6: 47–49.

Baker, Bo, Caitlin Shanley, and Lane Wilkinson. 2011. "Nightmare on Vine Street: Librarians, Zombies, and Information Literacy." In *Let the Games Begin! Engaging Students with Field-Tested Interactive Information Literacy Instruction*, edited by Theresa R. McDevitt, 30–32. New York: Neal-Schuman.

Bateman, Judith. 1999. "Modeling the Importance of End-User Relevance Criteria." *Proceedings of the 62nd ASIS Annual Meeting* 36: 396–406.

Bates, Marcia J. 1989. "The Design of Browsing and Berrypicking Techniques for the Online Search Interface." *Online Review* 13, no. 5: 407–24.

Battles, Jason, Valerie Glenn, and Lindley Shedd. 2011. "Rethinking the Library Game: Creating an Alternate Reality with Social Media." *Journal of Web Librarianship* 5, no. 2: 114–31.

Beck, Donna, Rachel Callison, John Fudrow, and Dan Hood. 2008. "Your Library Instruction Is in Another Castle: Developing Information Literacy Based Videogames at Carnegie Mellon University." In *Gaming in Academic Libraries: Collections, Marketing, and Information Literacy*, edited by Amy Harris and Scott E. Rice, 135–48. Chicago: Association of College and Research Libraries.

Becker, Nancy J. 2003. "Google in Perspective: Understanding and Enhancing Student Search Skills." *New Review of Academic Librarianship* 9, no. 1: 84–100.

Behrens, Shirley J. 1994. "A Conceptual Analysis and Historical Overview of Information Literacy." *College and Research Libraries* 55, no. 4: 309–22.

Beile, Penny M. 2003. "Effectiveness of Course-Integrated and Repeated Library Instruction on Library Skills of Education Students." *Journal of Educational Media and Library Sciences* 40, no. 3: 271–77.

Belkin, Nicholas J. 1980. "Anomalous States of Knowledge as a Basis for Information Retrieval." *Canadian Journal of Information Science* 5: 133–43.

Bell, Steven. 2011. "Bridging the Information Literacy Communication Gap." *Library Issues* 32, no. 2. Available at http://projectinfolit.org/pdfs/PIL_issue_11_2011.pdf.

"Bibliography-Building Game Exercise." 2011. Available at http://cra-w.org/Portals/Pdfs/CRAWBibliographyGame.pdf.

Bobish, Greg. 2011. "Participation and Pedagogy: Connecting the Social Web to ACRL Learning Outcomes." *Journal of Academic Librarianship* 37, no. 1: 54–63.

Boff, Colleen, and Kristin Johnson. 2002. "The Library and First-Year Experience Courses: A Nationwide Study." *Reference Services Review* 30, no. 4: 277–87.

Branston, Christy. 2006. "Game Studies to Bibliographic Gaming: Libraries Tap into the Video Game Culture." *Bulletin of the American Society for Information Science and Technology* 32, no. 4: 24–29.

Brathwaite, Brenda, and Ian Schreiber. 2009. *Challenges for Game Designers*. Boston: Course Technology.

Breivik, Patricia Senn, and Dan L. Jones. 1993. "Information Literacy: Liberal Education for the Information Age." *Liberal Education* 79, no. 1: 24–29.

Broussard, Mary J. Snyder. 2011a. "Digital Games in Academic Libraries: A Review of Games and Suggested Best Practices." *Reference Services Review* 40, no. 1: 75–89.

———. 2011b. "Goblin Threat." In *Let the Games Begin! Engaging Students with Field-Tested Interactive Information Literacy Instruction*, edited by Theresa R. McDevitt, 132–33. New York: Neal-Schuman.

———. 2011c. "It's Alive!" In *Let the Games Begin! Engaging Students with Field-Tested Interactive Information Literacy Instruction*, edited by Theresa R. McDevitt, 25–27. New York: Neal-Schuman.

———. 2013. "Secret Agents in the Library: Integrating Virtual and Physical Games in a Small Academic Library." *College and Undergraduate Libraries* 17, no. 1: 20–30.

Broussard, Mary J. Snyder, and Jessica Urich Oberlin. 2011. "Using Online Games to Fight Plagiarism: A Spoonful of Sugar Helps the Medicine Go Down." *Indiana Libraries* 30, no. 1: 28–39.

Brown, Ann, Paola Ceccarini, and Cathy Eisenhower. 2007. "Muckrakers: Engaging Students in the Research Process through an Online Game." In *Proceedings of the Thirteenth National Conference of the Association of College and Research Libraries*, edited by Hugh A. Thompson, 226–36. Chicago: Association of College and Research Libraries.

Bruce, Christine. 2000. "Information Literacy Research: Dimensions of the Emerging Collective Consciousness." *Australian Academic and Research Libraries* 31, no. 2: 91–109.

Bruce, Christine, Sylvia Edwards, and Mandy Lupton. 2006. "Six Frames of Information Literacy Education: A Conceptual Framework for Interpreting the Relationships between Theory and Practice." *ITALICS* 5, no. 1: 1–18.

Chaplin, Heather, and Aaron Ruby. 2006. *Smartbomb: The Quest for Art, Entertainment and Big Bucks in the Videogame Revolution.* Chapel Hill, NC: Algonquin Books.

Chen, Sin-Liang, and James Patrick Williams. 2009. "Use of Multi-Modal Media and Tools in an Online Information Literacy Course: College Students' Attitudes and Perceptions." *Journal of Academic Librarianship* 35, no. 1: 14–24.

Chung, Jin Soon, and Delia Neuman. 2007. "High School Students' Information Seeking and Use for Class Projects." *Journal of the American Society for Information Science and Technology* 58, no. 10: 1503–17.

Churkovich, M., and Christine Oughtred. 2002. "Can an Online Tutorial Pass the Test for Library Instruction? An Evaluation and Comparison of Library Skills Instruction Methods for First Year Students at Deakin University." *Australian Academic and Research Libraries* 33, no. 1: 25–38.

Clyde, Jerremie, and Chris Thomas. 2008. "Building an Information Literacy First-Person Shooter." *Reference Services Review* 36, no. 4: 366–80.

Colón-Aguirre, Mónica, and Rachel A. Fleming-May. 2012. "You Just Type in What You Are Looking For: Undergraduates' Use of Library Resources vs. Wikipedia." *Journal of Academic Librarianship* 38, no. 6: 391–99.

Common Core State Standards Initiative (CCSSI). 2010. "Common Core State Standards for English Language Arts and Literacy in History/Social Studies, Science, and Technical Subjects." Available at http://www.corestandards.org/assets/CCSSI_ELA%20Standards.pdf.

Cooke, Rachel, and Danielle Rosenthal. 2011. "Students Use More Books after Library Instruction: An Analysis of Undergraduate Paper Citations." *College and Research Libraries* 72, no. 4: 332–43.

Costello, Barbara, Robert Lenholt, and Judson Stryker. 2004. "Using Blackboard in Library Instruction: Addressing the Learning Styles of Generations X and Y." *Journal of Academic Librarianship* 30, no. 6: 452–60.

Crowston, Kevin, and Barbara H. Kwasnik. 2004. "A Framework for Creating a Faceted Classification for Genres: Addressing Issues of Multidimensionality." Syracuse: Syracuse University Library. Available at http://surface.syr.edu/cgi/viewcontent.cgi?article=1134&context=istpub.

Csíkszentmihályi, Mihály. 1975. *Beyond Boredom and Anxiety*. San Francisco, CA: Jossey-Bass.

Curtis, Susan Chandler. 2000. "Listening to Generation X." *Journal of Educational Media and Library Science* 38, no. 2: 122–32.

D'Angelo, Barbara J., and Barry M. Maid. 2004. "Moving beyond Definitions: Implementing Information Literacy across Curriculum." *Journal of Academic Librarianship* 30, no. 3: 212–17.

Daugherty, Alice L., and Michael F. Russo. 2011. "An Assessment of the Lasting Effects of a Stand-Alone Information Literacy Course: The Students' Perspective." *Journal of Academic Librarianship* 37, no. 4: 319–26.

Donald, Jeremy. 2008. "The 'Blood on the Stacks' ARG: Immersive Marketing Meets Library New Student Orientation." In *Gaming in Academic Libraries: Collections, Marketing, and Information Literacy*, edited by Amy Harris and Scott E. Rice, 189–211. Chicago: Association of College and Research Libraries.

Doshi, Ameet. 2006. "How Gaming Could Improve Information Literacy." *Computers in Libraries* 26, no. 5: 14–17.

Eisenberg, Michael, Carrie A. Lowe, and Kathleen L. Spitzer. 2004. *Information Literacy: Essential Skills for the Information Age*. 2nd ed. Westport, CT: Libraries Unlimited.

Eisenberg, Michael B., and Robert E. Berkowitz. 1988. *Curriculum Initiative: An Agenda and Strategy for Library Media Programs*. Norwood, NJ: Ablex.

———. 2003. *The Definitive Big 6 Workshop Handbook*. 3rd ed. Worthington, OH: Linworth Publishing.

Ellis, David. 1989. "A Behavioural Approach to Information Retrieval System Design." *Journal of Documentation* 45, no. 3: 171–212.

Farmer, Sandy. 2010. "Gaming 2.0." *American Libraries* 41, nos. 11/12: 32–34.

Fast, Karl V., and D. Grant Campbell. 2004. "'I Still Like Google': University Student Perceptions of Searching OPACs and the Web." *Proceedings of the ASIS Annual Meeting 2004* 41: 138–46.

Fitzgerald, Mary Ann, and Chad Galloway. 2001. "Relevance Judging, Evaluation, and Decision Making in Virtual Libraries: A Descriptive Study." *Journal of the American Society for Information Science and Technology* 52, no. 12: 989–1010.

Fitzpatrick, Maureen J., and Yvonne Nalani Meulemans. 2011. "Assessing an Information Literacy Assignment and Workshop Using a Quasi-Experimental Design." *College Teaching* 59, no. 4: 142–49.

Flanagan, Mary, and Peter Carini. 2012. "How Games Can Help Us Access and Understand Archival Images." *American Archivist* 75, no. 2: 514–37.

Flanagin, Andrew J., and Miriam J. Metzger. 2010. *Kids and Credibility: An Empirical Examination of Youth, Digital Media Use, and Information Credibility.* Cambridge, MA: MIT Press.

Fogg, B. J. 2003. *Persuasive Technology: Using Computers to Change What We Think and Do.* San Francisco, CA: Morgan Kaufmann.

Fullerton, Tracy. 2008. *Game Design Workshop: A Playcentric Approach to Creating Innovative Games.* Burlington, MA: Morgan Kaufmann.

Gallegos, Bee, and Tammy Allgood. 2008. "The Fletcher Library Game Project." In *Gaming in Academic Libraries*: *Collections, Marketing, and Information Literacy*, edited by Amy Harris and Scott E. Rice, 149–63. Chicago: Association of College and Research Libraries.

Gallegos, Bee, Tammy Allgood, and Karen Grondin. 2007. "Quarantined: The Fletcher Library Game Project." In *Uncharted Waters: Tapping the Depths of Our Community to Enhance Learning: Thirty-Fifth National LOEX Library Instruction Conference Proceedings, San Diego, California, May 3–5, 2007*, edited by Brad Seitz et al., 133–37. Ypsilanti, MI: LOEX Press.

Galloway, Beth. 2009. *Game On! Gaming at the Library.* New York: Neal-Schuman.

Garfield, Eugene. 1979. "2001: An Information Society?" *Journal of Information Science* 1, no. 4: 209–15.

Gasser, Uri, Sandra Cortesi, Momin Malik, and Ashley Lee. 2012. *Youth and Digital Media: From Credibility to Information Quality.* Cambridge, MA: Harvard University, Berkman Center for Internet and Society. Available at http://papers.ssrn.com/sol3/papers.cfm?abstract_id=2005272.

Gee, James Paul. 2003. *What Video Games Have to Teach Us about Learning and Literacy.* New York: Palgrave.

———. 2005. *Why Video Games Are Good for Your Soul.* Melbourne, Australia: Common Ground.

Gilton, Donna L. 2004. "Information Literary Instruction: A History in Context." University of Rhode Island. Available at http://www.uri.edu/artsci/lsc/Faculty/gilton/InformationLiteracyInstruction-AHistoryinContext.htm.

Gonzalez, Sara Russell, Valrie Davis, Chelsea Dinsmore, Cynthia Frey, Carrie Newsom, and Laurie Taylor. 2008. "Bioterrorism at UF: Exploring and Developing a Library Instruction Game for New Students." In *Gaming in Academic Libraries*: *Collections, Marketing, and Information Literacy*, edited by Amy Harris and Scott E. Rice, 164–74. Chicago: Association of College and Research Libraries.

Gordon, Carol. 2000. "The Effects of Concept Mapping on the Searching Behavior of Tenth Grade Students." *School Library Media Research* 3: 1–18.

Gross, Melissa, and Don Latham. 2007. "Attaining Information Literacy: An Investigation of the Relationship between Skill Level, Self-Estimates of Skill, and Library Anxiety." *Library and Information Science Research* 29, no. 3: 332–53.

Gumulak, Sabina, and Sheila Webber. 2011. "Playing Video Games: Learning and Information Literacy." *Aslib Proceedings* 63, nos. 2/3: 241–55.

Hardesty, Larry. 1995. "Faculty Culture and Bibliographic Instruction: An Exploratory Analysis." *Library Trends* 44, no. 2: 39–67.

Hargittai, Eszter, Lindsay Fullerton, Ericka Menchen-Trevino, and Kristin Yates Thomas. 2010. "Trust Online: Young Adults' Evaluation of Web Content." *International Journal of Communication* 4: 468–94.

Harris, Amy, and Scott E. Rice. 2008. *Gaming in Academic Libraries: Collections, Marketing, and Information Literacy.* Chicago: Association of College and Research Libraries.

Hays, Robert T. 2005. *The Effectiveness of Instructional Games: A Literature Review and Discussion.* Orlando, FL: Naval Air Warfare Center. Available at http://www.dtic.mil/cgi-bin/GetTRDoc?AD=ADA441935.

Head, Allison J. 2007. "How Do Students Conduct Academic Research?" *First Monday* 12, no. 8. Available at http://firstmonday.org/issues/issue12_8/head/index.html.

Head, Allison J., and Michael B. Eisenberg. 2010. "How Today's College Students Use Wikipedia for Course-Related Research" *First Monday* 15, no. 3. Available at http://firstmonday.org/htbin/cgiwrap/bin/ojs/index.php/fm/article/view/2830/2476.

Henderson, David E. 2010. "A Chemical Instrumentation Game for Teaching Critical Thinking and Information Literacy in Instrumental Analysis Courses." *Journal of Chemical Education* 87, no. 4: 412–15.

Herring, J. 2011. *Improving Students' Web Use and Information Literacy.* London: Facet Publishing.

Hohmann, Rebecca. 2011. "Jane McGonigal and the NYPL Present 'Find the Future: The Game.'" New York Public Library. Available at http://www.nypl.org/blog/2011/04/01/jane-mcgonigal-and-nypl-present-find-future-game.

Holder, Sara. 2010. "History and Evolution of Credit IL Courses in Higher Education." In *Best Practices for Credit-Bearing Information Literacy Courses*, edited by Christopher V. Hollister, 1–9. Chicago: Association of College and Research Libraries.

Hovland, Carl I., Irving L. Janis, and Harold H. Kelley. 1953. *Communication and Persuasion: Psychological Studies of Opinion Change.* New Haven, CT: Yale University Press.

Hrycaj, Paul, and Michael Russo. 2007. "Reflections on Surveys of Faculty Attitudes toward Collaboration with Librarians." *Journal of Academic Librarianship* 33, no. 6: 692–96.

International Society for Technology in Education (ISTE). 2007. "National Educational Technology Standards for Students." Available at http://www.iste.org/standards/nets-for-students.

Jacobson, Trudi E., and Beth L. Mark. 2000. "Separating Wheat from Chaff: Helping First-Year Students Become Information Savvy." *Journal of General Education* 49, no. 4: 256–78.

Johnson, Catherine, Thomas Arendall, Michael Shochet, and April Duncan. 2010. "Creating a Combination IL and English Composition Course in a College Setting." In *Best Practices for Credit-Bearing Information Literacy Courses*, edited by Christopher V. Hollister, 53–63. Chicago: Association of College and Research Libraries.

Johnson, Marggeaux, and Sara Russell Gonzalez. 2010. "Creating a Credit IL Course for Science Students." In *Best Practices for Credit-Bearing Information Literacy Courses*, edited by Christopher V. Hollister, 93–108. Chicago: Association of College and Research Libraries.

Johnson, Steven. 2006. *Everything Bad Is Good for You: How Today's Popular Culture Is Actually Making Us Smarter.* New York: Riverhead Books.

Johnston, Bill, and Sheila Webber. 2003. "Information Literacy in Higher Education: A Review and Case Study." *Studies in Higher Education* 28, no. 3: 335–52.

Julien, Heidi, and Susan Barker. 2009. "How High-School Students Find and Evaluate Scientific Information: A Basis for Information Literacy Skills Development." *Library and Information Science Research* 31, no. 1: 12–17.

Ke, Fengfeng. 2009. "A Qualitative Meta-Analysis of Computer Games as Learning Tools." *Handbook of Research on Effective Electronic Gaming in Education* 1: 1–32.

Kerr, Paulette A. 2010. "Conceptions and Practice of Information Literacy in Academic Libraries: Espoused Theories and Theories-in-Use." PhD diss., Rutgers University, New Brunswick, NJ.

Kim, Kyung-Sun, and Sei-Ching Joanna Sin. 2011. "Selecting Quality Sources: Bridging the Gap between the Perception and Use of Information Sources." *Journal of Information Science* 37, no. 2: 178–88.

Kirk, Thomas. 1974. "Problems in Library Instruction in Four-Year Colleges." In *Educating the Library User*, edited by John Lubans Jr., 83–103. New York: R. R. Bowker.

Kirriemuir, John. 2002. "Video Gaming, Education and Digital Learning Technologies." *D-Lib Magazine* 8, no. 2: 25–32.

———. 2008. "Teaching Information Literacy through Digital Games." In *Information Literacy Meets Library 2.0*, edited by Peter Godwin and Jo Parker, 153–64. London: Facet Publishing.

Kolowich, Steve. 2011. "What Students Don't Know." *Inside Higher Education.* Available at http://www.insidehighered.com/news/2011/08//22.

Koster, Ralph. 2005. *A Theory of Fun for Game Design.* Scottsdale, AZ: Paraglyph Press.

Kuhlthau, Carol. 2004. *Seeking Meaning: A Process Approach to Library and Information Services.* 2nd ed. Westport, CT: Libraries Unlimited.

———. 2013. "Information Search Process." Available at http://comminfo.rutgers.edu/~kuhlthau/information_search_process.htm.

Leach, Guy J., and Tammy S. Sugarman. 2006. "Play to Win! Using Games in Library Instruction to Enhance Student Learning." *Research Strategies* 20, no. 3: 191–203.

Leeder, Chris, Karen Markey, and Elizabeth Yakel. 2012. "Developing a Faceted Taxonomy for Rating Student Bibliographies." *College and Research Libraries* 73, no. 2: 115–33.

Leeder, Chris, Victor Rosenberg, and Chuck Severance. 2011. "Integrating the Online BiblioBouts Game to Teach Information Literacy in Academic Classes." Available at http://www.slideshare.net/csev/educause-bibliobouts.

Lenhart, Amanda, Sydney Jones, and Alexandra Macgill. 2008. "Adults and Video Games." *PEW Internet Project Data Memo.* Available at http://www.pewinternet.org/Reports/2008/Adults-and-Video-Games.aspx.

Levine, Jenny. 2006a. "Gaming and Libraries: Intersection of Services." *Library Technology Reports* 42, no. 5.

———. 2006b. "Why Gaming?" *Library Technology Reports* 42, no. 5: 10–17.

———. 2008. "Gaming and Libraries Update: Broadening the Intersections." *Library Technology Reports* 44, no. 3: 10–17.

Library Orientation Exchange (LOEX). 2013. "Welcome." Eastern Michigan University. Available at http://www.emich.edu/public/loex.

Limberg, Louise. 1999. "Experiencing Information Seeking and Learning: A Study of the Interaction between Two Phenomena." *Information Research* 5, no. 1. Available at http://informationr.net/ir/5-1/paper68.html.

Lin, Shin-Jeng, and Nicholas J. Belkin. 2000. "Modeling Multiple Information Seeking Episodes." *Proceedings of the ASIS Annual Meeting* 37: 133–47.

Lloyd, Annemaree. 2005. "Information Literacy: Different Contexts, Different Concepts, Different Truths?" *Journal of Librarianship and Information Science* 37: 82–88.

Luo, Lili. 2010. "Web 2.0 Integration in Information Literacy Instruction: An Overview." *Journal of Academic Librarianship* 36, no. 1: 32–40.

Lupton, Mandy. 2002. "The Getting of Wisdom: Reflections of a Teaching Librarian." *Australian Academic and Research Libraries* 33, no. 2: 75–85.

Maglaughlin, Kelly L., and Diane Sonnenwald. 2002. "User Perspectives on Relevance Criteria: A Comparison among Relevant, Partially Relevant, and Not-Relevant Judgments." *Journal of the American Society for Information Science and Technology* 53, no. 2: 327–42.

Manuel, Kate, Susan E. Beck, and Molly Molloy. 2005. "An Ethnographic Study of Attitudes Influencing Faculty Collaboration in Library Instruction." *Reference Librarian* 43: 89–90.

Markey, Karen. 2007. "Twenty-Five Years of Research on End-User Searching: Research Findings." *Journal of the American Society for Information Science and Technology* 58, no. 8: 1071–81. Available at http://hdl.handle.net/2027.42/56093.

Markey, Karen, Chris Leeder, and Soo Young Rieh. 2012. "Through a Game Darkly: Student Experiences with the Technology of the Library Research Process." *Library Hi Tech* 30, no. 1: 12–34.

Markey, Karen, Chris Leeder, and Charles Taylor. 2012. "Playing Games to Improve the Quality of the Sources Students Cite in Their Papers." *Reference and User Services Quarterly* 52, no. 2: 123–35.

Markey, Karen, Soo Young Rieh, Victor Rosenberg, Fritz Swanson, Gregory R. Peters Jr., Brian Jennings, Chris Leeder, Beth St. Jean, Andrew Calvetti, and Meredith Raymond. 2010. *Building the Games Students Want to Play: BiblioBouts Project Interim Report #3.* Ann Arbor, MI: School of Information. Available at http://hdl.handle.net/2027.42/69157.

Markey, Karen, Soo Young Rieh, Victor Rosenberg, Fritz Swanson, Gregory R. Peters Jr., Brian Jennings, Xingxing Yao, and Beth St. Jean. 2009. *Building the*

Games Students Want to Play: BiblioBouts Project Interim Report #1. Ann Arbor, MI: School of Information. Available at http://hdl.handle.net/2027.42/62072.

Markey, Karen, Soo Young Rieh, Victor Rosenberg, Fritz Swanson, Gregory R. Peters Jr., Michele Wong, Brian Jennings, Chris Leeder, and Beth St. Jean. 2012. *Building the Games Students Want to Play: BiblioBouts Final Performance Review.* Ann Arbor, MI: School of Information. Available at http://hdl.handle. net/2027.42/97036.

Markey, Karen, Fritz Swanson, Andrea Jenkins, Brian J. Jennings, Beth St. Jean, Victor Rosenberg, Xingxing Yao, and Robert L. Frost. 2008a. "The Effectiveness of a Web-Based Board Game for Teaching Undergraduate Students Information Literacy Concepts and Skills." *D-Lib Magazine* 14, nos. 9/10. Available at http:// www.dlib.org/dlib/september08/markey/09markey.html.

———. 2008b. *Engaging Undergraduates in Research through a Storytelling and Gaming Strategy: Final Report to the Delmas Foundation.* Ann Arbor, MI: School of Information. Available at http://hdl.handle.net/2027.42/58630.

Martin, Justine, and Robin Ewing. 2008. "Power Up! Using Digital Gaming Techniques to Enhance Library Instruction." *Internet Reference Services Quarterly* 13, no. 2/3: 209–25.

Mayer, Richard E. 2011. "Multimedia Learning and Games." In *Computer Games and Instruction*, edited by Sigmund Tobias and J. D. Fletcher, 281–305. Charlotte, NC: Information Age Publishing.

McCabe, Jennifer, and Steven Wise. 2009. "It's All Fun and Games until Someone Learns Something: Assessing the Learning Outcomes of Two Educational Games." *Evidence Based Library and Information Practice* 4, no. 4: 6–23.

McCarthy, Constance. 1985. "The Faculty Problem." *Journal of Academic Librarianship* 11, no. 3: 142–45.

McDevitt, Theresa R., ed. 2011. *Let the Games Begin! Engaging Students with Field-Tested Interactive Information Literacy Instruction.* New York: Neal-Schuman.

McGuinness, Claire. 2006. "What Faculty Think: Exploring the Barriers to Information Literacy Development in Undergraduate Education." *Journal of Academic Librarianship* 32, no. 6: 573–82.

Mellon, Constance. 1986. "Library Anxiety: A Grounded Theory and Its Development." *College and Research Libraries* 47, no. 2: 160–65.

Meola, Marc. 2004. "Chucking the Checklist: A Contextual Approach to Teaching Undergraduates Web-Site Evaluation." *portal: Libraries and the Academy* 4, no. 3: 331–44.

Mery, Yvonne, Rebecca Blakiston, Elizabeth Kline, Leslie Sult, and Michael M. Brewer. 2010. "Developing an Online Credit IL Course for a Freshman Writing Program in a University Setting." In *Best Practices for Credit-Bearing Information Literacy Courses*, edited by Christopher V. Hollister, 77–92. Chicago: Association of College and Research Libraries.

Mery, Yvonne, Jill Newby, and Ke Peng. 2012. "Why One-Shot Information Literacy Sessions Are Not the Future of Instruction: A Case for Online Credit Courses." *College and Research Libraries* 73, no. 4: 366–77.

Metzger, Miriam. J. 2007. "Making Sense of Credibility on the Web: Models for Evaluating Online Information and Recommendations for Future Research." *Journal of the American Society for Information Science and Technology* 58, no. 13: 2078–91.

Metzger, Miriam J., Andrew J. Flanagin, and Ryan B. Medders. 2010. "Social and Heuristic Approaches to Credibility Evaluation Online." *Journal of Communication* 60, no. 3: 413–39.

Michel, Stephanie. 2001. "'What Do They Really Think?' Assessing Student and Faculty Perspectives of a Web-Based Tutorial to Library Research." *College and Research Libraries* 62: 317–32.

Middleton, Anne. 2005. "An Attempt to Quantify the Quality of Student Bibliographies." *Performance Measurement and Metrics* 6, no. 1: 7–18.

Mokhtar, Intan Azura, Shaheen Majid, and Schubert Foo. 2008. "Information Literacy Education: Applications of Mediated Learning and Multiple Intelligences." *Library and Information Science Research* 30, no. 3: 195–206.

National Leadership Council for Liberal Education and America's Promise (NLCLEAP). 2007. *College Learning for the New Global Century.* Washington, DC: Association of American Colleges and Universities.

Neiburger, Eli. 2009. *Gamers . . . in the Library? The Why, What, and How of Videogame Tournaments for All Ages.* Chicago: American Library Association.

Neufeldt, Victoria, and David Guralnik. 1996. *Webster's New World College Dictionary.* New York: Macmillan.

Nicholson, Scott. 2010. *Everyone Plays at the Library: Creating Great Gaming Experiences for All Ages.* Medford, NJ: Information Today.

O'Hanlon, Nancy, Karen Diaz, and Fred Roecker. 2009. "A Game-Based Multimedia Approach to Library Orientation." In *Uncharted Waters: Tapping the Depths of Our Community to Enhance Learning: Thirty-Fifth National LOEX Library Instruction Conference Proceedings, San Diego, California, May 3–5, 2007*, edited by Brad Seitz et al., 105–9. Ypsilanti, MI: LOEX Press.

OCLC. 2002. *How Academic Librarians Can Influence Students' Web-Based Information Choices.* Dublin, OH: OCLC.

———. 2006. *College Students' Perceptions of the Librarians and Information Resources.* Dublin, OH: OCLC.

———. 2011. *Perceptions of Libraries, 2010: Context and Community.* Dublin, OH: OCLC.

Onwuegbuzie, Anthony J., and Qun G. Jiao. 2000. "I'll Go to the Library Later: The Relationship between Academic Procrastination and Library Anxiety." *College and Research Libraries* 61, no. 1: 45–54.

Onwuegbuzie, Anthony J., Qun G. Jiao, and Sharon L. Bostick. 2004. *Library Anxiety: Theory, Research, and Applications.* Lanham, MD: Scarecrow Press.

Owusu-Ansah, Edward K. 2004. "Information Literacy and Higher Education: Placing the Academic Library in the Center of a Comprehensive Solution." *Journal of Academic Librarianship* 30, no. 1: 3–16.

Palfrey, John, and Uri Gasser. 2008. *Born Digital: Understanding the First Generation of Digital Natives.* New York: Basic Books.

Partnership for 21st Century Skills. 2011. *Framework for 21st Century Learning.* Partnership for 21st Century Skills. Available at http://www.p21.org/overview/skills-framework.

Perrotta, Carlo, Gill Featherstone, Helen Aston, and Emily Houghton. 2013. *Game-Based Learning: Latest Evidence and Future Directions.* Slough, UK: National Foundation for Educational Research.

Petty, Richard E., and John T. Cacioppo. 1981. *Attitude and Persuasion: Classic and Contemporary Approaches.* Boulder, CO: Westview Press.

———. 1986. "The Elaboration Likelihood Model of Persuasion." *Advances in Experimental Social Psychology* 19: 123–205.

"Popular Games Support Literacy in Libraries." 2009. *American Libraries* 40, nos. 1/2: 18.

Prensky, Marc. 2001a. *Digital Game-Based Learning.* New York: McGraw-Hill.

———. 2001b. "Digital Natives, Digital Immigrants." *On the Horizon* 9, no. 5: 1–6.

Ren, Wen-Hua. 2000. "Library Instruction and College Student Self-Efficacy in Electronic Information Searching." *Journal of Academic Librarianship* 26, no. 5: 323–28.

Rice, Scott E. 2008. "Education on a Shoestring: Creating an Online Information Literacy Game." In *Gaming in Academic Libraries: Collections, Marketing, and Information Literacy*, edited by Amy Harris and Scott E. Rice, 175–88. Chicago: Association of College and Research Libraries.

Rieh, Soo Young. 2002. "Judgment of Information Quality and Cognitive Authority in the Web." *Journal of the American Society for Information Science and Technology* 53, no. 2: 145–61.

———. 2010. "Credibility and Cognitive Authority of Information." In *Encyclopedia of Library and Information Sciences*, edited by Marcia Bates and Mary Niles Maack, 1337–44. 3rd ed. New York: Taylor and Francis Group.

Rieh, Soo Young, and Brian Hilligoss. 2008. "College Students' Credibility Judgments in the Information Seeking Process." In *Digital Media, Youth, and Credibility*, edited by Miriam J. Metzger and Andrew J. Flanagin, 49–72. Cambridge, MA: MIT Press.

Rieh, Soo Young, Yong-Mi Kim, and Karen Markey. 2012. "Amount of Invested Mental Effort (AIME) in Online Searching." *Information Processing and Management* 48, no. 6: 1136–50.

Roberson, Julie, and Jenny Horton. 2010. "Creating a Combination IL and English Composition Course in a College Setting." In *Best Practices for Credit-Bearing Information Literacy Courses*, edited by Christopher V. Hollister, 64–76. Chicago: Association of College and Research Libraries.

Robertson, Michael J. 2009. "Identifying Digital Gaming Literature Relevant to the Library and Information Science Community." *Library Student Journal* 4. Available at http://www.librarystudentjournal.org/index.php/lsj/article/viewArticle/97.

Robertson, Michael J., and James G. Jones. 2009. "Exploring Academic Library Users' Preferences of Delivery Methods for Library Instruction: Webpage, Digital Game, and Other Modalities." *Reference and User Services Quarterly* 48, no. 3: 259–69.

Rogers, Scott. 2010. *Level Up: The Guide to Great Video Game Design.* Chichester, UK: Wiley.

Rosenberg, Victor. 1987. "Literature Management Software for the Scholar's Workstation." *Library Software Review* 16: 29–30.

Saracevic, Tefko. 2007. "Relevance: A Review of the Literature and a Framework for Thinking on the Notion in Information Science. Part II: Nature and Manifestations of Relevance." *Journal of the American Society for Information Science and Technology* 58, no. 13: 1915–33.

Saunders, Laura. 2012. "Faculty Perspectives on Information Literacy as a Student Learning Outcome." *Journal of Academic Librarianship* 38, no. 4: 226–36.

Schamber, Linda, and Judith Bateman. 1996. "User Criteria in Relevance Evaluation: Toward Development of a Measurement Scale." *Proceedings of the 59th ASIS Annual Meeting* 33: 218–25.

Schell, Eric. 2008. *The Art of Game Design: A Book of Lenses.* Boca Raton, FL: CRC Press.

Schilling, Katherine Lynne. 2002. *Information Literacy Skills Development in Undergraduate Medical Education: A Comparison Study of the Impact of Training Methodologies on Learning Outcomes.* PhD diss., Boston University.

Selegean, John Cornell, Martha Lou Thomas, and Marie Louise Richman. 1983. "Long-Range Effectiveness of Library Use Instruction." *College and Research Libraries* 44, no. 6: 476–80.

Shute, Valerie, and Matthew Ventura. 2013. *Stealth Assessment: Measuring and Supporting Learning in Video Games.* Cambridge, MA: MIT Press.

Silver, Susan L., and Lisa T. Nickel. 2005. "Are Online Tutorials Effective? A Comparison of Online and Classroom Library Instruction Methods." *Research Strategies* 20, no. 4: 389–96.

Sitler, Ryan L., Chad Sherman, David P. Keppel, Christine E. Schaeffer, Dana C. Hackley, and Laurie A. Grosik. 2011 "A Planet in Peril: Using Digital Games to Teach Information Literacy Skills." In *Let the Games Begin! Engaging Students with Field-Tested Interactive Information Literacy Instruction*, edited by Theresa R. McDevitt, 134–37. New York: Neal-Schuman.

Sitzmann, Traci. 2011. "A Meta-Analytic Examination of the Instructional Effectiveness of Computer-Based Simulation Games." *Personnel Psychology* 64: 489–528.

Smale, Maura A. 2011. "Learning through Quests and Contests: Games in Information Literacy Instruction." *Library Innovation* 2, no. 2: 36–55.

Smith, Anna-Lise, and Lesli Baker. 2011. "Getting a Clue: Creating Student Detectives and Dragon Slayers in Your Library." *Reference Services Review* 39, no. 4: 628–42.

Smith, Brena. 2008. "Twenty-First Century Game Studies in the Academy: Libraries and an Emerging Discipline." *Reference Services Review* 36, no. 2: 205–20.

Smith, Felicia A. 2007. "Games for Teaching Information Literacy Skills." *Library Philosophy and Practice* 9, no. 2: 12.

Smith, Susan. 2006. *Web-Based Instruction: A Guide for Libraries.* 2nd ed. Chicago: American Library Association.

Špiranec, Sonja, and Mihaela Banek Zorica. 2010. "Information Literacy 2.0: Hype or Discourse Refinement?" *Journal of Documentation* 66, no. 1: 140–53.

Squire, Kurt, and Henry Jenkins. 2003. "Harnessing the Power of Games in Education." *Insight* 3, no. 5: 7–33.

Steinkuhler, Constance. 2007. "Massively Multiplayer Online Gaming as a Constellation of Literary Practices." *E-Learning and Digital Media* 4, no. 3: 297–318.

Sundin, Olof. 2005. "Negotiations on Information-Seeking Expertise: A Study of Web-Based Tutorials for Information Literacy." *Journal of Documentation* 64, no. 1: 24–44.

Sundin, Olof, and Helena Francke. 2009. "In Search of Credibility: Pupils' Information Practices in Learning Environments." *Information Research* 14, no. 4: 6.

Swanson, Troy. 2005. "Teaching Students about Information: Information Literacy and Cognitive Authority." *Research Strategies* 20, no. 4: 322–33.

Tapscott, Don. 1998. *Growing Up Digital: The Rise of the Net Generation.* New York: McGraw-Hill.

Thistlethwaite, Polly J. 2001. "The Data Game: Colorado State University's Animated Library Research Tutorial." *Colorado Libraries* 27, no. 3: 12–15.

Thomas, Nancy Pickering. 2004. *Information Literacy and Information Skills Instruction: Applying Research to Practice in the School Library Media Center.* Westport, CT: Libraries Unlimited.

Todd, Ross. 2000. "A Theory of Information Literacy: In-Formation and Outward Looking." In *Information Literacy around the World: Advances in Programs and Research*, edited by Christine Bruce and Philip Candy, 163–65. New South Wales, Australia: Centre for Information Studies, Charles Stuart University.

van Meegen, Ana, and Imke Limpens. 2010. "How Serious Do We Need to Be? Improving Information Literacy Skills through Gaming and Interactive Elements." *LIBER Quarterly* 20, no. 2: 270–88. Available at http://www.religionandgender. org/index.php/lq/article/view/7993/8316.

Van Scoyoc, Anna M. 2003. "Reducing Library Anxiety in First-Year Students." *Reference and User Services Quarterly* 42, no. 4: 329–41.

VanLeer, Lynn. 2006. "Interactive Gaming vs. Library Tutorials for Information Literacy: A Resource Guide." *Indiana Libraries* 25, no. 4: 52–55.

Vogel, Jennifer J., David S. Vogel, Jan Cannon-Bowers, Clint A. Bowers, Kathryn Muse, and Michelle Wright. 2006. "Computer Gaming and Interactive Simulations for Learning: A Meta-Analysis." *Journal of Educational Computing Research* 34, no. 3: 229–43.

Waelchli, Paul. 2008. "Leveling Up: Increasing Information Literacy through Videogame Strategies." In *Gaming in Academic Libraries: Collections, Marketing, and Information Literacy*, edited by Amy Harris and Scott E. Rice, 212–28. Chicago: Association of College and Research Libraries.

Walsh, Andrew. 2009. "Information Literacy Assessment: Where Do We Start?" *Journal of Librarianship and Information Science* 41, no. 1: 19–28.

Wang, Rui. 2006. "The Lasting Impact of a Library Credit Course." *portal: Libraries and the Academy* 61: 79–92.

Ward, David. 2006. "Previsioning Information Literacy from Lifelong Meaning." *Journal of Academic Librarianship* 32, no. 4: 396–402.

Weiner, Sharon A. 2012. "Institutionalizing Information Literacy." *Journal of Academic Librarianship* 38, no. 5: 287–93.

Wheeler, Diana, Lia Vallardita, and Amy Kindschi. 2010. "Providing a Credit Information Literacy Course for an Engineering School." In *Best Practices for Credit-Bearing Information Literacy Courses*, edited by Christopher V. Hollister, 109–25. Chicago: Association of College and Research Libraries.

Whitton, Nicola. 2010. *Learning with Digital Games: A Practical Guide to Engaging Students in Higher Education*. New York: Routledge.

Wong, Gabrielle, Diana Chan, and Sam Chu. 2006. "Assessing the Enduring Impact of Library Instruction Programs." *Journal of Academic Librarianship* 32, no. 4: 384–95.

Wong, Shun Han Rebekah, and Dianne Cmor. 2011. "Measuring Association between Library Instruction and Graduation GPA." *College and Research Libraries* 72, no. 5: 464–73.

Wouters, Pieter, Christof van Nimwegen, Herre van Oostendorp, and Erik D. van der Spek. 2013. "A Meta-Analysis of the Cognitive and Motivational Effects of Serious Games." *Journal of Educational Psychology* 105, no. 2: 249–65.

Xie, Hong. 2007. "Shifts in Information-Seeking Strategies in Information Retrieval in the Digital Age: Planned-Situational Model." *Information Research* 12, no. 4. Available at http://informationr.net/ir/12-4/colis/colis22.html.

Zotero. 2013. "Zotero Home." Available at http://www.zotero.org.

Zurkowski, Paul. 1974. *The Information Service Environment: Relationships and Priorities*. Washington, DC: National Commission on Libraries and Information Science.

Index